ROUTLEDGE LIBRARY EDITIONS: EDUCATION AND GENDER

Volume 13

INTERNATIONAL FEMINIST PERSPECTIVES ON EDUCATIONAL REFORM

INTERNATIONAL FEMINIST PERSPECTIVES ON EDUCATIONAL REFORM
The Work of Gail Paradise Kelly

Edited by
DAVID H. KELLY

LONDON AND NEW YORK

First published in 1996 by Garland

This edition first published in 2017
by Routledge
2 Park Square, Milton Park, Abingdon, Oxon OX14 4RN

and by Routledge
711 Third Avenue, New York, NY 10017

Routledge is an imprint of the Taylor & Francis Group, an informa business

© 1996 David H. Kelly

All rights reserved. No part of this book may be reprinted or reproduced or utilised in any form or by any electronic, mechanical, or other means, now known or hereafter invented, including photocopying and recording, or in any information storage or retrieval system, without permission in writing from the publishers.

Trademark notice: Product or corporate names may be trademarks or registered trademarks, and are used only for identification and explanation without intent to infringe.

British Library Cataloguing in Publication Data
A catalogue record for this book is available from the British Library

ISBN: 978-1-138-73736-5 (Set)
ISBN: 978-1-315-18103-5 (Set) (ebk)
ISBN: 978-1-138-04077-9 (Volume 13) (hbk)
ISBN: 978-1-138-04078-6 (Volume 13) (pbk)
ISBN: 978-1-315-17478-5 (Volume 13) (ebk)

Publisher's Note
The publisher has gone to great lengths to ensure the quality of this reprint but points out that some imperfections in the original copies may be apparent.

Disclaimer
The publisher has made every effort to trace copyright holders and would welcome correspondence from those they have been unable to trace.

International Feminist Perspectives on Educational Reform
The Work of Gail Paradise Kelly

Edited by
David H. Kelly

Garland Publishing, Inc.
New York and London
1996

Copyright © 1996 by David H. Kelly
All rights reserved

Library of Congress Cataloging-in-Publication Data

Kelly, Gail Paradise.
    International feminist perspectives on educational reform : the work of Gail Paradise Kelly / edited by David H. Kelly.
        p.   cm. — (Garland reference library of social science ; vol. 1030)
    A collection of articles by Gail Paradise Kelly spanning a 20-year period.
    Includes bibliographical references and index.
    ISBN 0-8153-2005-1 (alk. paper)
    1. Feminism and education. 2. Educational change. 3. Educational equalization.   I. Kelly, David H. II. Title. III. Series: Garland reference library of social science ; v. 1030.
LC197.K45   1996
370.19'345—dc20   95-14664
                                                                                       CIP

Printed on acid-free, 250-year-life paper
Manufactured in the United States of America

Dedication

This volume is dedicated to the literally hundreds of men and women who collaborated with Gail Kelly as colleagues, students or just friends. Gail worked through interaction with others; her ideas were always tested, and her writing always revised through the process of discussion. I had thought to list as many of you as I could remember, but I would undoubtedly leave out many. Hence, while this dedication is to all who worked with Gail, I will list only a few fellow SUNY faculty members who worked longest and most directly with Gail—Philip Altbach, Elizabeth Kennedy, Hugh Petrie, Maxine Seller, Sheila Slaughter, Lois Weis (and so many more).

Contents

Acknowledgments 3

Feminist Agendas: An Introduction
    David Kelly 5

Women's Liberation and the New Left 9

Adult Education of Vietnamese Refugees: Commentary on
    Pluralism in America 17

Research on the Education of Women in the Third World:
    Problems and Perspectives 29

Schooling and the Reproduction of Patriarchy: Unequal
    Workloads, Unequal Rewards
    Gail P. Kelly and Ann S. Nihlen 41

New Directions for Research
    Carolyn M. Elliott and Gail P. Kelly 61

Failures of Androcentric Studies of Women's Education in
    the Third World 75

Comparative Education: Challenge and Response
    Gail P. Kelly and Philip G. Altbach 89

Dialogue: Response to Angus's "Conflict, Class, and the
    Nineteenth-Century Public High School in the
    Cities of the Midwest, 1845-1900" 113

Comparative Education and the Problem of Change: An
    Agenda for the 1980s 121

Vietnam 137

Education, Women and Change 163

Setting the Boundaries of Debate about Education 183

Center on Education in the Inner Cities
      Gail P. Kelly and Maxine S. Seller 197

The Education of Gail Paradise Kelly: A Memoir
      David Kelly 219

Works of Gail P. Kelly 233

Index 241

International Feminist Perspectives on Educational Reform

Acknowledgments

To begin I would like to thank the various journals and publishers who have allowed me to reprint Gail's essays. They include *Radical America*, the *Journal of Ethnic Studies*, Pergamon Press, Routledge and Kegan Paul, SUNY Press, University of Illinois Press, University of Chicago Press, John Wiley and Sons, Greenwood and Prometheus Books. I also would like to thank Ann Nihlen, Carolyn Elliott, Philip Altbach and Maxine Seller whose work with Gail has been reprinted here with their permission. Philip Altbach, as with many aspects of my life, provided the push to get me started, and he and Edith Hoshino Altbach were valuable critics of the initial prospectus. Ruth Kelly provided editorial assistance on the Introduction, and Lois Weis commented warmly on the Memoir. If the reader notices better grammar and syntax in the Memoir than in the Introduction the improvement is due to George Bishop of the D'Youville College English faculty who suggested numerous alterations. Finally, the computer lab at D'Youville College and particularly Daniel Lyman has guided a sometimes very frustrated neophyte through to the completion of this volume.

Feminist Agendas: An Introduction

David Kelly

In this volume I have brought together articles by Gail Paradise Kelly that span almost a twenty-year period. As such they represent an aspect of the history of the feminist movement as related to education. Gail generally defined feminism as the struggle to empower women to break down the patriarchal structures that limited their lives. Women needed to have the freedom of choice in their life styles and in their relations with men. Men were not the enemy, unless they consciously or unconsciously used the power of patriarchy to circumscribe the lives of women. Her feminism envisioned free women and men leading fuller, more complete lives in a situation that dismissed most gender roles as culturally determined and provided for equality of gender in all its aspects. While this definition is idealistic Gail was a total realist in viewing the contemporary position of women and its historical causes. Her aim was to establish goals, methods and questions which would illuminate women's position and suggest modes of change.

In the first article (from 1970), "Women's Liberation and the New Left," Gail looked at her own and other students' experience in the campus feminist movement of the late 1960s. She looked at the question of revolution or reform and saw a need for fundamental change. This would be driven by self-amelioration but would shake the system because feminism would question the basis of society. The article reflects the view of a radical movement that seems to be imploding.

The second article, "Adult Education of Vietnamese Refugees," (1977) described research on Vietnam refugees in this country. It demonstrated the absolute folly of ignoring culture, gender and social class issues when trying to educate. It also showed how such limited vision was built directly into the curriculum and that it was more than an individual teacher's misconception.

"Research on the Education of Women in the Third World" (1978) reviewed current scholarship on Third World women's education. Gail questioned some work as limited to the economic returns of education. She called for research on the relationship between the subjects taught and the lives of women with the focus on women's lives, not the education or even the economic system.

Writing with Ann Nihlen in the next article, "Schooling and the Reproduction of Patriarchy," (1982) Gail looked directly at school process as well as the work outcomes of school. The article examined staffing and authority patterns from a gender perspective, examined roles of women shown in textbooks, and classroom interaction patterns between males and females. It also examined the gendered tracking of various fields of intellectual pursuit. The authors concluded that the schools do reproduce patriarchy and the notion of reproduction, if not completely acceptable, was at least didactically sound.

In 1982 Gail also edited (with Carolyn Elliott) a volume on women's education in the Third World. The next selection, "New Directions for Research," both summarized that volume and attempted to establish agendas for further research. The article stressed how a wide range of difference in women's access to education has not been explained, nor was the impact of education on family patterns and health issues at all clear. The article summarized and lauded several chapters in the book which looked at educational process. It concluded with a call to look at education in the context of women's lives, not in comparison to men's occupations or roles, to see needed avenues of reform.

In "Failures of Androcentric Studies of Women's Education in the Third World" (1985) Gail was working out the definitions of feminist scholarship as opposed to those studies of women that assume a patriarchal family. Feminist scholarship should examine the role of women in all life patterns, child bearing and rearing, education and work, and should question how these patterns might change to improve the control of women over their lives.

In the next three articles Gail was writing as part of the continuing debate on how to study education and its meaning in society. In "Comparative Education: Challenge and Response" (1986 with Philip Altbach) she brought the history of her own narrower field, including comparative education, into focus and examined the impact of various challenges feminism had on that field of study. In "Dialogue: Response to Angus's 'Conflict, Class and the Nineteenth-Century Public High School...'" (1988) she defended the use of various paradigms that generate questions about education against the rather dry historicism that she saw applauded by Angus. In her presidential address to the Comparative and International Education Society, entitled "Comparative Education and the Problem of Change," (1987) she attacked what she considered undue pessimism about the value and impact of education. She was particularly concerned that issues of equity (including, of course, the question of equity for women) were being neglected and down played on the basis of very brief attempts at reform and change.

In 1988 Gail, long a scholar of Vietnam, visited that country for the first time. The article, "Vietnam," (1988) is a report of that visit. Gail returned to the whole question of the meaning of revolution in the context of women's lives and found both advancement and, in the long run, the continuing power of patriarchy.

The next article, "Education, Women and Change," has been edited by me. I have used the 1992 version of the article for its more up to date statistics and the more complete discussion of similar statistics and other material from a slightly earlier version of the article, "Education and Equality," (1990). In these articles Gail summarized the complexity of enrollment, access and outcomes data that has appeared for less developed countries.

Gail began in the late 1970s and early 1980s from an American perspective and then brought feminist concerns to an international context in articles about Third World women. In the late 1980s she returned to American reform perspectives. This return is represented in the last two articles included here. The first of these, "Setting the Boundaries of Debate about Education," contains nothing directly on feminism. However in the article Gail expressed serious questions about those national reports that put the blame on teachers (who are generally female) and was sharply critical of the reports for not focusing on the actual process of education; a theme she had referred to time and again in her critiques of educational research on women in the Third World. She saw the boundaries being established as excluding what needed to be considered.

The last selection by Gail in this book is not a finished article; rather it is a grant proposal on which Gail worked during the last portion of her life. (She certainly would never have published it in this form). I have included only those portions she was to be most responsible for but her ideas were critical in assembling and shaping the whole. The grant dealt with education in the inner city; it focused on how to empower groups to work with the schools to develop relevant curriculum and teaching processes to provide strength and hope to those schools. Her own pieces of the project (with Maxine Seller) involved immigrant organizations and their interest and potential impact on schools and a project on how to work with families to improve schools. (This latter proposal has implicit feminist roots when one considers that many families of the inner city are headed by women). These proposals represent the real grass roots direction that reform must include if education is to return to being the hope for America's future.

The volume concludes with a personal memoir by this author that depicts the background and formation of Gail's thought and gives a brief look at her entire career and intellectual interests. Also included is a bibliography of her work, including those materials that have been published since her death.

Women's Liberation and the New Left[†]

Gail Paradise Kelly is a graduate student in Education at the University of Wisconsin. She has been active in Women's Liberation since its beginning.

The past several years have seen the growth of a radical Women's Movement. It is widely accepted that this movement has its origins in the New Left. Beginning with a brief discussion of the transition from Old to New Left, this article will show how changes in the Left during the 1960's led to the alienation of women from the Left as a whole and helped to convince them of the need for an autonomous Women's Movement.

Developments on the Left

The American Left is said to fall into two phases—"Old" and "New." These terms are often used as simple chronological distinctions. However, the distinctions are ideological; the interplay of Old and New Left ideologies was much in evidence during the course of the Movement in the 1960's, and this process has continued on into the Women's Liberation Movement.

Most of the Old Left, from Trotskyites to members of the Communist Party, to Maoists, conceives of revolution as institutional change and the process of revolution as the process of one class obtaining power. Put another way, revolution has to do with political power relationships that will bring about institutional change. Old Leftists as a whole perceive that their first task is organizing a group capable of exerting power—e.g., the working class. They know intellectually, if not emotionally, that this is a long process and that, therefore, revolution in the foreseeable future is highly unlikely. Finally, to organize the working class, personal fulfillment had to be put aside as Leftists from a bourgeois background attempted to get jobs on the line, in auto plants, and in steel mills.

The Left in the late Fifties and early Sixties was still concerned primarily with changing power relationships, and it was helpless, isolated and irrelevant. The Old Left had just emerged from a period of

[†]Reprinted with permission from: *Radical America* 4:2 (February 1970), pp. 19-25.

justifiable paranoia—McCarthyism. The Movement, the traditional left sectarian parties and the newer organizations concerning themselves with liberal causes such as the arms race or civil rights were caught in an almost paralyzing dilemma: Should they work for liberal causes which would not destroy capitalism but which might at best raise some consciousness of the need for change, or should they withdraw from these activities because of the risk of cooption (which was real) and participate in only "true" pure revolutionary activity such as only those things "guaranteed" to bring the system down. The major activities of the Old Left usually consisted of interminable meetings, debates, and study sessions. In the early 1960's many leftists knew more about Russia, Hungary, and China than they did about the United States, more about the Paris Commune than the ghettos, poverty, the nature of American capitalism, or women's oppression.

At the same time, the New Left received a strong infusion of people upset with their own perceived oppression. They did not share the Old Left's perspective on the working class. In fact, they developed a decidedly anti working class bias. The working class, they argued, was racist and reactionary; capitalism had taken away its revolutionary potential. The constituency for revolution was composed of the dispossessed, the unemployed, the Blacks, the alienated middle class. Whoever felt oppression was potentially a revolutionary. The early SDS JOIN and Newark Projects, the SCEF projects in Kentucky and Appalachia, the Mississippi Voter Registration Projects were based on this new conception of a revolutionary class. So, the first element introduced was activism which believed that change was possible, which rejected the exclusive role assigned to the working class, and which, finally, saw elements of the middle class as one of the constituencies for revolution. Moreover, in another reaction against the Old Left, the New Left seemingly rejected not only Marxist ideology, but all ideology on the grounds that (a) capitalism, rather than Leftists with different ideological casts, is the enemy; (b) ideology is irrelevant, especially since so much of it is grounded on non-American (e.g., Russian, Chinese, Cuban) experiences and conditions and not on the American context; (c) ideology in-fighting leads to a de-emphasis on activism and an over-emphasis on faction-fighting and ideology construction. (Actually, one can question whether the distinction is valid today, especially given recent SDS fractionalizing and other instances of hostile confrontation between groups—now all the factions are highly ideological, rigidly Marxist, and strongly sectarian. Likewise, the "back to the worker" movement is still much in evidence among the Trotskyist SWP (Socialist Workers Party) and the Maoist PL

(Progressive Labor)—facts which show, again, that the distinction between Old and New Left is more ideological than chronological).

The second factor that accounts for changes in the Left is the subsequent disillusionment of the Left with the activism directed toward working within the framework of institutions traditionally used by the Left—e.g., politics, organizing, demonstrating. Whites soon learned they could neither organize Blacks nor poor whites. Despite a nuclear test ban treaty the U.S. had begun a bloody war in Asia, and while Cuba still survived, all of Latin America was in fact occupied. The war in Vietnam, more than anything else, helped shape the new movement. By the time the 1964 presidential campaign rolled around, it had become obvious to some that nothing short of armed revolution could end American imperialism, racism, and capitalism. So corrupt had the ruling class become that many Leftists no longer attempted to relate to what they considered "establishment groups"—defined often as labor unions, liberals, petit bourgeois, the poor—since most of them either supported the war or were racist, or voted Democratic.

Instead, large segments of the Left started to withdraw from political activism and rationalize that withdrawal as a form of revolution—e.g., the lifestyle revolution. The focus shifted to how revolutionaries lived, what their hang-ups were, how a new revolutionary man could be developed, how individual forms of oppression could be dealt with. Freud replaced Marx. Much of the lifestyle revolution was accompanied by the increasing use of drugs and by the development of a rock-blues counter-culture. Among New Leftists (more specifically, elements of the Weathermen, some members of the New University Conference [NUC], New Mobe types), revolution has taken on a cultural, almost existentialist character. First there is emphasis on adopting a revolutionary life style here and now, which is considered possible without institutional changes in capitalism. A good example of such thought is an article written by Bob Klawitter in the NUC newsletter last Fall. Revolution, Klawitter proclaims is "swiss pink-a-dots," or whatever else you personally groove. The formation of communes and collectives are steps in this direction. There are some who think that the adaptation of a new lifestyle in and of itself is the revolution, especially in the "green" communes that have taken up farming. The great majority see the lifestyle changes as fundamental to the creation of a revolutionary man. The change in lifestyles is supposed to serve the following functions: (a) to detach the individual from the comfort of capitalism (although often the lifestyle is supported by rich parents clipping coupons); (b) to rid individuals of hang-ups carried over from bourgeois upbringings; (c) to provide financial support for members of the commune so that only a few might work and the rest might be engaged in revolutionary action of some sort or another; (d) to develop a group capable of taking part in terrorist-disruptive activities; (e) to provide a ready-made "cell" when their actions bring repression into full swing. These goals tend to stress elements totally foreign to the Old Left and at first appears Narodnik rather than socialist. But it lacks a crucial Narodnik element: the Narodniks attempted to *go among the people and organize them*, while to some extent the New Left has abandoned organizing.

The cult of the lifestyle revolution has led to another emphasis on the Left which is by no means new, but which came to the fore with the New Left's politics—ego-tripping. The emphasis on lifestyle in the New Left, while it has established an *easy* role that revolutionaries from the middle-class can play, also tends to bring out romantic egotistical tendencies among its participants. The prime role is that of the individual revolutionary—his (or her) life, his or her act of revolution. It tends to stress revolution as an individual act rather than a class act; as a psychological purging rather than a change in political power relationships. To paraphrase a speech made by Mark Rudd at Indiana University in Fall 1969, middle-class revolutionaries have to show they have the balls to make revolution (the psychological dress rehearsal for the real thing? or an existentialist final act or meaning like Hugo's in Sartre's "Dirty Hands"?). The foregoing was not intended as a definitive discussion of the Old versus the New Left. Rather, it presents the perspective from which the relationship of Women's Liberation to New Left will be analyzed in the next section. The next section will comment on ways in which New Leftism influenced the growth of Women's Liberation as a separate movement and, at the same time, increased the alienation of women from Old and New Left alike.

Women's Liberation and the Cultural Revolution

Once the Left had taken the turn toward living the revolution, examining individual hang-ups, and developing alternative institutions in the present, it was inevitable that the sisters in the movement would gain greater consciousness of the oppression inherent in not only traditional relationships between men and women, but also in the so-called "revolutionary" relationships in which the women typed, cleaned, and were fucked and the men did "political work." Women began to understand how little the movement offered them. They began to understand some of the experience of the Blacks, that the only effective work for Blacks was done by exclusively Black groups. In order to deal with women's oppression, women had to form a distinct group.

Women in the Old Left did not form their own group, not because there was no oppression, but because they were not conscious of it. The ideology of the Old Left militated against such a consciousness with its emphasis on economic and political analysis of capitalism almost, if not entirely, to the exclusion of the psychological dimensions of oppression. It was, so to speak, Marxism devoid of human content. Male chauvinism was just as rampant in the movement ten years ago as it is today; those sisters who were active in the Old Left know all too well the remarks about "horizontal recruitment," the almost exclusively male leadership and the almost exclusively female office staff.

Those political groups today which have an Old Left orientation PL, SWP, YSA (Young Socialist Alliance)—have an ambivalent position on Women's Liberation. They think that the oppression of women is a phenomenon restricted to capitalism and that, therefore, if one wants to fight for Women's Liberation, one should not necessarily form a separate group, unless, of course, it is either to organize working class women to join the Left or recruit middle-class women out of Women's Liberation into the Left. Such a view appears condescending to most women who are not willing to sacrifice ameliorating their own lives to working for some amorphous "revolution" that only promises to put the working class (male only?) in control.

Like the New Left movement from which it broke away, Women's Liberation has a similar affinity for the "psychological" and "cultural" sides of revolution. This is apparent in the amount of time which Women's Liberation devotes to support groups. The purpose of these groups is to heighten the consciousness of women to their own hang-ups and the oppression which confronts them in day-to-day existence—from TV ads to job discrimination. Women in the group receive support in dealing with their jobs, their husbands or lovers, men on the Left, etc. The emphasis here is on personal oppression, not on class oppression, unless women are considered a class (which is the case with many theorists in Women's Liberation—to wit, Kate Millett in her book, *Sexual Politics*). The influence of the lifestyle revolution is apparent in the development of a women's counter-culture complete with Women's Communes, the destruction of symbols of oppression on an individual basis, the development of a body of prose and poetry about women written by women.

Although the Women's Liberation movement has a good reason to be hostile to both the Old and New Left it has not yet been able to solve the dilemmas of the Left as a whole Women's Liberation has vacillated between the psychological and social aspects of revolution and the political aspects. We have seen how political orthodoxy made the Old Left sterile and isolated. Yet, we have also seen that an exclusive preoccupation with the cultural revolution has led the New Left to a stalemate—changing psyches and individual lifestyles in and of themselves is not likely to bring about revolution. This approach has already created a sub-culture that can survive in peaceful harmony with male chauvinism, with capitalism, with imperialism, and with every other form of oppression. It can even give profits to capitalism, as the Woodstock rock festival has shown. The expansion of the Minnie Pearl Chicken Chain into day-care centers has shown Women's Liberation how easily one of its central demands can be turned into a profit-making business. Women's Liberation must rather seek to form a synthesis of the diverging sides to revolution.

As the Women's movement tries to solve this dilemma it must decide whether to organize constituencies for revolution or make revolution now. While this dilemma is not put in the language of Women's Liberation, it might well be—whether to seek to organize new constituencies of women for bread and butter, concrete political, economic, and social demands which may "radicalize" women for further actions—or whether to take the present constituency and further "steel it" for immediate direct attacks on capitalism. But immediate guerrilla tactics assume an elitist small group character. At this stage, the Weatherwoman"ish" tendencies are in a minor key, but their influence is strong and very capable of destroying Women's Liberation just by virtue of their secretiveness and their efforts to turn the movement into an underground elite.

There is a strong element of compassion for the condition of their sisters which has thus far protected Women's Liberation from being satisfied to remain within its own subculture. It was not only the ego-tripping, the chauvinism, and the refusal to take female oppression seriously that led to hostility between Women's Liberation and the Left. Much of the hostility was and is in reaction to the New Left's increasing refusal to engage in activities that might fall short of immediate revolution—i. e., its withdrawal out of community organizing, its withdrawal (at the insistence of the Blacks) out of the Black movement, the withdrawal out of student politics, etc. The New Left seemingly was trapped in its own sub-culture. Women, as Blacks, understood on a gut level that something *had to be done* about female oppression. They also understood that something short of revolution could be done that would make women's lives more bearable, e.g., abortion law repeal, formation of day care centers, inroads against job discrimination and work conditions. Women wanted a movement for themselves that would not sluff off their oppression as something to be dealt with after the revolution.

The majority of Women's Liberation which has begun to move toward *organizing* has bogged down on the question of whom to organize, on what basis to organize them, and for what purpose. Only organizing working class women, some maintain, is revolutionary; organizing middle-class women is not. Many have gotten so hung up in this discussion that *no organizing* at all has taken place, even among middle-class college women whose destiny unhappily appears to be that of sex kitten in suburbia. Even if the decision is made toward organizing, the problem then arises of how a group of middle-class women can relate to them. One possible way is through the establishment of day care centers. But even this has been limited by Women's Liberation itself over the insistence that any day care center that be established be run cooperatively by both parents regardless of whether both have to work from 9 to 5, five days a week. The purpose of the day care centers becomes confused—is their purpose to develop "revolutionary" children or are they a means of helping people realize that control of their own lives is a right? The insistence on "purity" may unfortunately tie us to the sub-culture rather than organize us for revolution. The same kind of problem is evident in the current ambivalence toward abortion law repeal. Many in Women's Liberation are opposed to the reforms now because legislators are voting to repeal the laws for the "wrong" reasons—i.e., because of over-population, especially among poor people, because middle class women want abortions—rather than because they believe that abortion is a woman's right. One can only wonder if this represents a tendency on the part of the sisters to be right, regardless of relevancy or effectiveness. This position is also indicative of another problem besetting the "organizers"—how to accept minor victories. There is a fear of "winning" anything based on the idea that: (a) if one's demands are accepted and capitalism does not fall, the demands were not revolutionary in the first place; and (b) if one's demands are accepted, then one is coopted and ends up supporting Sexism and capitalism. A comprehensive program could put small victories into perspective and could explain why it is worth fighting for legalized abortions even though sexism would still remain afterwards. Women's Liberation has accepted the political implications of its movement on an intellectual basis. However, the movement has not yet fully understood emotionally what such a comprehensive program would entail. Ultimately this means deferred fulfillment of individual desires; it means we must make demands that will be accepted. Ours should be a long-term program that encompasses the full range of psychological, social, economic, and political aspects of the revolution against capitalism and sexism.

What this article has tried to stress is the need of Women's Liberation to develop a program. It is no longer enough to know what we are against, we have to know what we are for. Only then can we engage in action, only then can we organize, impatient as we are, for a revolution that avoids the weaknesses of both Old and New Left ideologies.

Adult Education of Vietnamese Refugees: Commentary on Pluralism in America[†]

In late April 1975 when the war in Vietnam ended, from the territories that had once been French Indochina came over 200,000 Cambodians, Laotians, and Vietnamese refugees. Most were Vietnamese fleeing battle zones and/or the prospects of living under a new political order. Those who left Vietnam were a diverse population. Many were high ranking officials of the South Vietnamese government, military leaders, provincial and district chiefs or mayors; others had worked closely with American government agencies and private corporations in Vietnam in positions ranging from secretaries, translators and chauffeurs to intelligence and propaganda specialists. While close to half of all Vietnamese refugees were persons who had held power in South Vietnam or had worked for the Americans in lucrative jobs and were clearly members of Vietnam's urban elites, the remainder of the refugees were from less privileged and less urbanized groups which had little exposure to western culture and life styles. Among them were enlisted men in the army and navy, fishermen and farmers, and petty traders.[1] Of the 200,000 refugees that poured out of Indochina in April 1975, 130,000 entered the United States.

Neither members of the Vietnamese elite nor lower class Vietnamese, rural and urban alike, who came to the United States, were prepared to live in American society, culturally, psychologically, or in any other way. Some believed they could continue living as they had in Vietnam, working in jobs similar to those they had held at home and living in Vietnamese communities as they had known them with their status within a Vietnamese world kept intact. Others, like N.V.S., a forty-five-year-old ARVN officer whom we interviewed at a refugee camp on the U.S. mainland, firmly believed his life would need to change as he became integrated into American society.[2] However, he, like so many of his compatriots, had no knowledge of what that change would entail and what it would mean in terms of future relationships to Vietnamese culture and society. N.V.S. and refugees like him looked to Americans to point the way, informing them of what Vietnamese would have to know and the directions in which their lives would need to change in order to survive in the United States.

N. V. S. looked to Americans for information about U.S. life because there was no pre-existing Vietnamese community in this

---

[†]Reprinted with permission of Western Washington University for the *Journal of Ethnic Studies* (1977).

country to mediate between the refugees and American cultures. Further, Americans willingly assumed the role of introducing Vietnamese to America and suggesting how Vietnamese would have to live in the U. S. They did this within the four refugee camps which the U. S. Government established to house Vietnamese while they awaited clearance to enter the country. These camps—Fort Indian Town Gap, Pennsylvania; Camp Pendleton in southern California; Fort Chaffee, Arkansas; and Elgin Air Force base in Florida—were open from May through December 1975.

In them Americans taught the Vietnamese about the United States. What they taught Vietnamese is a significant subject and it is important to analyze the education of adults in the camps, specifically in terms of how that education presented American society and what kind of changes in Vietnamese life styles it promoted. Such an analysis suggests the types of demands for cultural change which Americans make on contemporary immigrants and enables us to explore the limits of cultural pluralism which the United States government promotes. The analysis which follows focuses solely on formal instruction in the English language. It is based on instructional materials used at Fort Indian Town Gap, observations of classroom instruction in that camp, and interviews conducted with teachers, curriculum specialists, school administrators, and refugees.

Teaching English, Teaching Survival, Teaching Culture

English instruction was by far the most widespread educational activity in the refugee camps. American authorities as well as Vietnamese refugees understood that Vietnamese would not be able to earn a living or cope with shopping, medical care, and finding places to live unless they could speak English. Over 50 percent of all refugees over age 18 spoke no English; another 25 percent spoke some English, but not enough to communicate effectively with Americans.[3] Thus, almost as soon as the refugee camps opened, English classes for adults were organized. At Fort Indian Town Gap, 9,700 adults attended 38 two-hour classes five days a week, beginning in May 1975, and were taught by about 320 American volunteers.[4] More people would have participated in English language education had it not been for the school authorities' decision to keep classes small by excluding women and children. While this decision was made on practical grounds—for teachers argued Vietnamese would not adequately learn English pronunciation if they were taught in classes of over thirty persons—it was also made on the grounds that including women and children in the classes would disrupt the immigrant's culture. School people reasoned that men would lose face if a woman learned English faster than they. As a result, they argued, the family, intrinsic to Vietnamese culture, would disintegrate.[5]

English instruction, before September 1975, at all refugee camps was based on "survival" and the course, consisting of 16 lessons in all, was called "Survival English."[6] It was developed by professional linguists from the Departments of Social and Health, Education and Welfare, assisted at Fort Indian Town Gap by the Pennsylvania State Department of Public Instruction. Emphasis was on oral English and not on reading and writing. The course taught what its authors believed would be the minimum of language skills necessary for functioning in the United States that would not impose on Vietnamese culture.[7]

The sixteen lessons in "Survival English" covered such topics as Meeting Strangers, Finding a Place to Live, Occupations, Renting Apartments, Shopping, Visiting the Library, and Applying for a Job. They taught Vietnamese about politeness in this country and how to talk about the weather with American friends or talk about food (Lesson #11, for example, was about Mr. Jones wanting black coffee or coffee with cream and how much he should eat for breakfast). This course did try to teach functional English, including words for food, parts of the body, occupations and numbers.

It is indeed ironic that although school authorities claimed they were anxious to preserve Vietnamese culture, the curriculum they designed and the vocabulary taught involved the teaching of cultural and social norms not necessarily congruent with those of the Vietnamese for whom the instruction was designed. The English curriculum, while it taught rudimentary vocabulary and phrases, also taught to the Vietnamese the American sex role divisions of labor and prepared the many members of Vietnam's former elite for new social and occupational roles. The lesson covering occupations illustrates this. Survival English lessons consisted of vocabulary introduced in isolation and then presented in sentences and phrases, usually in the form of a conversation between a Mr. Brown and a Mr. Jones. Mr. Jones was no doubt the refugee, for he was always asking Mr. Brown questions about shopping, finding a place to live, and job hunting. In the unit on jobs, Mr. Jones wanted to find a job that would allow him to support his wife and two children. The kinds of jobs he considered were, for the most part, on the lowest end of the American occupational structure: room clerk, salesman, cashier, laborer, cook, cleaning person, plumber, bricklayer, secretary, typist, seamstress, and nurses' aide. Mr. Brown assured the refugee he would make more than enough money in any of these jobs for his family to live comfortably.[8]

American stereotypic sex role divisions of labor were clearly presented in the English course. Women were almost totally absent from curricular materials as well as from the classrooms due to

American rather than Vietnamese initiatives. Women entered the lessons only twice in the sixteen-topic sequence: in a lesson called "Conversation," and in a lesson on budgeting and shopping. In the former, women appeared in but two sentences: "Miss Jones missed the bus to the Miss Universe competition," and "She is an attractive girl."[9] In the lesson on shopping, women went to the store only to purchase cosmetics, food, baby needs and aspirins; men shopped for shirts, houses, cars, and furniture. Women could purchase only small items without consulting their husbands.

While women were almost absent from course materials and when present were interested in beauty contests, in being pretty, and in purchasing small commodities, the Survival English course tended to place Vietnamese men in roles usually reserved for American women. In the lesson on occupations, men could be seamstresses, typists, cleaning persons, secretaries, and nurses' aides, traditionally women's occupations in the United States and, I might add, in Vietnam also. Further, the man in subsequent lessons and drills finds doctors for his family, locates stores for buying food and clothing, takes care of children's schooling, and selects a church. This variation on American sex role stereotypes may well have been tailor-made for Vietnamese. Americans designing the programs seemed to believe that effort should be made to preserve the sanctity of Vietnamese family by reinforcing patriarchal values assumed by Americans to be central to it. While Americans may have been well-intentioned on this score, they were incapable of reinforcing any Vietnamese values simply because they understood very little about Vietnamese culture or society. This was clear in the sex role division of labor in the curriculum which removed women from the labor force.

Most immigrant women had been part of the money economy in their own country.[10] Rural women, especially if from farming or fishing families, earned money through either petty trade, crafts, or working with the family plot or in fishing. Their economic importance to the household increased as a result of the war. Inflation was rampant over the past twenty years in Vietnam, forcing women into the cash economy. Further, the war changed the occupational structure of Vietnam significantly, opening up women's work while obliterating men's work. Farmers who had been relocated through the various rural programs aimed at rooting out the Viet Cong found themselves unemployed or unemployable except as soldiers. Their pay and disability benefits if wounded were notoriously low. Thus, many became dependent on their wives and daughters who could find work as prostitutes, bar girls, laundresses, maids—all war-created work, much of which until recently was related to the American presence.

Not only had rural women, even as urban immigrants, become an economic mainstay of Vietnamese families, so too had urban middle class women. War time inflation had forced them into wage-earning occupations. Middle class Saigon families found they could not survive without women working. Mrs. H., an immigrant with five young children, had worked as a teletype operator, while her husband had been manager of a radio network in South Vietnam.[11] The mother of N.T.D., another immigrant, opened a knitting shop in Saigon to help make ends meet, even though her husband was a highly paid government official, two sons were army officers, one was a custom's inspector, and another son a university professor.[12] The removal of Vietnamese women from the work force as depicted in American English language curriculum did not represent Vietnamese values and culture. Neither, for that matter, did it represent values universally accepted by all Americans, nor were the values typical of American families. Rather, they represented American preconceptions of Vietnamese cultural norms, resulting in part from the isolation of the school and its curriculum from the Vietnamese being taught. If Vietnamese had no hand in designing the course, how could it possibly have stood as the guardian of Vietnamese cultural norms as school authorities claimed it was?

The English language curriculum of the school was by no means consistent in its stance regarding preserving Vietnamese culture or in what aspects of American life and society it would present to Vietnamese. The Survival English curriculum at Fort Indian Town Gap was replaced in September 1975, when the Pennsylvania State Department of Public Instruction received a contract to set up an adult school from HEW. With HEW funding came a new curriculum taught by a group of teachers trained to work with foreigners and unlike the volunteer teachers of the summer, less interested in Vietnamese culture and its preservation. By Fall, 26 classrooms had been set up to teach English in three-hour lessons, three times a day, five days a week to between twenty and forty adults in each class. The classes were segregated as to ability level, with illiterate non-English speaking (about 120 Vietnamese in all), literate non-English speaking, literate persons who spoke a little English, and those who were literate and had substantial English language backgrounds taught in separate classes.[13]

The curricular materials used were not designed specifically for Vietnamese; rather, they were developed for all non-English speakers be they Arab, Italian, Chinese, German, French or Vietnamese. The text used was the three-volume Macmillan 900 Series. Fluency in the language—reading, speaking, and writing—was the goal, and the program was a long-term rather than a short-term affair. It was not designed to teach minimal language skills rapidly so that within six weeks a person could purchase food, ask directions, fill out job applications, or seek medical care. It focused on building a proper foundation for total English mastery. Thus, the texts were full of words for colors, enumerations, weights, measures; for objects, for making requests, getting information; for talking about family, relatives, and marriage; for chatting with neighbors and friends; and for talking about the future and the weather. Eight weeks into the course (assuming that the classes covered one unit per week, which most did not), the text introduced vocabulary on sickness and health. Vocabulary related to occupations, finding jobs, shopping, and dealing with school or government authorities was totally lacking in the texts and was absent in all classrooms where teachers felt obliged to follow strictly the prescribed medicine.

The Macmillan 900 Series taught social and cultural roles in a manner quite different from the Survival English course. The series made no attempt to adjust Vietnamese to a new and lower occupational and social status than they had held in their own country. The world of work did not appear. The series presented a personal life world—gift-giving, relations with neighbors, work around the house, getting married, family celebrations, the weather, getting dressed—all within the context of suburban middle class existence. While men work, women keep their suburban homes, have coffee breaks with neighbors, shop for and attend weddings and showers, and bake cakes. Much of the series dwells on depicting private social life and thus strongly delineates sex roles and social roles, not occupational roles. For this reason women are more visible in the series than they were in the Survival English courses. In every lesson women bake cakes, shop, chat with neighbors, get advice on children's health habits, and prepare parties. Men's roles are delineated only in terms of social behavior, leisure, and tasks (mowing the lawn, hammering nails in the wall, watching TV). Language curriculum based on these texts presented only one American life style.

While textual materials, whether organized as in the Survival English or in the Macmillan 900 format, seemed to teach Vietnamese how to act and think as Americans while learning English, the conduct of class, for the most part, emphasized this even more, although in more subtle ways, for teachers elaborated on the texts, trying to make them more "useful" to Vietnamese. Two adult classes that I observed at Fort Indian Town Gap exemplified this. One was a class for illiterate Vietnamese with equal numbers of men and women in it—which was quite unusual for most classes in which the overwhelming majority of students were men. The women in the class were among the most traditional in the camp. They were from rural extended families—all had lacquered teeth and were dressed in the black peasant *ao ba-ba*; several had fished for a living. The teacher, a former anti-Vietnam war activist, discarded the Macmillan text because his students couldn't read. He opted instead to teach his own version of Survival English centering on learning the English terms for parts of the body and pains, things to eat, and jobs. His classes where chaotic. Students rarely understood him; he, in turn, did not understand what they said. His method consisted of pointing at objects and naming them, and pantomime. To introduce the word "chicken," for example, he clucked and crowed for the class. He then drilled them in the sentence "I want some chicken to eat." [14]

This class established occupational/social choices for Vietnamese that also were not necessarily consonant with Vietnamese culture or with the culture Vietnamese were to face once resettled in America. This was apparent when it came to teaching about jobs. The instructor began the lesson with the phrase "What kind of work do you do?" He then drew stick figures on the blackboard showing different kinds of work–ditch digging, selling, etc.—naming them all. After introducing phrases like "I am a ditch digger," "I am a mechanic," he asked each of his thirty or more students: "What kind of work do you do?" The first student to respond was a young man who replied "I rat-a-tat-tat," pointing his fingers. The teacher corrected him with "I work with my hands," which the man repeated. Next to recite was a middle aged woman. She made a motion that looked like casting nets. The teacher retorted: "I am a housewife." The woman looked puzzled. The teacher then drew a stick figure holding a broom inside a home on the blackboard and repeated "I am a housewife." She and the women sitting with her began a lively discussion in Vietnamese and started laughing. The teacher then drilled these former fisherwomen and petty traders as a group with the phrase, "I am a housewife." [15]

A second class at Fort Indian Town Gap for students whose English was reasonably good was more subtle in imposing American cultural norms. The class had pretenses of being bicultural. Each session was divided into three one-hour segments. The first segment used the Macmillan 900 Series. Students read both individually and in unison phrases and conversations. The teacher interrupted to correct their pronunciation or some of the text's cultural biases. One evening, after students read a conversation aloud in which Mr. James purchases a new house, the teacher stopped the class to explain to her students that the book gave the impression that all houses in the U. S. were new houses and that it was desirable to buy a new home.[16] Vietnamese, she pointed out, probably wouldn't be able to afford to buy a new house. This, she added, was not a tragedy since old houses were nice too. Besides, she ended, most people from Fort Indian Town Gap would live in apartments and would be happy in their new apartments. Her message was clear: you don't need a new house to be happy.

The second hour of class tried to bring a bit of Vietnam into the classroom. Tea and cookies were served, the ban against speaking Vietnamese was lifted, and students socialized with one another and with their teacher. The teacher frequently invited refugees who owned guitars to class so that students could sing folk songs and Vietnamese popular ballads.

The third hour of class was devoted to student compositions. The teacher had students write about themselves in English and read these essays aloud in class. Two to three essays per night were covered. These autobiographical sketches were often emotional outpourings of despair. In one class a student, a former sailor, told how sad he was to have left Vietnam and how he wanted to kill himself. He read this to a rather stone-faced audience of fellow Vietnamese who disapproved his venting of emotions before strangers. More typical of the essays was one that told how the particular student was born in Saigon, went to school, and is now in the United States. The teacher suggested he rewrite his essay to include more of his feelings about being in the United States. In this class, the teacher presupposed that Vietnamese needed to express their feelings in the same manner as Americans. The teacher stated this explicitly, as did the counselor of the adult school, both of whom thought Vietnamese reserve to be "unhealthy." [17] English class became a way for Vietnamese to learn not only how to speak English but also to deal with their emotional lives on American terms.

English language classes were, in short, classes that taught American culture as they taught pronunciation and vocabulary. The teachers and programs were divorced from Vietnamese culture. They were American-run, with Americans determining what Vietnamese needed to know to live in this country. Because of the controlled curriculum and format, Vietnamese had no say as to what they were being prepared for, what they would learn, or how they would learn.

English for Immigrants and Cultural Pluralism

English language instruction in the camps was, without question, designed to prepare Vietnamese to live in America. On one level, it taught language, a skill necessary to Vietnamese living in the United States. Without knowledge of English, Vietnamese could find neither employment nor lodging, and be unable to cope with American governmental and bureaucratic structures, or to any degree control their lives in this country.

Undeniably English instruction for Vietnamese was both necessary and desirable. There remains the issue concerning the extent to which the language training necessitates the teaching of new cultural norms. To some extent, one can ask whether different languages involve thought and cultural patterns so diverse as to make bicultural modes impossible. To some degree, one can assert that there is no way Vietnamese can be taught English without their undergoing cultural transformation, given the hierarchical structure of the Vietnamese language versus the lack of such structures in English (in English, for example, we address all persons, regardless of sex as "you." In Vietnamese there is no equivalent for "you." Rather, the term of address one uses depends on individuals' age, sex, and status vis-a-vis the speaker).

Contrasting linguistic structures and the possibilities they present for cultural pluralism lie outside the boundaries of this discussion. If Vietnamese and English as languages convey two distinct cultural/conceptual systems, then English instruction at Fort Indian Town Gap, irrespective of its curricular content, precludes cultural pluralism. This may well be. However, the *content* of English language instruction as developed by American authorities working with refugees allowed little room for cultural differences. The curricular intent was to prepare Vietnamese to live within an American world, not a Vietnamese world. Vietnamese, insofar as most school people were concerned, knew their own culture, how to act within it, and what to expect from it. Most school people believed or hoped that American and Vietnamese society and culture had enough in common that behavior appropriate to both would not conflict. There was no way Americans could confirm this simply because Vietnamese immigrants were not involved in selecting what schools would teach. This was deliberate, and professional educators argued that Vietnamese had little place in setting the level of English language instruction simply because they were not native speakers. Technical expertise in essence ruled out Vietnamese input. School personnel also felt that Vietnamese knew little about the United States and would be of no use in selecting the elements of American life and culture to be taught. The lack of a pre-existing Vietnamese-American community was often pointed to as the reason why Americans alone set curricular content.

The school programs thus taught Vietnamese what Americans thought they would need to know to live in an American context. This was the only context with which curriculum coordinators, teachers, and linguistic specialists were familiar. They described to adults the types of behavior expected of them at work, in the family, the neighborhood, the restaurant, with the M.D., etc. This was all within an American society, not a Vietnamese-American society, for in the English classes no Vietnamese-American community existed.

The programs did more than inform immigrants about life in America. They tried to mold Vietnamese expectations of their futures in this country. English language classes were placed where Vietnamese learned about a range of occupations which Americans assumed Vietnamese would accept as contrasted with work which Vietnamese had done. Many former government ministers, lawyers, journalists, and businessmen were told that they could support their families working as dishwashers, cooks, and nurses' aides. The courses viewed these occupations as "respectable."

The kind of life styles for which English language classes prepared Vietnamese were not necessarily consistent. Survival English introduced immigrant men to a work world at the lowest end of the occupational structure, and women to the life a housewife. Other textual materials like the Macmillan 900 Series oriented refugees to suburban life styles and to the leisure befitting the American middle class. The English language program contained contradictions. They presented what various Americans thought newcomers had to know about the country to live in it. There was little agreement among Americans about the aspects of American life which Vietnamese needed to know. Americans were not clear about their own culture. There simply was no way to resolve contradictions.

It may be that Americans cannot possibly hope to set the terms of adjustment for persons who are not yet part of American society and who may prefer to join a Vietnamese-American culture within the U.S. Other immigrant groups to the United States have done this, and there is little reason to expect that Vietnamese will be different. Since the camps have closed, Vietnamese, regardless of government resettlement policies directed toward preventing the establishment of a Vietnamese community in this country, have begun to develop such communities. They have formed cultural and social associations as a means of relating to American society as Vietnamese-Americans.[18] This perhaps serves as a commentary on American policy toward cultural pluralism. The adult classes denied the possibility of pluralism—Vietnamese adjustment was to be on American terms—but insofar as Vietnamese were concerned, such an adjustment was impossible, regardless of what Americans wished for them.

While it is easy to pinpoint the shortcomings of the English language programs designed for Vietnamese immigrants, it is far more difficult to present alternatives. What kind of programs allow for cultural pluralism and enable immigrants to function within a society. Once English is taught, to what extent is it necessary to teach immigrants American cultural and social modes? Did they need to learn to eat American food; to chatter amicably with American neighbors; to shop in American supermarkets; to spend their leisure in the same manner as Americans? Clearly immigrants need not adopt all aspects of American life in order to live and work in this country, and allowing Vietnamese participation in curriculum development may well have produced a different type of instructional program more suitable to cultural and material survival.

Notes*

*Research for this paper was made possible by grants from the University of Buffalo Foundation; State University of New York at Buffalo Institutional Funds; the SUNY Foundation; and the New York State Council for the Humanities.

[1] For a complete background of the refugees who came to the United States, see Gail P. Kelly, *From Vietnam to America: A Chronicle of the Vietnamese Immigration to the United States* (Boulder: Westview Press, in press), Chapter 3, Tables 1-4.

[2] Interview with N.V.S., Fort Indian Town Gap, Pennsylvania, September 14, 1975, Vietnamese Immigration Collection, SUNY/Buffalo Archives, Tape #3, Side 2.

[3] Joint Message Form, Senior Civilian Coordinator, Fort Indian Town Gap, Pennsylvania, to Secstate, Washington, D.C., IATF, Unclassified Subject: Weekly Profile, November 14, 1975 (Mimeo), Vietnamese Immigration Collection, SUNY/Buffalo Archives, Box 2 .

[4] Interview with K. A., Superintendent, School, Fort Indian Town Gap, Pennsylvania, September 29, 1975, Vietnamese Immigration Collection, SUNY/Buffalo Archives, Tape #9, Side 2; Tape #10, Side 1.

[5] See especially, Interview with P. H., Curriculum Coordinator, Adult Education Program, Day School, Fort Indian Town Gap, October 29, 1975, Vietnamese Immigration Collection, SUNY/Buffalo Archives, Tape #29, Side 1.

[6] The entire Survival English Curriculum can be found in the Vietnamese Immigration Collection, SUNY/Buffalo Archives, Box #3.

[7] Interview with P. H., op . cit.

[8] Survival English, Lesson 7, "Occupations."

[9] Survival English, Level II, Intermediate, Lesson 4, p. 4.

[10] My discussion of women's roles in Vietnam is based on the following sources: Ngo Vinh Long (ed.), *Vietnamese Women in Society and Revolution: The French Colonial Period* (Cambridge: Vietnam Resource Center, 1974); Arlene Eisen Bergman, *Women of Vietnam* (San Francisco: People's Press, 1974). Changes in women's roles are discussed to some extent in Tiziano Terzani, *Giai Phong: The Fall and Liberation of Saigon* (New York: St. Martin's Press, 1976) and in several interviews I conducted. See particularly, interview with M.C., Fort Indian Town Gap, November 20, 1975, Vietnamese Immigration Collection, SUNY/Buffalo Archives, Tape #42.

[11] The case of Mrs. H. can be found in Interview with E. R., New York City, September 21, 1976, Vietnamese Immigration Collection, SUNY/Buffalo Archives, Tape #77, Side l; Tape #78, Sides 1 and 2.

[12] Interview with N. T. D., Fort Indian Town Gap, Pennsylvania, October 30, 1975, Vietnamese Immigration Collection, SUNY/Buffalo Archives, Tapes #32 and 33.

[13] Interview with P.H., op. cit.

[14] I taped one of these classes and it is available at the Vietnamese Immigration Collection, SUNY/Buffalo Archives, Tape #34, Sides 1 and 2. The development of this class' curriculum is discussed in an Interview with D. M., Teacher, Adult Education School, Day Program, Fort Indian Town Gap, Vietnamese Immigration Collection, SUNY/Buffalo Archives, Tape #34, Side 2.

[15] Vietnamese Immigration Collection, SUNY/Buffalo Archives, Tape #34, Side 1.

[16] See English Language Services, Inc. *English 900, Books 1-3* (New York: Collier Macmillan, Inc., 1974, 16th Ed.) Book 3, Unit 5, p. 49. This class was also taped. See Vietnamese Immigration Collection, SUNY/Buffalo Archives, Tape #25, Sides 1 and 2; Tape #35, Sides 1 and 2.

[17] Interview with P.D., Teacher, and E.W., Counselor, Adult Education Night Program, Fort Indian Town Gap, November 20, 1975, Vietnamese Immigration Collection, SUNY/Buffalo Archives, Tape #43, Sides 1 and 2.

[18] For a more detailed discussion of this, see Gail P. Kelly, *From Vietnam to America,* op. cit., Chapter 8.

Research on the Education of Women in the Third World: Problems and Perspectives[†]

Research on the education of women in the Third World nations of Africa, Asia, and Latin America is relatively new. When I was a graduate student in the early 1970s being trained to do research on education in Asia and Africa, not one "classic" in the field ever mentioned women. I read tomes on social change, on modernization, on pedagogical theories and on colonialism and their relation to schooling. Women simply did not exist. It was presumed that education affected women in the same ways as it did men. If there was any difference between the sexes in the impact of schooling, such differences were thought insignificant. The lack of research on the education of women was underscored to me 3 years ago when I helped develop a course on the education of women in cross-national perspective and found very little for my students to read. Most research that was available was written since 1970; much of it was descriptive rather than analytic. To teach a course on women's education cross-nationally meant creating new materials and asking questions that research has only begun to address.

My experience in teaching about the education of women in the Third World made me painfully aware of the dilemmas and problems of conducting cross-national research on education and of the policy implications of the questions we care to address in conducting research. It became clear to me that research on seemingly technical issues like how individuals learn, could become a means of reproducing relations between the sexes that are found in our own society in the Third World. Additionally, it seemed that research on women could follow paths that are not particularly fruitful, in the sense that it might fail to explain to us the significance of education to the lives of women and point to ways that women could begin to control their own lives.

In this paper I will share some of my concerns about the direction of research on the education of women in the Third World. I have organized the paper around four questions that seem to me important to

---

[†]Presented at Feminist Scholarship 1978, University of Illinois Urbana—Champaign, March 2, 1978. Reprinted from *Women's Studies International Quarterly* Vol. I (1978) pp. 365-373, with kind permission from Elsevier Science Ltd, The Boulevard, Langford Lane, Kidlington OX5 1GB, UK.

feminist scholars. These questions relate to the issues that have been asked in the research available to us now. They are: 1. To what extent can the study of the learning process result in reproducing the relations between the sexes that are found in American society in the Third World? 2. Can one study the education of women in the Third World independent of developments in the entire school system? 3. What are the implications of studying the expectations of women who are educated? 4. What limitations arise from studying women's education and its relation to the work force within the boundaries of nation states? I will end the paper with suggestions for further research.

Sex Differences in Learning: Reproduction of Sex Discrimination in Schooling?

Studies of the learning process usually serve as a basis for setting instruction within the classroom and for determining the allocation of resources within a school system. How we study the learning process reflects in large measure our concerns about who should be educated and what they should be educated for. It should come as little surprise to those of us who are students of the Third World that little research of any kind on learning occurred before the mid-1960s. It is only recently that Third World nations emerged from colonial domination. Colonial powers had limited interest in schooling those they ruled. In most countries, like in Vietnam, it was not until 1938 that a single study on the learning process occurred.[1] In Africa, research of this nature began earlier. None of it dealt with sex differences in learning. Rather, its concern was whether non-Westerners could learn as efficiently and in the same way as Europeans. Much of it substantiated colonizers' prejudices about the ineducability of the colonized and served as a basis for limiting educational efforts.[2]

Since independence, research about the learning process has developed. Very little of it has focused on sex differences.[3] Research on sex differences in learning in the Third World, however, is currently underway, funded by an American foundation. It seeks to determine whether the differences in school achievement between the sexes found in Western industrialized societies can be found in the Third World. What are the implications of undertaking research of this nature which is in the main stream of educational research in the United States and Western Europe? Supposed sex differences in learning have in this country been the basis for developing distinct and inequitable education for women.[4] It has provided the rationale for denying women access to educational institutions. Insofar as education is tied to the economic and political structure, it has also been a means of keeping women in inferior positions. Can such research herald a similar phenomenon in the Third World? The potential certainly is there.

Over the past decades Third World governments have invested heavily in education, assuming that by so doing it would bring about economic development. The rapid expansion of schooling, accompanied by unprecedented increases in the number of girls attending school, has cost these countries up to twenty-five percent of their yearly budgets.[5]

Meanwhile their economies have stagnated. In the fiscal crises of recent years many Third World nations, encouraged by the World Bank and foreign advisers, have begun rethinking their educational policies and have tried to curb educational expansion. Achievement and sex difference research in education in such an atmosphere may become a way to deny women access to education. It can provide a rationale for policy and thereby engender, if not exacerbate, inequalities between the sexes. This will become all the more true in the industrial sectors of the economy if and when they expand, since formal education is a major means of obtaining work in it. If women are denied education, they will be confined to subsistence economy and work within the lower echelons of service and industrial sectors of the economy. If sex role difference research leads to greater differentiation in education by sex, then women also will be allocated into the roles in the economy that women in Western capitalist society hold.[6]

My point here is not to deny the validity of such research on its own terms; rather, it is to point out that cross-cultural research of this kind can become a means of reproducing relations as they are in one society in another society. It should serve to remind us that educational research does not function within a vacuum and has its social uses.

To What Extent Can We Study Women's Education as a Thing unto Itself?

What can we study when we choose to investigate the education of women in the Third World, especially if we choose to avoid asking those questions which lead to the possibility of re-creating the Third World in the image of the United States? One path research has taken has been to study the education of women. Much of this type of research has documented the growth and development of western-style schooling introduced by colonial governments in the nineteenth century. The research consists either of histories of institutions educating women or of statistical compendiums that trace increases in the number of schools serving women and the number of women being educated.[7]

What is the significance of such studies? Research that limits itself to the study of women's education can at best have misleading results. Such research assumes that increases in the number of women educated and increases in the number of years that women remain in school are intrinsically significant. It fails to refer to trends within the school system as a whole or the uses that can be made of education in the society. Underlying it is the notion that increases in education are necessarily related to women's status or that women's productivity in the economy will somehow increase as a result of education. Both assumptions are somewhat dubious.

The significance of the expansion of women's education cannot be gauged without reference to changes in educational systems. School systems in the Third World have been rapidly expanding. As they expand two things happen. First, education has become devalued as a means for obtaining employment. No longer is secondary education a guarantee of white collar employment. Second, a status hierarchy has developed among educational institutions. No longer is all secondary education of the same value, either for entering higher education or the job market. Rather, differentiation between schools has occurred that grants graduates of some schools privileges that graduates from other schools do not get.[8] In short, the type of distinction between inner city American high schools and Philips Exeter Academy exists in most Third World countries. Without attention to the overall devaluation of education as more people receive it and the emerging status hierarchy of schools, both public and private, we have no idea what the increases in the education of women represent. It could be that women, like Alice in Wonderland, have to run faster to stay in the same place.

Few studies have tried to look at women's education in light of the overall development of education and because of this have concluded that increases in education represent real advances in women's status and roles within society both vis-à-vis men as well as vis-à-vis uneducated women. In short, these studies tell us that more women get more education, but we do not know what it means. It could be that education changes individuals who are schooled and that its significance lies in how schools change women's lives. Research that dwells on what schools teach and their impact on individual women who attend them has yet to be done.

Underlying much of the interest in increases in women's education is the assumption that education leads to increased productivity of labor and that increased productivity of labor is the key to economic development.[9] In this light, interest in the increases in women's education merely reflects an interest in development as a whole and serves, at least for several scholars, as an indication of the pace of modernization.[10] Women are seen as unemployed in the subsistence economies of the Third World or, if employed, not especially productive. Education is seen as the route for employing women and raising their productivity.

These assumptions are questionable. In the first place, the literature has yet to show that education is necessarily related to increases in anyone's productivity.[11] Secondly, women are productive within agriculture in Third World nations. Third, it is not at all clear that women who are educated engage in productive labor. It may be that education for women, as for men, becomes the means of entering bureaucracies in the Third World rather than industry or any other productive labor. Insofar as schools are a means for women leaving subsistence agriculture, they may in fact help decrease women's place in productive labor.[12]

My point here is that until we know what schools teach and what women do with their schooling, we cannot make any assumptions about the significance of increasing the number of women attending school, nor can we make any claims about the impact of extending the time women attend school on women's roles in the society.

What Do We Know about Women Who Are Educated?

To know the impact of schooling, many have maintained, is to know what people expect from schooling and what they do as a result of being schooled. Research on the education of women in the Third World has dwelt extensively on what women expect from schooling by focusing primarily on career and marriage expectations.[13] These studies deal only tangentially, if at all, with how school curriculum, organization, and place of the school within the educational status hierarchy influence these aspirations. None of the studies we have to date have explained women's aspirations by referring to employment possibilities for women within the society or the role of women within the family. The findings of this research, done predominantly on African school girls, are clear: girls who go to school expect to enter a profession and get married and have children. Unlike their western sisters, they see little conflict between marriage and careers. In addition, most girls go to school because they perceive education as the only route to professional employment in the urban economy. Some attend school to find husbands of a suitable class and ethnic background.

The research on aspirations and expectations may tell us women's motives in entering the school system. However, it tells us little about the effect of the schools on women or explains why educated women feel the way they do. Do their expectations reflect the roles that women can or have assumed in the society? Can women do what they expect to do with their education? Do educated women enter the work force at the same level as women who are uneducated or men who are educated? What does education mean in the context of social life and changing economies and family structures? In short, the study of career and marriage expectations of school girls may inform us of what school girls want out of life. It does not tell us what they get out of life, why they have such expectations, the role of the schools in forming these expectations, or whether these expectations represent a change from roles women in the society have traditionally had.

The Study of Women's Education and the Work Force: a Commentary on the Need for Women-Centric Measures

Things outside the school are as important to study as things within them. So wrote Michael Sadler, an early scholar in comparative education.[14] Sadler argued that the significance of the school lay in its impact on the nation. Some current research has tried to assess the effect of women's education on the work force and the role of women within it. These studies are correlational in nature, looking at increases in the number of women being educated at various levels of schooling and correlating these increases with changes in women's participation in the national labor force.[15] The data used in such studies are derived from national censuses and from education reports. The information supplied consists of the number of men and women in agriculture, manufacturing, and service sectors of the economy over a given time period taken against educational statistics relating to the number of years of education individuals receive and the number of individuals attending school broken down by sex.

Underlying much of this research is modernization theory, which posits that as a nation develops the manufacturing sector of the economy expands. This is accompanied by increasing differentiation within the labor force and a heightened demand for skilled labor, which schools train. As modernization proceeds, the rate of employment of educated individuals, regardless of gender, is supposed to increase. Women are expected to enter the labor force in growing numbers. As women receive more education, they should enter manufacturing either as managers or as skilled labor.

What research has shown is that the expectations borne out of modernization theory work for men, but not necessarily for women. While the education of women has increased, it has not resulted in women entering industry at levels their increases in education would have led us to believe. Rather, women are leaving agriculture to enter either the lower echelons of the service sector of the economy, becoming domestic labor and in some instances prostitutes, or are marginally employed in industry. As Van Allen has pointed out, modernization has meant more dependency for women.[16]

Why this trend? Explanations are varied. Some clearly have argued that modernization has not occurred and since it hasn't, women have been pushed out of the few jobs that are available for the educated and placed either out of work or into the lowest paying jobs within the economy.[17] This type of explanation implies that if modernization did occur, then the impact of education on women would be quite different vis-à-vis the work force. Such an analysis, however, begs the issue of whether in modernized countries education's impact has been any different than what has been noted in countries in which modernization has not taken place. For this reason, others have argued that the effect is due to the introduction of capitalism which reproduces a given set of relations between the sexes which the relative position of men and women in the Third World work force reflects. Education, they argue, is not a mediating factor.[18]

It is not my desire here to enter the debates and come up with a definitive explanation for a trend clearly identified in the research. However, I wish to point out some of the difficulties in making such statements about the relation between the education of women and the composition of the work force. These difficulties have to do with how one analyzes changes in women's roles in the work force and with the geographic boundaries within which analyses have taken place.

All the research we have to date documenting the changes in women's participation in the labor force consists of correlating population characteristics that have traditionally been used to study men. Such indicators—region, race, ethnicity, and sometimes social class origins—are presumed to be the only things that influence entry into the work force. They may well be the only factors that affect entry into the work force if one studies men. However, it is questionable that they are the only things that affect women.[19] To what extent does the structure of the family affect women and where they work? Would not a change in women's place in the work force be contingent not only on the number of women entering the work force in various sectors of the economy, but also on the types of women entering the work force? Are more married women withdrawing from economic activity? Are women with young children entering the economy or leaving it? Before we can make any statements about the relation between industrialization, the spread of capitalism, and women's position within the society, we need to develop indicators that will be sensitive to characteristics of women that influence their work. In short, only with the development of women-centric measures can we begin to assess changes in the lives and roles of women and understand if or how institutions like schools influence such changes.

A second problem with research on women's education and its relation to work force changes is the extent to which we can assess the impact of schooling through correlational data. Scholarship to date has tried to relate increases in the number of women within certain sectors of the economy and increases in the number of women educated, finding the two to have little relationship. It has not proceeded from a study of women who are educated, tracing their work and family lives. It could be that increases in the number of women in the work force at lower echelons of manufacturing and service industries reflect young single women entering the work force at an earlier age than their contemporaries who are in school until age 19 or 25. Third World populations are young; what may seem a trend now may not reflect the impact or lack of impact of education; it may reflect instead the problems of doing correlational research that does not take into account the ages of individuals at work. To assess the relation of education to the work force for women, we need to study educated women, something which scholarship has yet to do.

The research that we have on women, education, and the work force are for the most part one nation studies or studies which compare the extension of education for women and changes in the work force across several Third World nations. Comparisons of this sort have been used to show that the phenomena observed are characteristic of all nations as they develop.[20] The few comparative studies we have, for example, are of women in the Ivory Coast or the Cameroons or Chile and selected Middle Eastern countries. We have no idea of women's education and its impact on the work force in revolutionary socialist societies since no research of this nature has been done. We can only guess that what we have observed in non-socialist Third World societies results from modernization or the spread of capitalism until we compare these findings with those analyses of education and the work force in societies like China and Cuba.

Lack of comparative analysis between revolutionary and non-revolutionary Third World countries is not the only limitation of the research done to date on women's education and the work force. There have been no comparisons on whether the effects noted in Third World countries are found in the advanced industrial societies which in most instances control Third World economies. Most of the research has presumed that the factors influencing the roles of women and the use of education for women are to be found within the boundaries of a nation-state. Most deny the impact of neo-colonialism and the international market. The extent to which the economies of Third World nations are controlled by capitalists from the industrialized nations of Western Europe and the United States has been ignored in the literature.[21] Its importance cannot be understated, since it is entirely possible that the extent to which women can use educational institutions to gain control of their lives is dependent on the degree to which patriarchal institutions operating outside of the nation state allow women to use institutions in this manner. In other words, it may be that education's impact on women and their role in the society is tied to the relationship that education has to women's role in advanced capitalist societies which control the Third World. In this case, it is important to know whether the impact of the feminist movement in changing schooling and its uses in countries like the United States has any relation to changing the role of the schools for women in the Third World. Comparative studies can begin to deal with these questions.

The Study of Women and Feminist Scholarship

This review of research has raised more questions than it has answered about the education of women in the Third World. Throughout the review I have emphasized what we do not know rather than what we do know. If our knowledge in this area is sparse, it is because research on the education of women in the Third World has only recently begun. The kinds of questions research has addressed reflect the newness of the field. The questions that have been studied—and not studied—also are a reflection of the differences between the study of the education of women and feminist scholarship on the education of women. We will always have studies of women's education. The result of such research may have little to do with the emancipation of women or bettering women's lives. The study of women's education in the Third World, as I have pointed out, can mean substantiating research paradigms like modernization theory that do not necessarily relate to changing women's lives. The study of women can also be used to deny women education opportunities by finding supposed sex differences that make women "bad risks" in the school system.

Feminist scholarship, however, is distinguishable from the scholarship on women in its goals, its concerns, and in the questions that it asks, all of which have to do with changing women's lives and freeing women from oppression. For feminist scholars of education in the Third World, our goal is to find ways in which schools can be made a force to better women's lives. Our task is to find out what types of changes can be made in the schools to make a difference in women's lives. We can't know the effect of changing the numbers of women going to school, or the results of curricular innovations, until we develop ways we can assess those changes. The first step is to develop women-centric measures—measures that will be sensitive to changes in women's lives. This is no easy task, but it is essential before we can further understand education's, or any other institution's, impact on women.

Notes*

[1] In Vietnam the only articles published in the four pedagogical journals about learning appeared in 1938 in a series entitled "Inquiry into the Child," see "Enquête sur l'Enfant," *Bulletin General de l'Instruction Publique,* 18e Anneé, Nos. 1, 2, 3, 4, 5, 6 (June 1938-January 1939). Educational research and teacher training in colonial Vietnam are discussed in Gail P. Kelly, Franco-Vietnamese Schools, 1918-1938, Unpublished Ph.D. Dissertation, University of Wisconsin, 1975, especially pp. 230-4.

[2] Judith Evans, *Children in Africa: A Review of Psychological Research.* Teachers College Press, New York, 1970; Charles V. Lyons, *To Wash an Aethiop White.* Teachers College Press, New York, 1976.

[3] Evans, *op. cit.;* See also Millie Almy, *et al., Studying School Children in Uganda.* Teachers College Press, New York, 1970; John Gay and Michael Cole, *The New Mathematics and an Old Culture.* Holt, Rinehart & Winston, New York, 1970.

[4] Mabel Newcomer, *A Century of Higher Education for American Women.* Harper, New York, 1959; Merle Curti, *The Social Ideas of American Educators.* Littlefield, Adams & Co., Totowa, New Jersey, 1966, pp. 169-93; Charles Lyons, "The Colonial Mentality: Assessments of the Intelligence of Blacks and of Women in 19th Century America," in P. G. Altbach and G. P. Kelly, *Education and Colonialism.* Longmans, New York, 1978, pp. 181-206.

[5] See Ernest Stabkr, *Education Since Uhuru.* Wesleyan University Press, Middletown, Connecticut, 1969; David Abernethy, *The Political Dilemma of Popular Education: An African Case.* Stanford University Press, Stanford, California, 1969.

[6] This is the general tenor of research on educational expansion and the work force. See Elsa Chaney and Marianne Schmink, "Women and Modernization: Access to Tools," in June Nash and Helen I. Safa, *Sex and Class in Latin America.* Praeger, New York, 1975, pp. 160-82; Judith Van Allen, "African Women, Modernization and National Liberation," in Lynne B. Iglitzin and Ruth Ross, *Women in the World: A Comparative Study.* Clio Books, Stanford, California, 1976, pp. 25-54.

[7] See, for example, Ida Bell Lewis, *The Education of Girls in China.* Teachers College Press, New York, 1919; Marie Eliou, "Scolarisation et Promotion Feminines en Afrique Francophone" (Côte d'Ivoire, Haute-Volta, Senegal), *International Review of Education,* Vol. 19, No. I (1973) pp. 30-46; Jacqueline Chaubaud, *The Education and Advancement of Women.* UNESCO, Paris, 1970; UNESCO, *Women and Education.* UNESCO, Paris, 1953; Mary Ann Alkins

Pilain, *Women, Education and Equality: A Decade of Experiment*. UNESCO Press, Paris, 1975; Sandra Carol, The women of Chile and education for a contemporary society: a study of Chilean women, their history and present status and the new demands of a society in transition. Unpublished Ph.D., Brandeis University, 1973.

[8] Differentiation within the school system is well documented. See, for example, Philip Foster, *Education and Social Change in Ghana*. University of Chicago Press, Chicago, 1965; Abernethy, *op. cit.*, Joseph P. Farrell, "The Structural Differentiation of Developing Educational Systems: a Latin American Comparison," *Comparative Education Review*, Vol. 13, No. 3 (October 1969), pp. 294-311.

[9] See, for example, W. Arthur Lewis, "Economic Development with Unlimited Supplies of Labour," in A. N. Agarwala and S. P. Singh, *The Economics of Underdevelopment*. Oxford University Press, New York, 1963, pp. 400-50.

[10] See Don Adams, "The Study of Education and Social Development," *Comparative Education Review*, Vol. 9, No. 3 (October 1965), pp. 258-69; William H. Friedland, "A Sociological Approach to Modernization," in Morse *et al.*, *Modernization by Design: Social Change in the Twentieth Century*. The Free Press, Glencoe, 1969, pp. 31-84.

[11] W. G. Bowen, "Assessing the Economic Contribution of Education," in M. Blaug (ed.), *Economics of Education, 1*. Penguin, Baltimore, 1965; Nicholas Georgescu-Roegen, "Economics and Educational Development," *Journal of Educational Finance*, Vol. 2 (Summer 1976), pp. 1-15.

[12] Ester Boserup, *Women's Role in Economic Development*. St. Martin's Press, New York, 1970. See also Kenneth Little, *African Women in Towns: An Aspect of Africa's Social Revolution*. Cambridge University Press, 1973. This is also implied in several studies of women and the work force. See especially Norma S. Chinchilla, "Industrialization, Monopoly Capitalism, and Women's Work in Guatemala," *Signs*, Vol. 3, No. 1 (Autumn 1977), pp. 38-56; Glaura Vasques de Miranda, "Women's Labor Force Participation in a Developing Society," *Signs*, Vol. 3, No. I (Autumn 1977), pp. 261-74.

[13] Typical of such research is Rhoda L. Goldstein, *Indian Women in Transition: A Bangalore Case Study*. Scarecrow Press, Metuchen, New Jersey, 1972; Erma Muckelhirn, *Secondary Education and Girls in Western Nigeria*. University of Michigan School of Education, Ann Arbor, 1966; Marjorie Mbilinyi, *The Education of Girls in Tanzania*. Dar Es Salaam, University College, 1969; Vandra Maseman, The education of girls in a West African boarding school, Unpublished Ph.D. Dissertation, University of Toronto, 1975.

[14] Michael Sadler, "How Far Can We Learn Anything of Practical Value from the Study of Foreign Systems of Education?" reprinted in the *Comparative Education Review*, Vol. 7 (February 1964), pp. 307-14.

[15] See especially Remi Clignet, "Social Change and Sexual Differentiation in the Camerouns and Ivory Coast," *Signs*, Vol. 3, No. 1 (Autumn 1977), pp. 244-60; Nadia Haggag Yousseff; *Women and Work in Developing Societies*. University of California, Institute of International Studies, Berkeley, 1974; Barry N. Heyman, Urbanization and the status of women in Peru. Unpublished Ph.D. Dissertation, University of Wisconsin, 1974.

[16] Judith van Allen, "Modernization Means More Dependency," *The Center Magazine*. May/June 1974, pp. 60-7. See also Little, *op. cit.*; Chinchilla, *op. cit.*

[17] Chinchilla, *op. cit.*

[18] *Ibid.;* see also Clignet, *op. cit.*

[19] Several scholars have attempted to develop women-centric indicators of change. See Batya Weinbaum, "Women in Transition to Socialism: Perspectives on the Chinese Case," The *Review of Radical Political Economists*, Vol. 8, No. 1 (Spring 1976), pp. 3-58.

[20] Clignet, *op. cit.*; Yousseff, *op. cit.*

[21] See, for example, Janes D. Cockcroft, Andre Gunder Frank and Dale L. Johnson, *Dependence and Underdevelopment*. Anchor Books, Garden City, New York, 1972.

Acknowledgments—I wish to thank David Kelly, Elizabeth Kennedy, Carolyn Korsmeyer, Beverly Lindsay, Ann Nihlen, Maxine Seller, Lois Weis, and Roger Woock for their comments on an earlier draft of this paper.

Schooling and the Reproduction of Patriarchy: Unequal Workloads, Unequal Rewards[†]

Gail P. Kelly and Ann S. Nihlen

Reproduction theorists assert that the schools reinforce the division of labor in the society by maintaining class, race and gender inequalities. The argument states that schools do not mediate or seek to change the structures of society or the characteristics of individuals who occupy positions of wealth, status and power. The schools are static because they are a microcosm of the society, rather than an agent for change as some theorists maintain.

While there is a large literature documenting the schools' roles in the reproduction of inequality, for the most part, it has not dealt systematically with the issue of gender (Frazier and Sadker 1973; Sexton 1976; Stacy *et al.* 1974). Research on women's schooling sees a direct relation between women's education and the status of women, and seeks to reform school practices in the hope that the schools could be made a force for equality. Yet that literature has been extremely vague concerning several issues. First and foremost it has glossed over the nature of sex inequality and tended to see it unidimensionally in terms of the paid labor force (MacDonald 1980b). It has neglected issues of "private (or "domestic") life"—notably marriage and child-bearing and raising—and how it affects sexual inequality. Much of our evaluation of the school's role in reproduction of the division of labor within the society is framed in terms of wage and workforce status of women versus men. By so doing we deny the impact of the family in patriarchal society where women, regardless of class, ethnicity and race, and their wage and status, retain major responsibility for household chores and for bearing and raising children, which men do not.[1] Given this, an evaluation of the school's role in reproduction of the sex division of labor cannot proceed on the basis of whether the schools prepare women for the same "public" or work force roles as men.

[†]Reprinted with permission. Gail Kelly and Ann Nihlen from *Cultural and Economic Reproduction in Education.* Edited by Michael Apple. London: Routledge & Kegan Paul, 1982; and with the agreement of Ann Nihlen.

Rather, it must also deal with forms of inequality in terms of responsibility for domestic life. Thus, inequality can be seen not only in terms of public life, but in terms of the burdens of women versus men in private life. Women could conceivably have wage and status equity with men within the workforce, but inequality remains if women still work their job in the household.

A second problem which the literature has yet to address, which we believe crucial, relates to what students are taught as opposed to what students learn or choose to learn. Research on women's education, as we will show in this essay, has always presumed that (1), the schools impart a unitary message regarding appropriate division of labor between the sexes and (2), that whatever the schools teach, students learn. Many studies have taken curriculum or an analysis of staffing patterns of the school as the sum total of school knowledge. They have not asked whether contradictory messages exist within the school environment to be considered separately as formal and informal (or "hidden") curriculum. In addition, the presumption of student as passive agent persists without any understanding that students may not learn what schools teach by choice, or may filter knowledge and use it to their own advantage.[2] The circumstances under which "resistance" occurs and when it becomes significant in countering attempts of the schools is an area relatively untouched by the literature on women's schooling. It is one that needs to be developed, for there have been major changes in women's public and private lives historically which could not be explained if we presumed female students did not renegotiate the messages of the schools.

This essay reviews the evidence linking the schools to the reproduction of the sex role division of labor within U.S. society. The essay begins with a discussion of the nature of the sex role division of labor in the United States in public and private life. It then turns to an analysis of the schools and evidence linking them to this division of labor. Finally, we point to new ways of thinking about women's education and its significance for future research.

The Nature of Sex Inequality

Inequality between the sexes at its simplest level consists of separate spheres of work which result in differences in status, wealth and power. Much of it derives from the distinction between the value of work in private (or domestic) and public domains. The origins of this distinction are unknown; scholars have documented its intensification with the development of capitalism and industrialization, but have also shown that, in many socialist nations, notably the Soviet Union and China, the same distinctions and the inequalities implicit in them are maintained (Croll 1978; DuBois *et al.*, in press; Lapidus 1979; Rosaldo 1974; Sacks 1974; Weinbaum 1976).

What we know to be true is that industrialization means that the workplace is separated from the household and that production for surplus becomes differentiated from production for use value, although one does not extinguish the other. Put more simply, income generation is placed outside the family, yet the family remains as a social and economic unit dependent on the work performed both inside and outside the home. As industrialization increases, the separation of household from income generation becomes more intense as does the necessity for wage labor. The family as a unit is charged predominantly with reproduction (or procreation), and child-rearing and the division of labor becomes such that women, by and large, become responsible for the household and child-rearing dependent on income earned outside the home by men. In most societies this is structurally imposed; it is not a "natural" phenomenon, and it is directly related to the wage structure for males. Employers can pay men less if unpaid females labor in the household to prepare food, clean, clothe, and rear the children.[3]

Sex role divisions of labor within the society are not necessarily contingent on women versus men confined to domestic versus public spheres, but rather on primary responsibility within one sphere versus another. Women's work is to maintain the home and the family, bear and rear the child, buy, clean, and prepare the food, "make life beautiful," and to nurture man and child (DuBois *et al.:* chapter 3). Men's primary responsibility is work outside the home in wage labor. These definitions of sex role divisions are all but idealized; women's work has rarely been confined to the domestic sphere even if it is the female's prime responsibility.

The sex role division of labor relates not only to the division of labor between public and private, but also to the division of labor within public life. Women have always, and increasingly, worked outside the home at wage labor while retaining their jobs in the domestic sphere. Inequality between the sexes, then, can be seen as the double job wherein women work two full-time loads, while men do not.[4]

The division of labor between the sexes is also a division of labor that manifests itself in inequalities in wage labor. While approximately 45 percent of women in the U.S. are active in the American workforce— and this figure increases yearly, and varies as to whether women are working-class, minority, or white middle-class—women are in inferior positions to men in income-generation and status. Women earn less than 56 percent of male income, regardless of job categories; they are concentrated in the lowest paying jobs in both service and industrial sectors of the economy; they are segregated into occupations which permit very little upward mobility; and they are concentrated in the "marginal" areas of the workforce (Chafe 1972; Smuts 1971). Women are, in short, not stratified in the workforce as are men. A few statistics will make this clearer.

In 1972 less than 7 percent of all clerical workers were male while 25 percent of minority and 36 percent of white women worked at such jobs. Fifteen percent of white men (and 9 percent of minority males) were managers and administrators versus 2 percent of minority and 5 percent of white women. In blue-collar jobs, 16 percent of minority and 21 percent of white men were employed as skilled workers versus 1 percent of women, both white and minority. Thirty-seven percent of minority and 19 percent of white women were employed as service workers while only 15 percent of minority and 7 percent of white men held similar jobs (Allen 1979: 676-7).

The pattern of employment reflects a hierarchy wherein women are subordinate to men in income and status, compounded by race. Black men are in a subordinate position to white men, white women to men and black and minority women subordinate to white women and all men.

Workforce status inequality for women is a function both of discriminatory practices imposed by employers and the sex role division of labor that places prime responsibility of the family and child-rearing on women. Marriage and children tend to drive women out of the workforce or to reduce their wage labor to less than full time (Standing 1976). Working class and minority women stand as an exception, poverty drives women into the workforce regardless of marriage, age and number of children. As of 1974, of the 35.8 million women in the U.S. workforce, 14.8 million were single, either having never married, or having been divorced or widowed and 21 million were married. The workforce participation rates of women with children show the effects of child-rearing. About 10.5 million women in the workforce have children, of these 6.5 million have children between the age of 6 and 17; only 4 million have children under the age of 6 (U.S. Department of Labor 1975). Because of the structure of work and the family within the society, women's "double burden," coupled with discrimination, tends to produce both workforce status and wage inequalities between men and women (Seccombe, in press).

When one looks at education and the reproduction of inequality within the society there are several questions that need to be asked. First, to what extent does education normalize the separation of prime responsibility in public and private domains that we have discussed here? Does the school, through formal and informal instruction, seek consistently to portray domestic life as the female domain, with work outside the household as secondary, and the public domain as the male preserve? Second, does the school system provide ideological rationales for women's lesser status and income-producing role within the workforce? And, does it do so for all women, regardless of class, race and ethnicity? Third, how does the school prepare women for the workforce? Is the pattern of women's income and occupations a function of the double burden which the schools either normalize or mitigate, or is it a function of the schools channeling women away from occupational preparation that would qualify women for jobs within the workforce of higher status and income? These sets of questions will allow us to see if the schools reinforce the private/public division of labor within the society or seek to equalize male/female domestic roles which account in large part for the pattern of sex inequality. They will also allow us to see whether the schools seek to provide women with qualifications equal to those of men which might conceivably, at least for single women, women heads of households, or women with grown children, produce a stratification pattern equal to that of men if workforce discrimination were broken? Finally, and related to this last question, do schools, outside of occupational preparation, encourage or discourage women's resistance to the sex role division of labor? This latter question is particularly important, given the fact that historically women have sought, and sometimes have succeeded in breaking the pattern which we have described here. The current sex role division of labor, at least in the workforce, is not what it has always been. In the 1920s, the 1940s and since the 1960s women have resisted and to some extent renegotiated their roles both within domestic and public life (Chafe 1972). Has this been a school produced phenomenon or a phenomenon that functions independent of, or despite, education?

Schooling and Sexual Inequality

School knowledge consists of both formal and informal curriculum. The formal curriculum is the knowledge transmitted through textbooks and curriculum guides, certified by school examinations. The informal curriculum, sometimes referred to as the "hidden" curriculum, is not always sanctioned by examination or congruent with the knowledge prescribed by the formal curriculum. Rather, it is the "noise" of the school—the messages implicit in the authority structure of the school, its staffing patterns, and the ways in which the curriculum is transmitted, and the systems of rewards and "correct" behavior. In the discussion which follows, we will focus on both the "hidden" and formal curricula of the schools, beginning first with the formal sex role division of labor in the schools in authority and staffing patterns and then the formal curriculum and the ways it is transmitted. Finally, we will turn to the issue of whether the messages transmitted in the school, however consistent or inconsistent they may be, are internalized by female students.

Authority Patterns and Staffing

The schools in the U.S. are staffed predominantly by women. Superficially, one could argue that the high visibility of women in the school system stands as encouragement for girls to enter the workforce. While this may well be the case, and explains why so many girls see teaching as a desirable occupation, entry into paid labor is not necessarily the key to ending sex inequalities. As we pointed out earlier, the nature of sex inequality has to do with not only women's roles in public life, but also the responsibility for domestic life and its relation to inequality.

School authority patterns represent a microcosm of the relative status of women in the workforce, despite the large number of women on school staffs. The school system places males in positions of authority and women in subordinate roles, and it does this regardless of qualification. A few statistics will illustrate this. In the early 1970s, out of 14,379 district superintendents, 90 were female; 55 out of 731 associate superintendents were women; and women accounted for 126 out of 4,402 assistant superintendents. Women fared better as administrative assistants to superintendents where they numbered 356 out of a total 2,345 persons. This is the case despite the fact that women hold over 20 percent of doctoral degrees of individuals employed at this level (Estler 1975: 364-5).

The pattern of male authority over females holds in each school in the United States where 67.2 percent of all teachers are women, yet women are less than 16 percent of all principals or assistant principals. These figures mask the status and wage hierarchies of education institutions. Female principals are elementary school principals. Twenty percent of all elementary school principals are women; less than 7 percent of middle school and secondary school principals are female (Estler 1975).

The underrepresentation of women in positions of authority in public school is relatively new, for in 1928 women were 55 percent of elementary school principals (Estler 1975). The pattern does mirror women's place in the contemporary workforce. In the school system women are segregated into the lowest status jobs. The higher the level of education the fewer the number of women in administrative and teaching positions. Women, when in positions of authority, supervise, for the most part, women rather than men. This reflects the vertical segregation of the American workforce where the few women in management positions are found in predominantly female occupations.

Women, as classroom teachers, dominate the elementary school where they constitute close to 90 percent of the teaching force (Frazier and Sadker 1973; Simpson 1974). In the junior and senior high schools the percentage of women teachers declines. The more adult the student becomes and the closer he or she is to entering the workforce, the less visible women workers become. This pattern is often a product of conscious hiring practices of school districts (Estler 1975: 364).

In higher education the dominance of male over female intensifies. Less than 3 percent of all top-level college and university administrators in 1972 were women (versus 11 percent in 1969/70). Most women college presidents are presidents of all or predominantly female institutions. Women form but 22 percent of the faculties of institutions of higher education. They are concentrated in the lower ranks of instructional staffs and underrepresented in the higher ranks. The lower the status of the institution (e.g., two-year colleges versus four-year colleges versus universities), the greater the number of women administrators, women faculty, and women full professors (Kilson 1976; Sexton 1976: 124). These statistics tell a simple tale: schools mirror gender inequalities in status and income of the workforce at large.

The schools perhaps may also reflect inequality which has less to do with status wage differentials and positions of authority in the workforce. Adult work in the school may also promote the separation of public and private domains and the concept that while women may work, work for a wage is secondary to them if they are married or have children. They may also imply that in order to work women cannot be married and have families. There are, to our knowledge, almost no studies which deal with the characteristics of women school staffs beyond those depicting educational backgrounds, income and positions within the hierarchy. We do not know whether, for example, the few women who are in positions of authority are women who are single or are married with small children. If they are single, this may serve to remind all that women can choose to work for a wage, but that choice involves forsaking marriage and children, which it does not for men. If women in positions of authority are single and childless and women in subordinate positions are not, then the school's messages may be even stronger.

Another dimension that has yet to be examined is the extent to which school authority patterns and personnel policies preclude "motherhood." School systems have traditionally enforced leaves for pregnant women, in some districts from the moment a woman begins to "show." This normalizes the concept that maternity and work are incompatible.

Systematic research on female teachers and staff and the extent to which messages normalizing inequality either in terms of the primacy of the domestic domain for women versus men or the choice between family and women's work is sorely needed.

Subject Matter Staff Segregation

One dimension of school staffing patterns that relates to inequality within public life is the segregation of teaching staffs by subject matter, which occurs predominantly in post-primary education and which both normalizes occupational segregation and transmits messages about "appropriate" knowledge for women versus men.

In the U.S. school system women are teachers of some subjects and not others (Simpson 1974). They are, by and large, concentrated in language arts, foreign languages, and, to a lesser extent, social studies. They become rare in mathematics and the sciences (except for biology). In higher education women constitute less than 1.9 percent of the Business faculties; 0.4 percent of Engineering teachers, 4.3 percent of teachers of Physical Sciences, Mathematics and Computer Science faculties. They are, however, 20.6 percent of teaching faculties in Education and 10.2 percent in Health Sciences (concentrated in nursing and health-related professions) (Sexton 1976: 124).

The concentration of female teaching staffs in these fields parallels women's workforce participation patterns. The subjects taught predominantly by female teachers correspond to preparation for occupations in which women are represented. Conversely, the absence of women in business administration, the sciences and mathematics related fields corresponds with the low number of female teachers in them. The gender of a teacher, when sex-segregated by subject-area, may well tell students that particular subject matter is legitimate knowledge for one sex, rather than both sexes.

The authority and staffing patterns of the school, in sum, represent the type of inequality between the sexes that exists in the workforce in terms of status and income distribution. Women are segregated into lower, less prestigious positions and into specific institutions (the primary school) and specific subject areas mirroring the vertical and horizontal segregation in the workforce. This is well documented. What we do not know is the extent to which the school staffing patterns transmit messages about the division of labor between the sexes in domestic and public spheres. Does the staffing pattern promote domestic life as primary to women who work and not primary to men who work? Does it normalize the concept of women's double job? By virtue of which women are placed in positions of authority does the school "teach" all that women who wish to succeed in work must not marry or have children—a choice which men, given the structure of work and the family, do not have to make?

Formal Curriculum

A formal curriculum does not represent all "school knowledge," but it does represent what schools purport to teach. Who the knowledge is distributed to is yet another question; here we will treat solely sex differentiation within curricular materials, taking textbooks as our example. We will ask whether the messages transmitted in the formal curriculum of the school are similar to those reflected in the authority structure and staffing patterns. Does the formal curriculum reinforce the primacy of the domestic sphere for women? Does it legitimate occupational segregation and the position of women in the workforce? Does it present women's role in public life as opposed to the ability to marry and have children?

There have been numerous analyses of school textbooks, predominantly beginning reading primers and children's literature.[5] They show that, for the most part, women are ignored in the curricular materials. Women either do not exist or, if they exist, they are confined to domestic life, although this varies by grade level. Primary school texts, more often than secondary and college level books, depict women. In some, 25 percent of textual space and illustrations contain females (Weitzman *et al.* 1972). Women, however, are background figures and not central to the numerous readings. Adult women are almost never depicted outside the house; they also engage predominantly in domestic chores—cleaning, cooking, sewing, nurturing. In some illustrations women are shown cooking dinner while the male (father) sits in an easy chair smoking his pipe and reading the newspaper. In the primary texts few women work outside the home for a wage. The few who do are in nursing, teaching or secretarial jobs. Interestingly enough, those who work are not portrayed either as married or having children.

While women are present in elementary primers, albeit in a minority, they are scarcer in secondary and college level books. Treckler, who studied secondary school history texts found that in the rare instances in which they mentioned women, they deliberately distorted women despite the advancements in knowledge about women's history since the mid 1960s (Treckler 1973). Women were sidelined to roles of pioneer wife, sewer of flags, social worker, nurse, presidential helpmates and the like. The women's suffrage movement, women's trade unionism, etc. were either ignored or relegated to one line. Women simply did not shape history; rather, Treckler points out, they simply were present and their contributions were ancillary to men's and domestic in nature.

The rigid stereotyping in the texts is well documented as is their language, which invariably uses the generic "he" (which also appears on school report cards which read: "The information contained in this report card will show you how well your child is succeeding with *his* school work") (Buffalo, New York, Public Schools 1980). The use of male pronouns and nouns conveys the message that only males act or are important; "she" is not. This point is made cogently by the studies of mathematics texts where "he" always solves the problem (Kepner and Koehn 1977; Jay and Schminke 1975).

The studies of school texts underscore the presence of curricular messages that deny women major roles in public life and emphasize the primacy of women in the domestic domain. Current research has suggested that these messages change by level of education, but it has not documented how thoroughly. Nor has attention been paid to whether they are consistent across all subject matter. In addition, we do not know whether the same images are conveyed in the multitude of workbooks and dittoed handouts used in the classroom.

While current school texts reinforce inequality between the sexes, their messages differ from those transmitted by school staffing patterns and authority structures in which women are actively involved in work outside the home. The texts deny such roles, but that denial is one which legitimates women's secondary status in public life and within the school system. Women are subordinate to men in society because, according to the texts, public life is "unnatural" for women. The texts also contain implicit rationalization of occupational segregation within the labor force. They depict "traits" of women appropriate to certain occupational roles. For example, women are portrayed as nurturing, passive and dependent. Nurses, elementary school teachers and secretaries are considered good workers then they embody these characteristics. Finally, the texts normalize the double job for women. Women may work for a wage (which the texts rarely mention), but they must take primary responsibility for rearing children, cooking and maintaining the home.

Channeling and Counseling

Formal instruction and hiring practices are not the only elements in the schools that correspond with inequality between male and female in society. Counseling procedures also do. There is an extensive literature which points to vocational testing and guidance procedures as active agents in sex role reproduction.[6] Until recently, the Strang Vocational Inventory had pink and blue forms, proposing different ranges of occupations for males and females. Females, for example, could choose to be stewardesses and nowhere could indicate preferences to become pilots, engineers or mechanics. They could opt to be "businessmen" though. On the basis of these tests high school counselors have been accused of actively channeling girls into educational programs that prepare girls only for such occupational roles.

The recently developed Vocational Awareness programs for elementary schools similarly channel men and women. These programs do not counsel or test students; rather, they expose students to the world of work through visits to local factories and businesses. This "reality of work" is an object lesson of male/female roles. No longer does the school feel the need to mediate, it merely exposes students to patriarchal relations in work without comment. The texts normalize separate and unequal relations between the sexes by omission and commission regardless of reality; counseling programs, in the attempt to be realistic, normalize these relations by bringing students to witness them.

Formalized curriculum and programs, school staffing patterns and authority structures as well as counseling are easily identifiable elements in the school. More subtle and perhaps more critical are the ways in which knowledge is transmitted in the classroom where it is distributed through regularities in classroom interactions. These interactions may or may not be consonant with the formalized aspects of the school.

Knowledge Distribution in the Classroom

Reproduction theorists and scholars of women's education have focused their efforts on analyzing the formal curriculum and school authority patterns. There is a relative paucity of research that deals with differential knowledge distribution within the classroom between the sexes except as it relates to access. We know, for example, that women are systematically denied certain knowledge because they are channeled in the high school away from it; in higher education they are often simply denied admission into certain programs. Women are thus schooled in subject matter which carries gender weight. Mathematics and science are "male" provinces; education, nursing, social work, literature, and English are "female" domains. While Title IX of the 1965 Civil Rights Act has attempted to remove access barriers, albeit somewhat unsuccessfully in higher education, those who have assessed its impact have not tackled the issue of differential distribution of knowledge within the classroom in which both males and females are present.

Are there regularities in the classroom that reinforce sex role divisions of labor? There are a few studies which suggest that through schooling, teachers, regardless of their gender, tend to interact less with girls than with boys and that this pattern intensifies at secondary and college levels.[7] This may well mean that the female student is taught that education is not as important for her as it is for her male peers. Research has shown us that teachers do not interact with girls as frequently as with boys. When they do, they tend to respond to them either neutrally or negatively, although this varies by a girl's class and race. Students in a SUNY/Buffalo Sociology of Education course found that teachers in all black secondary school classes tended to interact more and more positively with female than with male students; the reverse was the case in a predominantly white working class school. In classes in heterogeneous integrated schools teachers followed the regularities of the white working-class school with some exceptions; they responded more positively to white middle-class girls than to black males or females or white working-class girls or boys.

While teachers tend to reinforce girls less frequently than boys, with variations by class and race, what they reinforce girls for is in and of itself important. Reinforcement tends to be for passivity and neatness, not for "getting the right answer." Nihlen (1976) found in her study of a working-class primary class that teachers did not attempt to change girls' emphasis on "sociability" which meant that the girls began deemphasizing academic performance and achieved below their capabilities. These working-class girls literally began doing different kinds of work in the school room from their working-class male peers and a similar group of middle-class children, and were systematically positively reinforced for not learning academic tasks by their teachers.

The few studies that we have on classroom knowledge distribution by gender suggest that teachers do not take female students seriously and that, within the classroom, girls' academic performance is systematically devaluated. This implies that the school is not "for keeps" for the female. While fragmentary data suggest such conclusions, we have far too little hard data. We do not know, for example, whether these patterns vary by school subjects. Do female students receive greater reinforcement for academic performance in "female" subjects like English and foreign languages than in "male" subjects like mathematics and physical sciences? Are there differences in these regularities among black women, white working-class women and middle-class females by subject matter and are they dependent on the class or racial mix of the schools? Are there differences in these patterns between co-educational and sex-segregated schools, between traditional classrooms and open classrooms, in various tracks within the schools? These questions are yet to be answered and are essential to a deeper understanding of the school's roles in reproducing sex inequality.

Reproduction and Resistance

There is much evidence to suggest that the schools do not mitigate and may indeed actively reinforce inequality by gender and that the dimensions of this inequality extend beyond occupational channeling and stratification to inequalities in workload. Thus far, we, as have most who investigate education in the framework of the reproduction of inequality, have been guilty of presuming that students internalize the schools' messages or that student rejection of school knowledge, if it exists, makes very little difference. Such assumptions may not be warranted.

We wish, for the remainder of this essay, to turn our attention to the issue of whether girls in fact do become what the messages of the school would have them become. This question may be crucial to understanding the ways in which schools operate to reinforce sexual inequality and the ways in which other questions about women's schooling may be posed.

So much research has gone into examining how school staffing and curriculum differentiate male from female, that we have very little real knowledge about whether girls accept what the schools teach. Instead we find a confusing literature examining whether girls internalize school messages which is inconclusive and rests on an assortment of evidential bases. Some of it suggests that girls either ignore the sex role messages of the schools, or renegotiate them.

For example, if, as the regularities in the classroom suggest, school achievement is "not for girls," we would expect to find that girls systematically underachieve. And, achievement studies that base themselves on standardized tests indicate that girls out-achieve boys across the board until tenth grade; thereafter boys score higher (Finn 1980; Finn, Dulberg and Reis 1979). This would seem to indicate that it takes the schools ten years to teach girls to learn to live down to expectations. However, if one takes actual school grades as a basis for assessing achievement, a different result emerges (Ellis and Peterson 1971). Girls get higher marks than boys throughout the primary and secondary schools regardless of subject area. This contradiction is not resolved in the research literature.

If girls are not interested in success, we would expect that they would not enter higher education at the same rate as males, and this is somewhat the case. Since 1973 women form 44 percent of the full time student population in higher education. This is an aggregate increase both numerically and proportionally since the 1960s. But while women enter institutions of higher education, not all institutions have the same status, nor do they provide credentials of equal currency in the society. Women make up 52 percent of the population in public two-year post-secondary institutions and only 41 percent of the population in major public universities and 37 percent of students in private research universities (Fitzpatrick 1976: 8-9). This pattern is certainly quite different from that of white males. It replicates, although not on as gross a level, the pattern of minority groups in education. White middle-class women get a "better shake" in access to the status hierarchy than minorities, both male and female, but are still inferior to the educational patterns of white males. This concentration of women in lower status institutions is a function of scholarship distribution and parental unwillingness to invest much in their daughter's education as much, if not more than it is a function of school channeling (Fitzpatrick 1976: chapter 2).

In addition, it has been amply documented that women do seek entry into fields that are supposedly "all male," such as engineering, business, mathematics, law and medicine, and have been prevented from so doing only by discriminatory admissions policies. As soon as the force of law has been brought, women have enrolled in such fields. Obviously the "messages" did not get through, suggesting that the pattern of enrollments that persist may be due to discrimination rather than women internalizing the messages of the school. Likewise, the workforce patterns too may be employer imposed rather than school induced, and family induced rather than school imposed.

While the above suggests that women may not necessarily incorporate all "school knowledge," it should not be taken by any means to deny what school knowledge in fact is or its attempted transmission in the classroom. Rather, it is to point out that within the classroom sets of knowledge renegotiation and/or active filtering occurs that may counter what the schools consider legitimate. How this renegotiation occurs we do not know, yet there is ample evidence to suggest its existence.

Matina Horner's (1972) controversial "fear of success" study shows us that women don't fully internalize school teachings. The women she studied were in higher education preparing for professions. Horner attributes their exit at the point when they are about to succeed as ambivalence to becoming "unfeminine" as schools and society have defined successful professional women. Scholars like Levine and Tressemer acknowledge that women exit from the professions but they dispute Horner's conclusion with evidence that demonstrates that women are pushed out of professions by discrimination and by the structure of work and the family, not by their own internalized fear (Levine and Crumrine 1975; Tressemer 1976).

Many autobiographical sketches of women also point to a "filtering" of the school's messages and women using knowledge not intended for them. Several, like Naomi Weisstein, said they did not expect the discrimination they experienced once in the workforce or the impact that marriage and the family had on their work. Said Weisstein after all those years in school, "I didn't know I wasn't supposed to succeed" (Ruddick and Daniels 1977). Weisstein's case is interesting in that she went through the U.S. school system at the time when there were the fewest women administrators, the most rigid sex differentiated curriculum and the heyday of the Strang pink and blue vocational interest inventories.

Clearly some women escape the messages of the schools in sex roles as they do the messages of race and class. Do groups of women slip through the cracks of socialization? How many actually do? And, at what cost? We have not yet studied these questions systematically, despite the fact that emerging feminist scholarship has shown women's resistance to very real oppression. Both the power and the contradictions of these forms of resistance need much greater attention. As McRobbie's (1978) study of working class girls so clearly documents, these resistances do have real costs as well as benefits.

The difficulty with the reproduction framework as it has been used thus far is that it fails both to deal with "deviations" and chart how and when they occur or become significant. Part of the difficulty lies with the ahistoric nature of the literature and its assumption that social protest movements have little impact on those who attend school. Most of our data on the schools and the reproduction of gender inequality states simply that because the school's authority and staffing pattern and curriculum are what they are women are not of equal status with men. Yet, this denies the structure of work and the family and it ignores history. We know that women have entered and exited the workforce in waves through American history, just as their educational attainments have had their ups and downs. But we do not know to what extent the schools have been responsible for this, or whether the schools have been affected by the development, strength and ebbing of the women's movement. The current upswing in women's workforce participation rates and status as well as educational levels (since the 1950s) has accelerated, with the onset of the women's movement (as did the wave of the 1920s) and its organization in the schools and development of women's studies programs on the secondary and college levels. It well may be—and more research is needed—that the presence of a women's movement provides a means of making resistance "count" and sets a tenor for the renegotiation of knowledge within the classroom.

Notes

[1] See especially the special issue, "The Labor of Women: Work and the Family," *Signs* IV (Summer 1979), Boulding (1976) and Safilios-Rothschild (1976).

[2] This is suggested by, for example, Wax (1970) in the case of Native Americans.

[3] An excellent review essay on women's housework and male wage structures can be found in Glazer-Mablin (1976). See also Seccombe (in press).

[4] This is clearest in male/female time budget studies. See, for example, Boulding (1976) and Lapidus (1979).

[5]Examples of this growing literature include Children's Rights Workshop (1976), Frasher and Walker (1972), Jay and Schminke (1975), Kepner and Koehn (1977), National Organization of Women (1972), Pottker (1977), Treckler (1973), and Weitzman et al. (1972). For further theoretical work on this, see MacDonald (1980a).

[6]A number of studies might be mentioned here, including Boring (1973), Frazier and Sadker (1973) especially chapters 4 and 5, Piotrofesa and Schlossbert (1977), Saario, Jacklin and Tittle (1973), Thomas and Steward (1971), Tittle (1974), and Verheyden-Hilliard (1977).

[7]Among these investigations are Gaite (1977), Levy (1972), Levitin and Chananie (1972), Meyer and Thompson (1956), Palardy (1969), Saario, Jacklin and Tittle (1973), and Seewald, Leinhard and Engel (1977).

Bibliography

Allen, Walter R. (1979), "Family Roles, Occupational Statuses and Achievement Orientations among Black Women in the United States," *Signs* 4 (Summer), 676-7.

Boring, P. Z. (1973), "Sex Stereotyping in Educational Guidance," National Education Association (ed.), *Sex Role Stereotyping in the Schools,* Washington, D.C.: NEA, pp. 14-22.

Boulding Elsie (1976), "Familial Constraints on Women's Work Roles," *Signs* 1 (Spring), 95-118.

Chafe, William H. (1972), *The American Woman: Her Changing Social, Economic and Political Roles, 1920-1970,* New York: Oxford University Press.

Children's Rights Workshop (1976), *Sexism in Children's Books: Facts, Figures and Guidelines,* New York: McGraw-Hill.

Croll, Elisabeth (1978), *Feminism and Socialism in China,* London: Routledge & Kegan Paul.

DuBois, Ellen, Gail P. Kelly, Elizabeth Kennedy, Carolyn Korsmeyer and Lillian Robinson (in press), *The Impact of Feminism on the Disciplines,* Urbana: University of Illinois Press.

Elementary School Report Card (1980), Buffalo, New York Public Schools.

Ellis, Joseph R., and Joan L. Peterson (1971), "Effects of Same Sex Class Organization on Junior High School Students' Academic Achievement, Self-Discipline, Self Concept, Sex Role Identification and Attitude Toward School," *Journal of Educational Research* 64 (July-August), 455-64.

Estler, Suzanne E. (1975), "Women as Leaders in Public Education," *Signs* 1 (Winter), 364-5.

Finn, Jeremy D. (1980), "Sex Differences in Educational Outcomes: A Cross National Study," *Sex Roles* 6 (February), 9-26.

Finn, Jeremy, Loretta Dulberg and Janet Reis (1979), "Sex Differences in Educational Attainment: A Cross National Perspective," *Harvard Educational Review* 49 (November), 477-503.

Fitzpatrick, Blanche (1976), *Women's Inferior Education: An Economic Analysis*, New York: Praeger.

Frasher, Ramona, and Annabelle Walker (1972), "Sex Roles in Early Reading Textbooks," *The Reading Teacher* 25 (May), 741-9.

Frazier, Nancy, and Myra Sadker (1973), *Sexism in School and Society*, New York: Harper & Row.

Gaite, A.J.H. (1977), "Teachers' Perceptions of Ideal Male and Female Students: Male Chauvinism in the School," in J. Pottker and A. Fishel (eds.), *Sex Bias in the Schools*, Teaneck, New Jersey: Fairleigh Dickinson University Press.

Glazer-Mablin, Nona (1976), "Housework," *Signs* 1 (Summer), 905-22.

Horner, Matina (1972), "Toward an Understanding of Achievement-Related Conflicts in Women," *Journal of Social Issues* 25, 157-75.

Jay, W.T., and Clarence W. Schminke (1975), "Sex Stereotyping in Elementary School Mathematics Texts," *The Arithmetic Teacher* 22 (March), 242-6.

Kepner, Henry S., and Lilane R. Koehn (1977), "Sex Roles in Mathematics: A Study of Sex Stereotypes in Elementary Mathematics Texts," *The Arithmetic Teacher* 24 (May), 379-85.

Kilson, Marion (1976), "The Status of Women in Higher Education," *Signs* 1 (Summer), 935-42.

Lapidus, Gail Warshofsky (1979), *Women in Soviet Society*, Berkeley: University of California Press.

Levine, A., and J. Crumrine (1975), "Women and the Fear of Success: A Problem in Replication," *American Journal of Sociology* 80, 964-74.

Levitin, Teresa A., and J. D. Chananie (1972), "Response of Female Primary School Teachers to Sex Typed Behaviors in Male and Female Children," *Child Development* 43 (December), 1309-16.

Levy, Betty (1972), "The School's Role in the Sex Role Stereotyping of Girls: A Feminist Review of the Literature," *Feminist Studies* 1 (Summer).

MacDonald, Madeleine (1980a), "Schooling and the Reproduction of Class and Gender Relations," in Roger Dale, Geoff Esland and Madeleine MacDonald (eds.), *Education and the State*, London: Routledge & Kegan Paul.

MacDonald, Madeleine (1980b), "Socio-Cultural Reproduction and Women's Education," in Rosemary Deem (ed.), *Schooling for Women's Work*, London: Routledge & Kegan Paul.

Meyer, William J., and George G. Thompson (1956), "Sex Differences in the Distribution of Teacher Approval and Disapproval Among Sixth Grade Children," *Journal of Educational Psychology* 47 (November), 385-96.

National Organization of Women (1972), *Dick and Jane as Victims*, Princeton, New Jersey: Central New Jersey National Organization of Women.

Nihlen, Ann (1976), "The White Working Class in School: A Study of First Grade Girls and Their Parents," unpublished Ph.D. dissertation, University of New Mexico.

Palaldy, J. Michael (1969), "What Teachers Believe—What Children Achieve," *Elementary School Journal* 69 (April), 370-4.

Pietrofesa, J. J., and N. K. Schlossbert (1977), "Counselor Bias and the Female Occupational Role," in J. Pottker and A. Fishel (eds.), *Sex Bias in the Schools*, Teaneck, New Jersey: Fairleigh Dickinson University Press, pp. 221-9.

Pottker, J. (1977), "Psychological and Occupational Sex Stereotypes in Elementary School Readers," in J. Pottker and A. Fishel (eds.) *Sex Bias in the Schools*, Teaneck, New Jersey: Fairleigh Dickinson University Press, pp. 111-25.

Rosaldo, Michelle Zimbalist (1974), "Women, Culture and Society: A Theoretical Overview," in Michelle Rosaldo and Louise Lamphere (eds.), *Women, Culture and Society*, Stanford: Stanford University Press, pp. 1742.

Ruddick, Sara, and Pamela Daniels (eds.) (1977), *Working It Out: 23 Women Writers, Artists, Scientists and Scholars Talk about Their Lives and Work*, New York: Pantheon.

Saario, Terry N., Carolyn N. Jacklin and Carol Tittle (1973), "Sex Role Stereotyping in the Public Schools," *Harvard Educational Review* 43 (August), 386-416.

Sacks, Karen (1974), "Engels Revisited: Women, the Organization of Production and Private Property," in Michelle Rosaldo and Louise Lamphere (eds.), *Women, Culture and Society*, Stanford: Stanford University Press, pp. 207-22.

Safilios-Rothschild, Constantina (1976), "Dual Linkages Between Occupational and Family Systems: A Macrosociological Analysis," *Signs* 1 (Spring), 51-60.

Seccombe, Wally (in press), *Domestic Labour and the Working Class Household*, Toronto: Canadian Women's Press.

Seewald, Andrea M., Gaea Leinhard and Mary Engel (1977), *Learning What's Taught: Sex Differences in Instruction*, Pittsburgh:

University of Pittsburgh, Learning Research and Development Center, report no. 15.

Sexton, Patricia (1976), *Women in Education,* Bloomington, Indiana: Phi Delta Kappa.

Simpson, Richard L. (1974), "Sex Stereotypes of Secondary School Teaching Subjects," *Sociology of Education* 47 (Summer), 388-98.

Smuts, Robert W. (1971), *Women and Work in America,* New York: Schocken.

Stacey, Judith, *et al.* (eds.) (1974), *And Jill Came Tumbling After: Sexism in American Education,* New York: Dell.

Standing, Guy (1976), "Education and Female Participation in the Labor Force," *International Labor Review* 114 (November-December), 281-97.

Thomas, Arthur and Norman Steward (1971), "Counselors' Response to Female Clients with Deviate and Conforming Career Goals," *Journal of Counseling Psychology* 18 (July), 352-7.

Tittle, Carol (1974), "The Use and Abuse of Vocational Tests," in Judith Stacey, *et al.* (eds.), *And Jill Came Tumbling After: Sexism in American Education,* New York: Dell, pp. 241-8.

Treckler, Janice L. (1973), "Women in U.S. History High School Textbooks," *International Review of Education* 19, 133-9.

Tressemer, David (1976), "Do Women Fear Success?" *Signs* 1 (Summer), 963-74.

U.S. Department of Labor (1975), *U.S. Working Women: A Chartbook,* Washington: Bureau of Labor Statistics, Bulletin 1880.

Verheyden-Hilliard, Mary E. (1977), "Counseling Potential Superbomb Against Sexism," *American Education,* 13 (April), 12-15.

Wax, Rosalie (1970), "The Warrior Dropouts," in H. Lindquist (ed.) *Education: Readings in the Processes of Cultural Transmission,* Boston: Houghton Mifflin, pp. 207-17.

Weinbaum, Batya (1976), "Chinese Women in the Transition to Socialism," *Review of Radical Political Economists* 8 (Spring), 34-58.

Weitzman, Lenore J., Deborah Eifler, Elizabeth Hodaka and Catherine Ross (1972), "Sex Role Socialization in Picture Books for Pre-School Children," *American Journal of Sociology* 77 (May), 1125-50.

New Directions for Research[†]

Carolyn M. Elliott and Gail P. Kelly

What has research to tell us about the existing patterns of education of women and the possibilities of improving them? We know most at the descriptive level. As Bowman and Anderson* underscore in their review essay, fewer girls than boys go to school, but there is considerable variation among Third World countries in their participation and educational attainment. A UNESCO study cited by Isabelle Deble in her comparable review of women's educational patterns states it even more strongly, that there is no relation between the intensity of enrollment and the percentage of students who are girls. Numerical equality among boys and girls is found in countries with low total enrollment, and girls may form a low percentage of pupils in countries with comparatively high enrollments.[1] The differences within countries are as great, making it very difficult to use broad national averages as the basis for hypothesis building regarding the reasons for sex differences. One finding does appear firm: Girls in school tend to be from families of higher socioeconomic status than boys, and this difference is compounded at higher levels of education. Thus girls from less privileged families are less likely to be in school than their brothers. Smith and Cheung* demonstrate how persistent this pattern is by showing it to be true even in the Philippines where sex equality in education is widely thought to have been achieved. Fathers with little schooling are found to provide more education to sons than to daughters. Equal allocation of education to sons and daughters is a recent phenomenon among relatively well educated urban families.

Efforts to explain these variations among and within countries start with relating education to levels of economic development. Bowman and Anderson explore whether, as economic development proceeds, women tend to receive educational parity with men. They find that this is sometimes true, but they also cite many cases where development has so far produced even greater disparities. Whether this is a transitional phenomenon, whereby boys' education levels lead that of girls' but girls later catch up, or whether modernization is producing long-term relative disabilities for girls, is a question that has concerned many students of modernization. Bowman and Anderson see girls

[†]Reprinted from Gail P. Kelly and Carolyn M. Elliott, eds. *Women's Education in the Third World: Comparative Perspectives.* Albany: SUNY Press, by permission of the State University of New York Press and Carolyn Elliott.

approaching parity with boys in pretertiary schooling in an impressive number of poor countries. Deble's analysis for UNESCO is, however, more pessimistic. While acknowledging that relative sex disparities in primary education are decreasing somewhat, she emphasizes that in absolute numbers the gap between the number of boys and girls in school is widening at all age groups and levels of instruction.[2] The Philippine data on the persistence of the father's education as a determinant of educational attainment despite the progress of modernization is a case in point. It reflects a rigidity in that society's valuation of girls that is unaffected by general patterns of social change.

Tracing the effects of broad cultural patterns on women's access to education represents another important attempt to account for sex differences in education. Some scholars have argued that women's access to institutions like schools depends on the extent to which cultural and religious beliefs accord women a role in life outside the family. Thus we should expect to find that, in cultures where female seclusion is widespread (e.g., in Islamic societies), women would have less access to schools than elsewhere. Similarly, we would expect to find that in Latin America, where constraints on women's equality appear to be embedded in core cultural values, women's participation in education would be lower than it is, for example, in non-Islamic African cultures where values differ.

Such hypotheses do not hold when taken against the broad array of data Bowman and Anderson present. While in some Islamic nations women's participation in education lags considerably behind that of women in societies that do not practice female seclusion, this pattern is not evident in all Muslim nations, nor is Islam always a barrier to women's schooling. Jones's article in this volume* shows that in Tunisia women's access to schools has grown appreciably over the past decades. Similarly, Schiefelbein and Farrell's contribution in this volume* demonstrates that in Chile, women's rates of participation in education at all levels is nearly equal to that of men, the tradition of machismo not withstanding. Their rates of participation transcend many of those in Western Europe and, in higher education, the more industrialized United States. Farrell and Schiefelbein explain these high rates as a function of the peculiar historical development of Chile. Whether one could identify in the Chilean experience factors that could serve as a basis for broader generalization must await further research.

Even if one could establish clear correlations between girls' education and levels of development or cultural patterns, little would be known about causation. A basic issue is how the provision of schools relates to utilization. Do wealthier countries generally get higher female participation rates because they provide more schools for girls, or are families in these countries more willing to send daughters to school? Alternatively, should we attribute low rates of female education to lack of school places for girls or to cultural and other factors making parents withhold their daughters from school?

The authors in this volume explore several dimensions of this argument. Marie Thourson Jones's work on educational policy in Tunisia emphasizes the importance of the supply side of the equation. She attributes the slackening of female enrollment to the low quality and poor accessibility of schools and to the government's growing disinclination to make schooling attractive to the reluctant portions of the population. Effectively supplying schooling to families who do not readily come forward to place daughters in schools requires a different and more expensive kind of investment in education.

The findings of this case study are supported by a survey of 62 governments made by UNESCO. These governments readily admitted to difficulties in providing even primary education to all children. Lack of transportation, lack of teachers, and lack of canteens were mentioned most frequently as critical constraints on the supply of education opportunity.[3] Except for Latin America, where enrollments are comparatively equal for boys and girls, the governments expressed particular concern about the wastage among girls. However, many saw no need for government attention to girls dropping out of school. They were inclined to see unsatisfactory levels of girls' enrollment as a result of cultural norms and parental decisions, rather than a result of omissions in educational planning. Such attitudes do not promise a willingness to look for, and pay for, the innovations needed to make schooling effectively available to girls, for example, child care, continuing education for married women, night classes for working children, and so on.

To understand the demand for education, we need to know why girls go to school and why they are prevented from doing so. Research in this area has so far concentrated largely on parental and daughters' aspirations for marriage and careers. Although none of these studies is included in this volume, surveys in Latin America and Africa have shown that a principal motivation among girls to remain in school is to have more say in the choice of a husband. Girls' education is now valued in many circles as a positive factor in the securing of husbands of high status, as reported by 65 percent of persons interviewed in an Indian study, or of high marriage settlements, as in Africa.[4] Bowman and Anderson review a number of other factors that must also be considered: early marriage, seclusion of girls at puberty, and the opportunity costs of schooling relative to more traditional forms of training for adulthood at home.

Studies in this volume concentrate on two key factors that have been widely discussed but not previously submitted to systematic examination: the time constraints on women's capacity to pursue schooling and the perceived economic rewards that influence family desires to invest in the education of daughters. McSweeney and Freedman* show us that the work load of women and girls in rural communities, such as those they studied in Upper Volta, allows females of all ages little time to pursue education. Both school-age boys and adult men have spare time that can be used to go to school or participate in nonformal educational programs. But, as McSweeney and Freedman point out, time alone is not the only barrier between women and an education. In the United Nations project they describe, which was designed to lighten female work loads, adult women did not use the time they gained to attend literacy and other nonformal educational programs. Rather, they chose to use the free time to increase their families' well-being, ignoring educational programs unless there was a tangible economic or health benefit for their families. The lightening of women's work, however, did result in greater participation of school-aged girls in the educational system.

Naik's* experience with night classes for working children in India bears this out. She has found that adjusting school hours to the time available to these children elicited a broad interest in girls' education. This is a fine example of how a policy innovation negated common assumptions about families' reluctance to educate girls and their unwillingness to allow girls out at night.

Perception of rewards for education is the second major factor explored here. Scholars of education have frequently speculated on how the labor market's inequalities may depress girls' interest in education or families' willingness to invest less in their daughters' education than in their sons'. Since sex-role socialization and family background are such strong factors in occupational choice, however, it has been difficult for researchers to get clear evidence for the independent effect of occupational irregularity.

Bee-Lan Chan Wang* utilizes the opportunity of the government's preferential hiring policies in Malaysia to sort out these variables. In a situation where the government is skewing employment opportunities toward groups with less advantaged backgrounds, students from these groups express higher educational aspirations than do students of advantaged backgrounds. Because women in the now favored groups continue to experience more job discrimination, however, they are less likely than their brothers to invest in further education. In Chile, on the other hand, women were motivated by job discrimination to continue education in order to compete effectively. Thus, an understanding of rewards and incentive structures can tell us much about sex differences in educational attainment.

Process of Education

From access and utilization we turn to the equality of women's participation in education. Finn, Reis, and Dulberg* pose the question most directly: What is the role of the schooling process in creating or exacerbating sex differences? They argue that it is a denial of equal opportunity in education to fail to expose both sexes not only to the full range of course contents and adult sex-role models, but also to the highest expectations and support for their performance. Their review argues that formal schooling is not equal for girls and boys. Differential interaction patterns between teachers and students by gender, "messages" implicit in curricular materials, lack of role models within the schools, schools' authority structures, and the like may all teach girls that to achieve is "unfeminine" or imply that girls will receive little reward for superior academic performance. Finn, Reis, and Dulberg's article is suggestive and can be nothing more, for most of the studies they cite were carried out in Western Europe and the United States. But three studies in this volume suggest much that is similar in the Third World.

Historically, equal participation was often not a goal of educators. Yates's* study of the Belgian Congo describes the interest of colonial and mission educators there to train good Christian wives and mothers, requiring a very different curriculum for girls than boys. Guided by Western conceptions of the proper woman's role, educators discouraged Congolese girls from pursuits outside the home, particularly their traditional role in agriculture, and denied them skills for effective participation in any but the most stereotypically female among modern occupations. A parallel study in India by Gail Minault shows how indigenous groups often had a similar view of women's education. Minault chronicles the movement for education of aristocratic Muslim girls at the major center of modern Muslim education in nineteenth-century India, Aligarh University. This movement was explicitly devoted to educating wives for the male university graduates, a continuation of traditional women's roles in new circumstances. In this case, the school even rigidified such customs as *purdah* by codifying and sanctioning it for modern families.[5]

The sobering fact of these historical experiences is the shadow they cast on the life chances for contemporary women. As Yates argues, it is difficult to equalize opportunity once some groups have established an initial lead, and even more so with current constraints on increasing educational investment and government employment. After actively discriminatory policies have set inequalities in motion, sex-neutral policies are sufficient to maintain established patterns. Thus the educational gap continues, as does the clustering of women in low-paid service occupations.

Two studies in this volume reveal how the legacy is passed along. In a study of school textbooks, Kalia* shows that instructional materials in India differentiate male from female. They praise the female for passivity, unscholarly attributes, and her dependence on others, while they show males as active agents and achievers. Kalia's study is important in beginning to demonstrate that "school knowledge" may be differentially imparted and directed at one sex rather than both sexes. We do not know whether the sex stereotypes presented in Indian primers are derived from Indian culture and colonial experience, or pervade curricula of all Third World countries. Finn, Reis, and Dulberg imply they do, and several unpublished studies of Latin American school texts would support their contention, with some minor variations. The extent to which Kalia's findings replicate analyses of texts carried out in the United States is striking.

It is important to know how the messages implicit in the formal curriculum of textbooks may be reinforced by other messages in the "hidden" curriculum of schools—authority structures, staffing patterns, and regularities in classroom interactions by gender. This hidden curriculum of a school may be as significant, or even more so, than the formal curriculum in molding educational outcomes. Biraimah's* research on a coeducational secondary school in Togo, reported in this volume, is an important step in tracing such impacts. She suggests that the schools reproduce, in their authority, staffing, and classroom interaction patterns, the sex differentiation Kalia found in Indian texts. Furthermore, Biraimah found that teachers themselves shared such stereotypical notions, regardless of actual student performance.

How the school environment affects what children learn remains a question. At the most extreme, it may prevent them even from going to school. One doesn't know whether the reluctance of Congolese families to send girls to school, as reported by Yates, was because they disapproved of the curriculum or for other reasons. But Chitra Naik, in her report on alternative schooling in India, reveals her conviction that the curriculum and the process of teaching have a major impact in children's attending school. Many drop out, she finds, because of bad experiences with teachers, or boredom. Thus, her project to universalize primary education involves not only altering time schedules, but making fundamental changes in the recruitment of teachers, the conduct of classes, and the content of materials. Early results show a marked change in girls' self-presentation, as well as their school attendance and achievement.

Where the classroom experience differed for boys and girls, however, Biraimah found no sex differences in achievement. Girls did as well as boys on tests and did not share teachers' attitudes about their personal and career goals. Thus we cannot assume that students internalize the messages of their textbooks and teachers; under the worst conditions, they resist internalization of sex-stereotyped attitudes. To explain her Togo findings, Biraimah provides several speculations, which may be generalizable. She suggests that where school teachings diverge from the actual roles of women in the society, girls may understand full well the school's messages and "tune out," choosing neither to interact with their teachers nor to take them as significant role models. The relative absence of female teachers in the classroom may decrease the girls' identification with their teachers. Finally, where the organization of the classroom favors lectures, this may limit the transmittal of teachers' personal attitudes.

These exploratory studies raise more questions than they answer, for research on the process and impact of different kinds of educational experiences is only beginning. Traditionally scholars have turned to such out-of-school variables as class, gender, or race to explain educational outcomes. Or they have reduced school variables to quantifiable but relatively indirect factors, such as class size, level of teachers' education, amount of time spent in subject-matter instruction, and expenditures per student. None of these help us to see factors that directly determine a student's experience in school and her performance. All too often scholars have led us to conclude that "schools make no difference," an unwarranted conclusion given the present state of our knowledge about what goes on within schools.

Women's Education and the Work Force

Research on the outcomes of women's education has concentrated on women's participation in the labor force. Does such participation rise with educational level? Does education yield similar occupational rewards for both women and men? For the most part, education does not correlate with labor force participation in Third World countries in the same way for women as it does for men. Rati Ram's* review essay shows us that there is great variation in women's labor force participation in the Third World. Part of the variation may be explained by inconsistencies in how work force participation is measured—counting women employed in the traditional sectors of the economy or solely in the modern industrial and service sectors. Nevertheless, it appears clear that women's participation in the modern sector of the labor force is less than males' and that women are, for the most part, in the lower-status, lower-paying jobs. Increases in women's educational levels have not altered this pattern.

Ram explores two explanations for this phenomenon: Either discrimination in hiring precludes women from using their education to full advantage, or women, by virtue of their roles as wives and mothers, are constrained from maximum work force participation because they have a "comparative advantage" in child rearing. While Ram believes the two interpretations are not mutually exclusive, he follows the human capital approach. He posits that childbearing and marriage, rather than discrimination, are the primary sources of differential labor force participation rates among educated men and women. Ram's analysis is controversial, for many would argue that women's decision to stay at home to rear children rests on an assessment of how much they might earn in the labor force relative to their husbands, rather than on a natural advantage in child raising. Ram emphasizes, however, that data to support either theory are weak for Third World countries and that much more research is needed to discern patterns.

Three studies in this volume bear on this problem. By introducing new types of data and modes of analysis, these studies may serve to break the stalemate between interpretations of women's labor market behavior.

Schiefelbein and Farrell examine how women's education relates to labor force participation in Chile, an unusual case because female participation there is very high in comparison to other societies. They examine whether the differences between women's and men's participation in the labor force are connected to the quality of education or the status of schools, and they reach a conclusion quite opposite from patterns prevailing elsewhere. Women in Chile attend schools of higher quality than do men, achieve equally by national measures, and show no evidence of experiencing educational discrimination. But, because they anticipate discrimination in the labor market, they tend to remain in school longer than men in order to compete for the same jobs. Thus, their answer to Ram's question is that labor market practices do affect decisions in education, for women as well as for men. Where women have access to nondiscriminatory education, they prepare themselves to compete in the labor market, even to the extent of enduring longer preparation time despite cultural anticipation of their future roles as wives and mothers. While it is too much to conclude that adoption of truly nondiscriminatory education would have such an impact elsewhere, the Chilean experience attests to the strength of women's chances for equal labor force participation in that country.

A contrasting case of countries with low labor force participation for women is presented by Wainerman.* Through a careful study of women in Argentina and Paraguay, in which levels of economic and educational development differ considerably, she shows that marriage, childbearing, and child rearing drive women from the work force.

However, education reverses this trend. In both countries, educated women tended to maintain their labor force participation rates: They did not leave the work force upon marriage or raising a family, which their uneducated peers with children did. This also modifies Ram's argument regarding a natural advantage of women in childbearing. It shows that marriage and child rearing are social facts, rather than natural ones, which have varying impacts on women, depending on educational and class status.

Raj's* study of well-educated women in India deepens this analysis by probing into the quality of the impacts. In her interviews of women scientists, she finds that their career aspirations are mitigated by involvement in family life. Because they derive much satisfaction from contributions to the family, they accept lack of career advancement and fail to detect discrimination. She points as well to the impact of generational change (complementing the report of Smith and Cheung) whereby first generation employed women may respond differently to job discrimination than others. Her conclusion echoes the theme announced in the introduction, that educational outcomes for women must be seen in terms of women's lives, not only in comparison to men. The women she studied compare themselves, not with men, but with the women in their families who preceded them, and they assess their work advancement as just one component of the full range of the daily reality they experience.

Education and the Family

The impact of education on the private sphere of marriage, family, and self is the subject of the final three papers. The effect on fertility has attracted the greatest attention of scholars, making possible several somewhat firm conclusions. It is now quite clear that women's education does reduce fertility in the majority of cases, but the number of instances where it does not is large and suggestive. Countries and rural groups within countries where low literacy prevails are the populations in which women's education increases fertility.

Efforts to explain the causal relationship have identified a large number of intermediate mechanisms by which education might affect fertility. Cochrane* provides a model that shows how the effects of education in reducing both infant mortality and the demand for children may be countered by its increasing not only the ability to afford children but also women's ability to conceive. Countries where education does not decrease fertility are those where poor health and traditional practices limit births, these being factors that education is likely to remove.

LeVine* takes us from fertility to mothering, with the question of whether educated women make better mothers. This is clearly one of the most important concerns motivating the education of women, but it is so value-laden that few scholars have dared to address it directly. LeVine brings a very useful orientation, which enables him to set aside ideology and examine research evidence. He begins, with the assumption that indigenous patterns of infant and child care represent largely successful adaptations to the conditions of life in different societies, and that nonliterate women have been very effective transmitters of these patterns. The question he poses is whether educated mothers are better able to prepare children for participation in a new socioeconomic order that involves schooling and employment. In effect, are educated mothers better able to prepare their children to be successful in school and the modern labor market?

As we have tried to do throughout this volume, LeVine attempts to distinguish the independent effects of education. This means sorting out the impact of education from confounding factors usually associated with education, such as family income, urban residence, and media exposure. He finds that one cannot make clear statements because the available research was not designed to answer this question. There is substantial evidence, however, that mothering behavior does change among educated women, so that their children perform better on Western preschool tests. Just how schooling causes this change in mothering behavior remains an unanswered question. LeVine provides interesting speculations, but answers must await investigation of the many linkages in the complex path of schooling to motherhood. Raj provides partial answers from her Indian interviews, which indicate that educated women utilize modern knowledge more effectively for family health and nutrition.

Perhaps the most difficult problem is the one with which this volume began, namely the impact of education on a woman's view of herself and her world. This has not been a fashionable question recently, for world interest in education has shifted from a humanitarian interest in enlightenment to more practical concerns with jobs and national development. Yet one cannot ignore the testimony of individuals from all parts of the world to the intellectual and personal liberation that education has brought to their lives. Ultimately these issues are philosophical ones, which is perhaps why researchers have shied away.

Raj reminds us, however, that one must come to terms with these hopes for education in order to assess whether educational goals are being accomplished. As a member of a poor country where customary practices act as a severe drag on urgently needed progress in many areas affecting human welfare, she holds high expectations of scientific education to overcome them. Although her expectations are largely disappointed, they cannot be dismissed, for they serve as a strong critique of the educational systems we have settled for, and a goal toward which we must strive in the education of both women and men.

Reflections from India

Since beginning work on this volume, one of the editors, Carolyn Elliott, has moved to India with the Ford Foundation. There one senses several attitudes affecting women's education which, if true elsewhere, suggest the need for a rededication to education.

Early naive faith in education as the key to national progress has been belied. Growing numbers of unemployed graduates emphasize the need for creating employment before skills can be utilized. It is also widely recognized that India's system of formal education does not impart the skills and attitudes needed for development, and that it is ineffective—and certainly inefficient—even in teaching basic literacy. Educators over the years have proposed many schemes to reshape the educational system, but these have yielded largely mechanistic exercises, such as juggling the years assigned to each level of schooling. Meanwhile the very visible success of other approaches to development, most notably the green revolution, have turned attention away from education to more promising avenues to progress. One senses the nation's intellectuals are bored with trying to reform education.

Without a more adequately financed and stronger political commitment to education, efforts to change it are likely to come to naught in any case. India currently invests just 2.2% of its budget on education, low compared to the U.S. and even compared to developing countries. Within the educational spending pattern is a very top-heavy investment in higher education, 20 times the expenditure per student in primary and secondary schooling, compared to a ratio of 3 to 1 in the U.S.[6] This pattern suits local rural power structures well, for it draws ambitious youth out of the countryside to urban colleges and does little to raise the aspirations of those left behind. Efforts under a recent populist government to change this power equation by a significant investment in adult education have now been withdrawn, as the potential of adult education for social mobilization and partisan political activity have become apparent.

Despite clearly established relationships between women's education and India's national policy goals in health and family planning, there appears to be little political will behind women's education. Although the new national plan cites the need for special measures to increase the enrollment and retention of girls in school—

child care centers at schools, women teachers and night classes—there is no national program for women's education. In school there is a widespread recourse to cultural explanations for the lack of activity. One finds in talking with educational administrators a full circle of explanations accounting for low enrollment rates of girls—sibling care, early marriage, parental unwillingness to invest in girls, women teachers' reluctance to work in villages, parental reluctance to allow girls to attend classes at night—which makes improvement seem impossible without long-term evolutionary social change. This proclivity to attribute women's lack of participation in education, and in all development programs, to family and culture is a major obstacle to creative thinking about policy innovations that would increase women's participation. And they mask the reluctance of policy makers to make the required financial investments in the levels of both primary and adult education that would reach the large proportion (75%) of Indian women who remain illiterate.

In higher education, India has a relatively strong ratio of girls to boys and a good stock of well-educated women, as the Raj paper demonstrates. However, the sex stereotyping of fields is marked, with consequences both for individual career choices and for development programs. Women's enrollments for an agricultural degree are still minuscule, and nonexistent in forestry. This means that development programs in critical areas of women's work—agriculture, fuel, and fodder—are designed, directed, and evaluated by male experts who, because of customary practices prevalent in most of India, can have no direct access to village women. There is some official reluctance to encourage women to enter agricultural colleges, because home economics is seen as a more suitable course and because there is unemployment among male agricultural graduates. Medicine is another critical area in which trained women are needed because of the reluctance of women patients to consult male doctors. India has a large stock of women doctors, but enrollments in medical colleges are declining, a worrisome trend. The probable reason is the rise of private medical colleges with capitation fees that parents are unwilling to pay for a daughter's education.

Persons concerned with women and development have not largely been a source of thinking or energy on behalf of women's education. Because the income needs of poor women are so obvious and urgent, they have emphasized income-generating programs. No one can question the need for these programs, nor the importance of integrating literacy with economic and health improvement. Without such linkages, previous literacy schemes have often failed to sustain participation. It is a matter of concern, however, that educational needs are often neglected. All too many income schemes stabilize or marginally improve the economic position of participants, but do not provide the skills and knowledge that would enable poor women to manage their own organizations or secure further mobility.

How might research help to develop a renewed zeal for women's education? The various studies in this volume show many possibilities—by documenting improvement and identifying groups falling behind, by clarifying motivations and effective incentives, and by demonstrating social pay-offs to investment in education. Perhaps most important, however, is to put cultural stereotypes in their place and demonstrate how improvement can be made.

Studies focusing on what can be changed, such as the distribution of schools, rather than on cultural values, such as religion or early marriage, that are difficult to affect, may raise the sense of possibility, and thus the commitment to education. Chitra Naik's description of night classes for working children may be the most important piece in the volume.

Notes

[1] Isabelle Deble, *The School Education of Girls* (New York: UNESCO, 1980) p. 29.

[2] Deble, *School Education of Girls.*

[3] Deble, *School Education of Girls,* p. 83.

[4] Government of India, *Towards Equality: Report of the Committee on the Status of Women* (New Dehli, 1976).

[5] Gail Minault, "Shaikh Abdullah, Begum Abdullah, and Sharef Education for Girls at Aligarh," unpublished manuscript, 1981.

[6] Calculated for 1977-8 from figures provided in The Planning Commission, Government of India, "Draft Sixth Five-Year Plan, 1978-83," rev., pp. 423, 429.

*This is a summary article of *Women's Education in the Third World: Comparative Perspectives*, edited by Gail P. Kelly and Carolyn M. Elliott, (Albany: SUNY Press, 1982). The asterisked articles are to be found in that volume and are listed below in order of first appearance in the summary.

Bowman, Mary Jean, and C. Arnold Anderson, "The Participation of Women in Education in the Third World," pp. 11-30.

Smith, Peter, and Paul P. L. Cheung, "Social Origins and Sex-differential Schooling in the Philippines," pp. 51-67.

Jones, Marie Thourson, "Educating Girls in Tunisia: Issues Generated by the Drive for Universal Enrollment," pp. 31-50.

Schiefelbein, Ernesto, and Joseph P. Farrell, "Women, Schooling and Work in Chile: Evidence from a Longitudinal Study," pp. 228-248.

McSweeney, Brenda Gael, and Marion Freedman, "Lack of Time as an Obstacle to Women's Education: The Case of Upper Volta," pp. 88-103.

Naik, Chitra, "An Action Project on Universal Primary Education: The Plan and the Process," pp. 152-172.

Wang, Bee-Lan Chan, "Sex and Ethnic Differences in Educational Investment in Malaysia: The Effect of Reward Structures," pp. 68-87.

Finn, Jeremy D., Janet Reis and Loretta Dulberg, "Sex Differences in Educational Attainment: The Process," pp. 107-126.

Yates, Barbara A., "Church, State and Edication in Belgian Africa: Implications for Contemporary Third World Women," pp. 127-151.

Kalia, Narendra Nath, "Images of Men and Women in Indian Textbooks," pp. 173-187.

Biraimah, Karen Coffyn, "The Impact of Western Schools on Girls' Expectations: A Togolese Case," pp. 188-200.

Ram, Rati, "Sex Differences in the Labor Market Outcomes of Education," pp. 203-227.

Wainerman, Catalina H., "The Impact of Education on the Female Labor Force in Argentina and Paraguay," pp. 264-279.

Raj, Maithreyi Krishna, "Women, Work and Science in India," pp. 249-263.

Cochrane, Susan H., "Education and Fertility: An Expanded Examination of the Evidence," pp. 311-330.

LeVine, Robert A., "Influences of Women's Schooling on Maternal Behavior in the Third World," pp. 283-310.

Failures of Androcentric Studies of Women's Education in the Third World[†]

Before 1970, scholars virtually ignored the study of women's education in the Third World nations of Africa, Asia, Latin America, and the Middle East. They did so despite the vast proliferation of research on these countries throughout the 1960s, which sought to trace the relation between school expansion; economic, social, and political development; and social justice and welfare. The absence of scholarship on women is even more shocking in view of the dramatic growth, since the 1950s, of female enrollments at all educational levels in most of the Third World nations.

Beginning in the early 1970s, research on the education of women in the Third World first challenged the assumption that the determinants, patterns, and outcomes of female education could be studied in the same manner as men's. More recently, this scholarship has raised new questions about the effect of education on women's lives and society, and has led to new methodologies for studying women's education.

Acknowledgment of Gender Roles, but not Gender Systems

The reason research on women's education was neglected until the 1970s is obvious. Most scholars believed it was not worth studying because women's roles were presumed immutable, confined to the domestic sphere, notably the family, which admitted but one type of organization and sex role division of labor. The few sketchy studies of women's schooling available indicated that women had lesser access to education, dropped out of school more frequently than men, achieved less well than men, and did not appear to enter the workforce in the modern sector of the economy in as great a proportion as men in jobs commensurate with their training.[1]

Studies of actual school achievement were almost nonexistent. It was presumed that the pattern of female versus male scholastic achievement identified in Western capitalist societies—notably the United States, Great Britain, Germany, and Sweden—held also in the Third World.[2] The few studies actually carried out seemed to bolster

[†]©1985 by the Board of Trustees of the University of Illinois. Used with Permission from the University of Illinois Press.

such assumptions with the notable exception of the largely ignored studies of Chile. Few scholars asked whether variations both within and among Third World nations existed; instead, they focused on establishing differences between males and females and assumed the differential outcomes of education were not likely to be modified.

In short, most researchers did not even consider the existence of patriarchy. They studied complex issues surrounding access to education, educational processes, and educational outcomes the same way for women as for men, and refused to recognize the gender-linked social relationships through which women are defined.

Studies conducted in this fashion, in current as well as past research, have a host of policy ramifications, given the present political activities in Third World countries. In the 1960s, most governments in these areas had allocated considerable sums of money to expanding educational opportunity. In countries like Kenya and Nigeria, up to 25 percent of the national budget was earmarked for schooling.[3] In other Third World nations, the percent was smaller, but still very large. Most government officials considered education an investment in economic development and assumed that schooling increased individual productivity, made industrialization possible by training a skilled labor force, and encouraged economic entrepreneurship.[4] By the late 1960s, the literature was dominated by correlational studies indicating that in countries with the greatest diffusion of formal education, the GNP per capita was highest, and that schooled individuals earned higher wages than those who were unschooled.[5] Despite the confusion between correlation and causation in this research literature, it became the basis for unprecedented government education expenditures and school expansion in Asia, Africa, and Latin America.

By the mid 1970s, it became clear that education had not produced the desired results. In most countries, educational expansion seemed totally unrelated to economic development, and in some countries it became associated with economic stagnation.[6] Government officials in Tunisia, for example, actually cut back educational expenditures and considered abandoning plans for universal primary education.[7] In the process, women's education was seen as an unnecessary "frill," even a "bad risk," given the scarcity in resources and the differences in male/female educational outcomes research had documented.

Thus the research of the past, shaky though it was, has provided government officials a rationale for denying women an education, thereby often creating greater gender inequalities in income and power.[8] In many Third World nations, women traditionally have been employed in subsistence agriculture, petty trade, and handicrafts. Mechanization of agriculture, the spread of industrial production, and new marketing mechanisms have displaced women's work and/or changed its nature.[9] Since education has become the only avenue to employment in the new economic structures, women are often barred from employment or confined to unskilled, low-paying work, often at wages below subsistence. This fosters their increased economic dependence on men and has undermined their power and authority within domestic as well as public life. In short, the old patriarchal tradition of Western capitalist economies is being transferred to many Third World countries, aided and abetted by educational research which acknowledges different work experiences of women and men but not hierarchical gender systems.

Problems with Traditional Research

Traditional research begins with the proposition that women's lives naturally center on domestic, private life to the exclusion of public (social, political, and economic) life. Much of this scholarship perceives, implicitly or explicitly, public life as secondary, or "unnatural," for women, for example, as a product of poverty or broken marriage. It limits itself to determination of whether education affects or improves "domestic" life.[10] The research nexus therefore becomes that of marriage, fertility or reproductive patterns, children's nutrition and health, and children's achievement in the schools.

While research on these issues acknowledges the differing experiences of women and men, it does so in ways quite different from scholarship generated by feminists. Women are not at the center of such research; rather, the family as traditionally defined is. The research is not necessarily concerned with whether education improves women's lives nor how or whether education gives women greater control over their lives; rather, it asks questions about the impact of women's formal education on the family. These studies have found at best a tenuous relationship between the number of years of education on the one hand and, on the other, marriage choice, marriage age, number of children, children's nutrition and health, and children's subsequent educational attainment and achievement. While it is the case that the more education a woman receives the older she is likely to be when she marries, it is also the case that the marriage age for all women is rising, and it is not clear that increased schooling is responsible for this trend. Once class is taken into account, educated women do not always have fewer children who are better nourished or better achievers in school. There are, of course, enormous variations among and within Third World nations and, because of them and the limitations of the research questions, this research has been unable to draw conclusions about the overall impact of women's formal education on the family.

The Recognition of Patriarchy or Pitfalls of Scholarship

Studies of women's education which either ignore or uncritically accept patriarchy and presuppose a strict dichotomized domestic/public division for women and men make unwarranted assumptions about women and about schools. Both kinds of scholarship basically ignore the realities of most women's lives, for women are neither totally confined to the domestic sphere, nor totally free of it when they enter public life. Marriage, reproduction, and child rearing are but some, although important, aspects of women's lives; their primacy in women's experiences varies widely by culture, social class, and economic organization in the Third World. Women's participation in public life is profoundly affected by marriage, child bearing, and child rearing in ways different from men's.[11] Because of this, one cannot assume, as do many of the researchers on women's education, the bifurcation of public and private spheres. Any research which rests on one to the exclusion of the other cannot help but be inconclusive and inaccurate, for it denies women's reality. Second, the acceptance, by white researchers in particular, of a bifurcation between public and private of necessity places the heterosexual family or the society at the center of research, which is tantamount to posing patriarchal institutions and their maintenance as a central research focus. Women are not, and cannot be, the center of research that begins with the fundamental question of how education affects institutions that women do not control and which, in most instances, oppress women.

This is one of the pitfalls of research on women's education in the Third World that rises from either denial or unquestioning acceptance of patriarchy. The research also presumes that schools are neutral in situations divorced from gender systems. Nowhere does the research acknowledge that schools, through their locations, curriculum, and structure, may in fact produce the kinds of asymmetrical outcomes that have been described in the research. Perhaps women do not go to schools because schools are not available to them; perhaps they do not achieve well in schools because the schools to which they have access are of lower quality than those which males attend; perhaps they do not achieve well in school because they are taught not to achieve through years of in-school socialization. In short, the research has tended to treat the school as a neutral institution that makes no distinction between males and females. Differences in outcomes, consequently, can only be seen as "natural."[12] The assumption of neutrality has been made with little knowledge of the types of education given to women versus men and the processes associated with them. Research has considered only the number of years in school, not the quality and content of the education. As long as the school is presumed "neutral," one need not study what goes on in school and how that affects the outcomes of education. The acceptance of the school as a Skinnerian "black box" may account for inconclusive results regarding the effects of educating women.

Recent research, influenced greatly by feminism, has begun to place women at the center of research and has sought to determine how education changes women's lives rather than how education affects "society" or "the family." Recognition of patriarchy and its consequences is the key to such scholarship: the new research assumes women's roles are socially rather than biologically derived. It inquires whether social institutions like schools contribute to maintaining sex gender systems and how schools might be changed to counter them.

Women at the Center of Research

Putting women at the center of research on schooling, combined with understanding sex-gender systems, has shown more fully why the pattern of women's educational attainment and achievement exists and how it might be changed. Research that does this is new. What follows will highlight the major differences between it and previous approaches.

For example, traditional scholarship never adequately explained why women go to school, or fail to go. Some scholars argued that social or cultural constraints accounted for lack of female education. More specifically, it has been posited, for example, that *purdah* (seclusion of women), practiced in Islamic nations and embedded in those cultures, explained why women's education rates were so low. But variation in women's educational enrollments is greater among nations that practice *purdah* than between those that do and those that do not, and women's enrollments in school have grown markedly in these countries since 1965.[13] Women have greater participation rates at all levels of education in Kuwait, Iran, and Tunisia, than they do in much of non-Islamic Asia and Africa. In fact, *purdah* in some cases has meant greater, rather than lesser, educational opportunities for women despite the fact that such participation does not necessarily imply equality for women in the society. Second, there is great variation among women within any given Islamic nation. To some extent, this variation can be explained by class: daughters of the middle class attend school more often than daughters of urban and rural poor. This is not always the case, for girls more often go to school, regardless of parents' occupations, when schools are available to them, culture and class not withstanding. In short, recent scholarship has demonstrated that a general "cultural constraint" explanation tells us very little; rather, it has shown that the way in which policy planners make schools available to women is more crucial. Third, if general culture constraints are not taken as major explanatory factors, one can also see how the quality of education, also a function of government choice, affects female enrollments. When high-quality schools are opened to women, women attend; they do not choose to go to third-rate schools. Also, clearly established is the fact that women's educational participation is dependent on the *type* of education offered to them. Schools which prepare women for prescribed familial roles tend not to be attended for they are redundant.[14] Finally, recent scholarship has found that, if education is related to a tangible reward structure, even if sex-segregated and in the context of *purdah,* women will attend school in increasing numbers.[15]

Recent scholarship also shows that the level of economic development, or industrialization, does not predict levels of female school enrollments, as some past scholarship has suggested. In Chile, for example, women are more equitably represented at all levels of the school system than they are in the U.S., Japan, or Canada, where per capita income and the contribution of manufacturing to the GNP is higher.[16]

In fact, in Chile, the quality of women's education is better than men's. The more highly educated a woman is in Chile, the more likely it is that she can enter high-paying professional and technical occupations. This is not to say that discrimination does not exist in the labor force; rather, because of discrimination, women need more schooling than men to enter those sectors of the labor force where qualification becomes more critical than prejudice. Women, given these circumstances, stay in school longer than men in order to reap the same economic rewards.

While for feminists it comes as no great surprise that social institutions such as schools support hierarchical gender systems, for scholars of education in the Third World it came as a revelation. Studies have begun to show that not only is the education offered to women in most parts of the Third World qualitatively inferior to that offered men, but that schools impart different social messages to their male and female students. Two studies of school textbooks, one carried out in Brazil, the other in India, have shown women portrayed as subservient to men, confined to domestic chores, and unable to benefit from education.[17] The Indian study found that these images are not always based on Indian traditions, and over time have become stronger in the texts, despite avowed government policies to correct sex inequality in education. Why this is the case is open to conjecture, but the trend, found also in Brazil and the United States, suggests some school materials used in the Third World are reproducing in those countries some of the patriarchal relations of Western capitalist societies. This linkage needs to be explored in greater depth, given the extensive aid programs in text book development between industrialized and Third World nations.

Not only has current research documented that schools impart different messages to females than to males through the formal curriculum, it has begun to show that the "hidden" curriculum operates similarly. Such work was pioneered by Vandra Masemann in her study of a Ghanaian secondary school.[18] Western-style schools reproduced in their staffing patterns the authority structures and social organization found in the West. Biraimah's study of a Togolese secondary school, conducted in 1979, found similar results; however, Biraimah went one step further. In extensive interviews with students, she found that girls resisted the roles proffered by the schools. While aware of the schools' messages, they did not internalize them. Rather, the more educated they became, the more they dismissed the schools' teachings.[19] We do not yet know the significance of such resistance, but its existence raises major issues about whether schools, despite their structural and curricular attributes, can be used by women to better their own lives, regardless of the imposition of new sex-gender systems. Biraimah's work has allowed scholars to see women not as passive victims, but rather as active agents who attempt to shape their own destinies.

While such studies direct our attention to the study of schooling—especially what is taught in school—and the ways in which girls renegotiate knowledge transmitted in the institution, they also contribute to our understanding of the ways in which we might view the impact of education on women. Traditionally, scholarship has shown that women's education has not led in the same way as men's to participation and status in public life. This is undeniable, but instead of concluding that because of this women are "bad risks" as far as education is concerned, feminist scholars have begun to ask whether women use schooling to mediate the impact of domestic life on public life and vice versa. Feminist scholarship has not accepted the bifurcation between the two presumed by previous scholarship. The research question becomes, instead, how does education change the impact of marriage, reproduction, and child-rearing on women's roles in society. Does education allow women to obtain greater power and authority in both spheres? One study, conducted in Upper Volta, showed that women would not participate in educational programs unless such programs were likely to have a tangible effect on their domestic burdens.[20] Literacy and numeracy skills were irrelevant; rather, women chose to attend only those classes that would introduce technologies that would free them from the tedium of household tasks. Otherwise, women had no time for education. The Upper Volta study begins with women's reality and shows not only how women's daily lives, given patriarchal family structures and unequal burdens, affect whether they or their daughters will attend school, but also that women chose to be educated, or remain uneducated, on the basis of their assessment of whether education helps them to ameliorate their domestic as well as public lives.

Traditionally the only distinctions researchers made among women were the same as were made among men: class, region, and ethnicity.[21] While these represent important distinctions, they presume that marriage, reproduction, and child bearing have the same impact on men as they do on women; feminist scholars have shown that this is not the case. Those who have studied women's participation in public life, notably in the workforce, know that marriage drives women from the workforce; child bearing and rearing have a similar effect unless productive employment is integrated into the household. This trend operates differently for different categories of women. Poverty tends to drive women into the workforce. Single women or female heads of households, regardless of class, are represented in greater numbers within the workforce than married women or married women with small children. Scholars, like Wainerman,[22] have begun to assess the impact of education, not in terms of whether it is the same for women as for men, but rather in terms of whether education changes the pattern of women's withdrawal from public life at times of marriage, child bearing, and child rearing. She has found, in her groundbreaking 1980 study, that women of all classes who are educated tend to sustain themselves in the workforce and resist the usual pattern of increased dependency on male income and the erosion of their status that has accompanied industrialization. Education, as she suggests, mediates the impact of domestic relations and restrictions on women's participation in public life. Her findings are very much in agreement with those of Biraimah and McSweeney and Freedman, for they highlight the fact that women use education to mediate the impact of patriarchy and its intensification due to economic trends. We still do not know, however, from any of these studies why and how education seems to have this effect. More research is needed that relates what schools teach and what girls learn in school to understand how women use the education they receive.

New Directions

Recent research suggests that women want to, and individual women are in some cases able to, use schooling to better their lives, but it has not been able to show whether education does so for all women and can be used in and of itself to improve women's position in society. Study after study has shown that despite the expansion of schooling for women, their position, relative to men, especially in the economy and workforce has not improved; rather, in many countries it has deteriorated.[23] Why this is the case is not easily explained without further research, and that research cannot limit itself to considering schools and their relation to society in a one-nation perspective.

Some scholars have argued that the deteriorating status of women, despite their increases in educational attainments, is directly traceable to the failure of individual nations to industrialize.[24] They claim that if industrialization were to occur, then women's status relative to men's would improve, especially given the gains in women's education. Such analyses assume, without evidential bases, that the status of women in relation to men in already industrialized nations of Western Europe and North America where education is universal for both males and females on the primary, and often on the secondary levels, is substantially better than that of women in the Third World. This is somewhat debatable. Because of this, others have argued that the deterioration of women's status within the workforce of the Third World nations is a necessary concomitant of capitalist development that education cannot mediate.[25]

It is impossible, given the present state of research, to arrive at a definitive explanation for the deterioration of women's status within the economies of most Third World nations as industrialization has progressed, or the role of women's education in this process. It is important, though, to point out some of the difficulties involved in making statements about the relationship between increases in the education of women and their status in the workforce. These difficulties have to do with how one analyzes changes in women's roles and with the geographic boundaries within which most analyses have been based.

Most of the research documenting the changes in women's participation in the economy consists of correlations of population characteristics that have been used to study men. A few studies, like Wainerman's, depart and consider the structure of the family and child rearing and how they influence women's participation in a nation's economy. Wainerman suggests, in a study confined to Paraguay and Argentina (both with capitalist economies and differing levels of industrialization), that education increases women's labor force participation and lessens their dependency on males. But Wainerman says nothing about women's *status,* relative to men's, within the economy. Clearly, scholarship needs to explore, through the use of women-centric measures, whether the mediating effect Wainerman found relates to changes in their status within the workforce.

We have little ability to assess, through correlational data, the impact of schooling, and this presents a second difficulty in the existing research on women's education and its relationship both to their participation in and status within the economy. Scholarship to date has related increases in the number of women within certain sectors of the economy and increases in the number of women educated, finding the two have little to do with one another. *It has not studied women who are educated* and traced their work and family lives. It could be that increases in the number of women entering the workforce, or failing to enter the workforce, reflect young single women who seek jobs at an earlier age than their contemporaries who are in school until age nineteen or twenty-five. Third World populations are young; what may seem a trend now may not reflect the impact or lack of impact of education; the research findings may reflect instead the inadequacy of correlational data to detect new trends. To assess the relation of women's education to changes in their status, we need to study the social and economic realities of the lives of *educated* women relative to educated men, something which scholarship has yet to do.

The research studies that we have on women's education and the workforce are, for the most part, one-nation studies. These studies, and a very limited range of them, have been used to argue that the phenomena observed are characteristic of all nations as they develop. However, we have no idea of the impact of women's education on the position of women in the workforce in revolutionary socialist societies, since no such research has been done. We can only guess that what we have observed in non-socialist Third World nations results from modernization or the spread of capitalism until we compare these findings with those from Third World countries like China, Cuba, and Tanzania.

Comparative research has not only neglected analysis of the impact of education on women's position in socialist and non-socialist Third World countries; it has also failed to assess whether changes in women's position noted in Third World countries exist in advanced industrial societies, which in most instances control Third World economies. Most of the research has presumed that the factors influencing the roles of women and the use women can make of education exist solely within the boundaries of a single nation-state. Most deny the impact of neo-colonialism and the international market. The extent to which the economies of Third World nations are controlled by capitalists from the industrialized nations of Western Europe and the United States has been ignored in the literature.[26] The importance of extending our analyses of the impact of education on women beyond national boundaries cannot be overstated, since it is entirely possible that the extent to which women can use educational institutions to gain control of their lives is dependent on the degree to which patriarchal institutions operating *outside* of the nation-state allow women to use institutions in this manner. In other words, the content of and opportunities for schooling for Third World women may be closely tied to education systems for women in the advanced capitalist societies which control the Third World. In this case, it is important to know whether the changes feminists are making in the educational systems in countries like the United States have any role in changing the schooling available to women in the Third World. Comparative studies can begin to deal with these questions.

Feminist Scholarship and the Study of Women

This review of research has raised more questions than it has answered about the education of women in the Third World. Throughout, I have emphasized the vast gains in knowledge, research perspectives, and methods developed over the past decade. Yet our knowledge is sparse because research in this area has only recently begun. The kind of questions researchers have addressed reflects the newness of the field. The questions that have been studied—and not studied—also reflect the differences between traditional and feminist research on the study of the education of women. Unless future research is conducted in full recognition of patriarchy as an institution that can and ought to be changed, and takes women's lives and realities as its starting point, the results may have little to do with emancipating women or bettering their lives. Research, as I have pointed out, can serve to oppress women. In the past it has been used to provide a rationale to deny them education on the grounds of supposed sex differences that make them "bad risks" in school.

Feminist scholarship, however, is distinguishable from other scholarship on women in that its methods, frameworks, concerns, and questions are directed to changing women's lives and freeing them from oppression. For feminist scholars of education in the Third World, our goal is to find ways in which schools can be made a force to better women's private and public lives. We cannot know the effects of changing the numbers of women going to school, the length of time they remain in school, or the results of curricular innovations, until we develop ways to assess those changes. The first step is to orient our study toward women's realities.

Notes

[1] See, for example, Marie Eliou, "Scolarisation et promotion feminines en Afrique francophone" (Côte d'Ivoire, Haute-Volta, Senegal), *International Review of Education* 19, no. I (1973): 30-46; Jacqueline Chaubaud, *The Education and Advancement of Women* (Paris: UNESCO, 1970). Excellent review articles include Mary Jean Bowman and C. Arnold Anderson, "The Participation of Women in Education in the Third World," *Comparative Education Review* 24, no.2, pt. 2 (Summer 1980):S13-31("S" indicates special issue here and subsequently); Jeremy D. Finn, Loretta Dulberg, and Janet Reis, "Sex Differences in Educational Attainment: A Cross National Perspective,"

Harvard Educational Review 49 (Nov. 1979): 477-503; Rati Ram, "Sex Differences in the Labor Market Outcomes of Education," *Comparative Education Review* 24, no. 2, pt. 2 (Summer 1980): S53-77; M. Kotwal, "Inequalities in the Distribution of Education Between Countries, Sexes, Generations, and Individuals," in *Education, Inequality and Life Chances* I (Paris: OECD, 1975): 31-109. The term *Third World,* used in many of these publications, is itself problematic and needs editorial attention.

[2] For a review of this research, see Jeremy D. Finn, "Sex Differences in Educational Outcomes: A Cross National Study," *Sex Roles* 6 (Feb. 1980): 9-26.

[3] See Ernest Stabler, *Education since Uhuru* (Middletown, Conn.: Wesleyan University Press, 1969); David Abernethy, *The Political Dilemma of Popular Education: An African Case* (Stanford: Stanford University Press, 1969).

[4] There is a vast literature on this subject. An excellent review article is Irvin Sobel, "The Human Capital Revolution in Economic Development," *Comparative Education Review* 22, no. 2 (June 1978): 278-308.

[5] See, for example, William S. Bennett, Jr., "Educational Change and Economic Development," *Sociology of Education* 40 (Spring 1967): 101-14; David C. McClelland, "Does Education Accelerate Economic Growth," *Economic Development and Cultural Change* 14 (April 1966): 257-78; George Psacharopoulous and Keith Hinchliffe, *Returns to Education: An International Comparison* (San Francisco: Jossey-Bass, 1973).

[6] See Sobel, "Human Capital"; Abernethy, *Political Dilemma;* Donald K. Adams, "Development Education," *Comparative Education Review* 21 (June/October 1977): 296-310.

[7] Marie Thourson Jones, "Education of Girls in Tunisia: Policy Implications of the Drive for Universal Enrollment," *Comparative Education Review* 24, no. 2, pt. 2 (Summer; 1980): S106-23.

[8] Ester Boserup, *Women's Role in Economic Development* (New York: St. Martin's, 1969).

[9] Ibid.; Norma S. Chinchilla, "Industrialization, Monopoly Capitalism and Women's Work in Guatemala," *Signs* 3, no. 1 (Autumn 1977): 38-56; Glaura Vasques de Miranda, "Women's Labor Force Participation in a Developing Society," ibid., pp. 261-74.

[10] Two excellent reviews of such research are: S. H. Cochrane, *Education and Fertility: What Do We Know?* (Baltimore: Johns Hopkins University Press, 1979); Robert Levine, "Influences of Women's Schooling on Maternal Behavior in the Third World,"

Comparative Education Review 24, no. 2, pt. 2 (Summer 1980): S78-105.

[11] See Guy Standing, "Education and Female Participation in the Labor Force," *International Lahore Review* 114 (Nov./Dec. 1976): 281-97; Catalina H. Wainerman, "The Impact of Education on the Female Labor Force in Argentina and Paraguay," *Comparative Education Review* 24, no. 2, pt. 2 (Summer 1980): S180-95.

[12] A good example of such research is Bowman and Anderson, "Participation of Women"; Boserup, *Women's Role*.

[13] Audrey Smock, *Women's Education in Developing Countries* (New York: Praeger, 1981).

[14] Bowman and Anderson, "Participation of Women"; see also, G. McSweeney and Marion Freedman, "Lack of Time as an Obstacle to Women's Education: The Case of Upper Volta," *Comparative Education Review* 24, no. 2, pt. 2 (Summer 1980): S124-39.

[15] Ernesto Schiefelbein and Joseph Farrell, "Women, Schooling and Work in Chile: Evidence from a Longitudinal Study," *Comparative Education Review* 24, no. 2, pt. 2 (Summer 1980): S160-79; Bee-Lan-Chan Wang, "Sex and Ethnic Differences in Educational Investment in Malaysia: The Effect of Reward Structures," *Comparative Education Review* 24, no. 2, pt. 2 (Summer 1980): S140-59.

[16] Schiefelbein and Farrell, "Women, Schooling and Work."

[17] Narendra Nath Kalia, "Images of Men and Women in Indian Text books," *Comparative Education Review* 24, no. 2, pt. 2 (Summer 1980): S209-23; Patricia Greenleaf, "Sexism in School Texts in Brazil," unpublished paper, Indiana University, 1979.

[18] Vandra Masemann, "The Education of Girls in a West African Boarding School" (unpublished Ph.D. dissertation, University of Toronto, 1975).

[19] Karen Coffyn Biraimah, "The Impact of Western Schools on Girls' Expectations: A Togolese Case," *Comparative Education Review* 24, no. 2, pt. 2 (Summer 1980): S196-208.

[20] McSweeney and Freedman, "Lack of Time."

[21] See, for example, Remi Clignet, "Social Change and Sexual Differentiation in the Camerouns and Ivory Coast," *Signs* 3, no. 1 (Autumn 1977): 244-60; Bowman and Anderson, "Participation of Women."

[22] Wainerman, "Impact of Education."

[23] Chinchilla, "Industrialization, Monopoly Capitalism"; Martha Maldonado Van Zuiden, "Participation of Women in Education and the Peruvian Labor Force," (Ph.D. dissertation, State University of New York at Buffalo, 1980); Boserup, *Women's Role;* Judith Van Allen,

"Modernization Means More Dependency," *The Center Magazine* (May/June 1974), pp. 60-67; Nadia Yousseff, *Women and Work in Developing Societies* (Berkeley: University of California, Institute of International Studies, 1974). See also, Isabelle Deblé, *The School Education of Girls* (Paris: UNESCO, 1981).

[24]See, for example, Elsa Chaney and Marianne Schmink, "Women and Modernization: Access to Tools," in *Sex and Class in Latin America,* ed. J. Nash and Helen I. Safa (New York: Praeger, 1975), pp. 160-82; Yousseff, *Women and Work.*

[25]See, for example, Chinchilla, "Industrialization, Monopoly Capitalism."

26. James D. Cockcroft, Andre Gunder Frank, and Dale L. Johnson, *Dependency and Underdevelopment* (New York: Anchor Books, 1972); "Introduction," P. G. Altbach and Gail P. Kelly, eds., *Education and Colonialism* (New York: Longmans, 1978); Robert P. Arnove, "Comparative Education and World Systems Analysis," *Comparative Education Review* 24, no. 1 (February 1980): 48-62; Philip G. Altbach, "Servitude of the Mind?'Education, Dependency and Neocolonialism," *Teachers' College Record* 72 (December 1977): 188-204. Only Chinchilla, "Industrialization, Monopoly Capitalism," attempts to make this connection for women in the case of Guatemala.

Comparative Education: Challenge and Response[†]

Gail P. Kelly and Philip G. Altbach

Comparative education is characterized today by a wide diversity of views, lively debates, and varying theoretical perspectives. Since *Comparative Education Review* and *Comparative Education* published their retrospective "state of the art" issues in 1977, the field has changed. In this essay, we will discuss some of these changes and the debates and research trends that have arisen since that date. Our interest is in the challenges posed to the field and the field's response.

It is our view that since 1977 many of the approaches that underlay the field, articulated so perceptively in the British and American appraisals in *Comparative Education* and the *Comparative Education Review* have come under criticism. Some have questioned the national comparisons that have traditionally characterized research and have argued cogently for world systems and regional analyses. Others have challenged the field to move beyond quantitative studies of school outcomes to qualitative research on educational processes. The theoretical assumptions that had guided the field, especially in the United States and particularly structural functionalism, have also emerged as subjects of intense debate. Some scholars have begun to explore alternative perspectives such as conflict theory, legitimation theory, and Marxism. Simultaneously, scholars challenged the field to consider subjects of inquiry that it had hitherto ignored. Among these are women'' education, the concrete study of social and political institutions and the question of how knowledge is disseminated, produced, and used. In the past decade, scholars in comparative education have also turned to reconsidering old questions, especially the role of education in bringing about modernization and social change.

The authors wish to thank Joseph Farrell and Stephen Klees for their criticism of an earlier draft of this article.

[†]©1986 by the Comparative and International Education Society. Reprinted with permission from *Comparative Education Review,* Vol. 30, No. 1, published by the University of Chicago Press, and Philip Altbach.

The pages that follow first consider the new challenges posited to the field since 1977 and then look at the field's response. Our discussion is based on an analysis of research that has appeared in the major journals in the field, such as *Comparative Education Review,* the *International Review of Education, Compare,* and *Comparative Education,* as well as in some of the major books published on the field in the United States and Great Britain, including those in the series issued by Pergamon and Praeger. Our discussion is limited to the English language literature, which, for the most part, is a British and North American literature. We make no pretenses of representing the developments in the field in Third World nations or anywhere but in the United States, Great Britain, and, to a lesser extent, Canada.

Our focus here is on new directions in the field. We will not dwell at length on traditional approaches or modes of analysis, which continue to dominate comparative education. Our purpose is to highlight challenges and to direct the field's attention to perspectives that have yet to be fully considered and that we believe are important to its vitality.

Challenges and New Directions

Since 1977, four kinds of challenges to established research traditions in comparative education have emerged. These are (1) those that question the nation-state or national characteristics as the major parameter in defining comparative study; (2) those that question the use of input-output models and exclusive reliance on quantification in the conduct of comparative research; (3) those that challenge structural functionalism as the major theoretical premise undergirding scholarship; and (4) those that direct attention to new subjects of inquiry. Some of these challenges began prior to 1977; however, before that time they scarcely entered the discourse of the field and were not promoted through the major journals or texts in comparative education. After 1977, they were increasingly and more directly articulated.

Although we have grouped the challenges to the field into four categories, we are aware that there is some overlap among them. For example, world systems analysis, which looks at international inequalities between nation-states in examining educational expansion, is guided by conflict theory and, in some instances, by Marxism. This is also the case with research that has arisen on women and sex differences in education cross nationally, on knowledge distribution and control, and on the politics of educational planning. Regardless of the overlap, we believe it useful to discuss the challenges.

Challenges to the Nation-State as the Exclusive Research Framework

Until recently, most research in comparative education focused on the nation-state, and/or characteristics of nation-states, treated as an autonomous unit. Indeed, much of the field was comprised of studies that applied a method derived from the social sciences to the study of education in a particular nation or that simply described education in a specific country. Often research asked how education contributed to the development and maintenance of social structures within that nation-state and compared education's role in one country with its role in another.[1] When the focus was on individual attitudes, research was situated in the context of school systems in a single nation presumed to be autonomous and coequal with others. This framework predominated in region-wide studies that, while dealing with Southeast Asia, Africa, Latin America, or Eastern Europe, focused on education in individual nation-states within that region that presumably shared similar cultures, histories, and economic or political structures. Topically based studies also were situated in national frameworks, asking, for example, if one national school system was more conducive to economic growth than another.

Scholars such as John Meyer, John Boliennet, Francisco Ramirez, Mathew Zachariah, Martin Carnoy, Robert Arnove, and Philip Altbach challenge the use of the nation-state as the dominant category guiding comparative research. They argue that educational systems in one country are often affected more by factors outside that country than they are by factors inside it and urge research to focus on identifying these external forces. Martin Carnoy's 1974 book, *Education as Culture Imperialism*, marked the beginning of such scholarship in the field. After 1977, the number of works of this nature in comparative education increased markedly.[2]

In 1979, John Meyer and Michael T. Hannon published *National Development and the World System*.[3] They point out that educational expansion in the post-World War II period could not be explained by reference to a single nation-state or its political structure, to the way in which it organized power, to how its economy was controlled, or to its peculiar social structure. The drive for universal primary education and the unparalleled expansion of education on the secondary and tertiary levels had little to do with national educational policies, either. Meyer and Hannon maintain that given changes in technology and communications and the internationalization of the labor market, education functions within a transnational context. They call on the field to reorient its inquiry by looking at what they call the world system rather than merely at the nation-state.

Meyer and his colleagues, as well as other scholars who focus on world systems analysis, use a range of perspectives in their work. Meyer, and his co-authors, for example, argue that an individual nation's political and economic systems have relatively little to do with either how education is organized and distributed or its content. Immanuel Wallerstein, on the other hand, discusses the nature of the world system by using Marxian frameworks, although his work is not directly dealing with education.[4] Most of the scholars directly in the field of comparative education utilize a range of explanatory frameworks in their work on specific aspects of how relationships between nations, regions, classes, or groups within and among societies affect schooling and its social, economic, and political outcomes. Altbach, Arnove, Carnoy, Zachariah, and Silva all argue that national school systems exist within the context of unequal power relations among nations.[5] They argue that either through design, historical circumstance, or the contemporary distribution of resources, including intellectual resources, the Western industrialized capitalist nations dominate the economic and educational systems of the less industrialized countries. Silva argues that educational dominance patterns parallel trading blocks. Altbach discusses how the knowledge that schools distribute in the Third World is generated, controlled, and distributed by the United States, Great Britain, and France. Carnoy contends that such controls seek to maintain existing international inequalities and keep the Third World dependent.

World systems analysis challenges comparative education to go beyond the nation-state as the major analytical category guiding research and to look at regional variations, social groups, classes, and others that are not necessarily bound to the nation. Other scholars who have not used the world systems approach have come to similar conclusions, frequently based on microanalytic research. Notable among these are those scholars who have focused on regional variation.

Research in comparative education before 1977 focused on schooling within a nation-state; rare was the scholar whose work centered on regional variation beyond urban/rural distinctions that were applied to Third World nations and, in the case of a few studies of African nations, beyond ethnically based distinctions. Comparative work took the nation-state as the boundary for comparison and referred to it in tracing school/society relations. Comparative research did not inquire as to whether there were major regional variations in the pattern of educational diffusion or in the determinants of educational access and outcomes within a nation-state. Proponents of the analysis of regional variation argue that comparison among regions within nation-states is as significant as comparison between nations. The challenge to pursue such a line of analysis was developed by John Craig and Margaret Archer in their works tracing the spread of education in the nineteenth century.[6] It was also advanced by Mary Jean Bowman, Phyllis Goldblatt, and David Plank.[7] All of these scholars showed that educational variance often is as great if not greater, between regions within a nation as between nations. The determinants of women's education, for example, is not the same in northeast Brazil as in the dominant south of that country; class and ethnicity may not operate similarly in regard to educational access and outcome throughout a single nation. They have pointed to the obvious—the necessity of looking at regional variation given growing trends to decentralization of education and deconcentration of educational decision making in much of the world.

Although scholars working in the newly emergent tradition of world systems analysis and analysis of regional variation challenge established research traditions, their questions represent but one kind among those to emerge since 1977.

Challenges to Input/Output Models and Dominant Reliance on Quantification

Much research in comparative education tended to focus almost exclusively on the quantitative analysis of educational inputs and outcomes, mostly the outcomes. Research assumed that the outcomes—such as modern attitudes or mathematics achievement levels—could be attributed to whatever schools taught. With some exceptions, research—following Sadlerian traditions—assumed that whatever went on in the school was unimportant and not worthy of study. The only studies of school processes—if one could call them that—were descriptions of curricular guides, analyses of texts, and a few ethnographic studies—considered anthropology—that treated the classroom as part of the broader social order, reflecting a social consensus.

Before 1977, there were some criticisms of the field for presuming that school processes were unimportant. More recently, this criticism was extended to research such as the international achievement studies (IEA) that focused only on the quantitative measurement of outcomes and inputs (such as test scores, number of hours in the classroom, years of teacher training, and the like) to stand for the study of the educational process. Scholars such as Masemann, Weis, Heyman, and Pfau argued cogently that reliance on school outcome data failed to relate outcomes to the processes of schooling and suggested that only through qualitative methods could the nature of educational processes and their outcomes be understood.[8] They pointed out that what schools teach cannot be reduced only to the formal curriculum texts and teacher attributes; rather, student and teacher interaction, the structure of educational institutions, and the "lived culture" of the schools represented a very powerful element in producing the social, cultural, and political outcomes of schooling. Their call was for the use of qualitative means of research that focused on educational processes.

Heyman and Pfau urge comparative education to adopt ethnomethodological techniques derived exclusively from anthropology; Masemann and Weis, in their respective works, challenge the field to go beyond anthropological traditions and to relate educational processes to broader theories of school/society relations. Weis points out that such scholarship could adopt varying theoretical perspectives, including either structural functionalism or Marxism.[9]

Although the challenge to engage in qualitative research on educational processes in light of social theory does not necessarily entail a paradigm shift for the field, paralleling interest in such studies has increased questioning of the dominance of structural functionalism in guiding research in comparative education.

Challenges to Structural Functionalism

Until the 1970s, comparative education in North America was largely influenced by structural functionalism. This is not surprising given the domination of this perspective in many of the social sciences. The "state-of-the-art" volumes of *Comparative Education Review* and of *Comparative Education* are largely in this tradition.[10] The field asked either how education functioned to maintain the social fabric or how it could be made to function, in the case of the Third World, to develop a nation-state generally along Western models. It was assumed that what was good for the nation also benefited all of society. In this context, conflict, as John Bock and Rolland Paulston so aptly point out, was considered dysfunctional at best.[11] Although many questions about functionalism were raised outside comparative education before 1977, few within the field paid much attention to debates in sociology and political science. Kazamias and Schwartz, in their essay that prefaces *Comparative Education Review's* state-of-the-art issue, note the dominance of structural functionalism in the field and urge that scholars inform their works with different perspectives.[12] Other voices joined them. Martin Carnoy, Philip Altbach, Robert Arnove, Michael Apple, and Henry Levin began to look at how educational systems serve societal groups differentially and how social inequalities are played out at the regional and international levels.[13] Carnoy, Apple, and Levin emphasize the relationship between education and the development of capitalist relations and argue that the nature of economic systems and of state control make a difference as to what schools teach and as to the outcomes of education.

Rolland Paulston argues that reliance on functionalism has led the field away from correctly analyzing education in most social settings and places too much stress on the national setting and not on the roles that education might play in society and its myriad institutions.[14] John Bock makes a similar point.[15] He asserts that most developing societies are plural societies characterized by conflict, where dominant groups seek to legitimize their control over the state. At the same time, minorities attempt to use education to assert themselves and sometimes to unseat the dominant groups. Bock shows us that education assumes contradictory roles—it is at once oppressive and liberating. Paulston and Bock and, more recently, Hans Weiler see alternatives to functionalism in conflict theory and in legitimation theory;[16] others have adopted a classical Marxian perspective.

It is not our intention in this essay to explore in-depth these alternative theories; rather, our point here is to show that alternatives to structural functionalism have been articulated in the field. These alternatives have also led to changes in research concerns, as we will now explore.

The Emergence of New Research Concerns

Comparative education until recently was a field that focused mainly on issues of education and development, on educational planning, on the individual outcomes of schooling in the context of the nation-state, and on a range of descriptive analyses and discussions of educational systems and issues. Most of the research was informed by structural functionalism or was basically atheoretical and descriptive. Few qualitative studies appeared in the field's journal that sought to understand what schools taught and that related educational processes to outcomes of education. Over the past decade the field has been challenged to study subjects that it had hitherto ignored. These ranged from including women both as a category in and as a central concern of research; to looking at the ways in which knowledge was disseminated, produced, and used; to new ways of looking at educational institutions and their relation to society. A major research challenge in all instances has been to reorient study away from preoccupation with individual outcomes and attitudes toward looking at institutions ranging from schools to the state to international agencies and finally to the relationships among them. The research challenge that emerged was to chart institutional content—that is, how institutions such as schools, planning agencies, the government, and so forth are organized and controlled and what the effect is that these institutional arrangements have on educational outcomes. We will discuss some of these challenges that have arisen in the past decade in the form of an interest in how education is planned and controlled, how educational contents are structured and distributed, and how schools shape the social reality of their pupils.

Although comparative education has a substantial literature on educational planning, much of that literature focuses on the technical aspects of planning and its outcomes—whether goals were or were not fulfilled. New scholarship has appeared that looks at the institutional context of planning—who plans what in whose interest and the relation between planning and structured inequality. Studies like Urwick's on Nigeria; McGinn, Schiefelbein, and Warwick's on planners in Chile; and Salvador's and McGinn and Street's on Mexico are in this vein.[17] Others have looked at institutional capacity to plan, the mechanisms by which plans are put into practice, and the role of political parties with distinctly different ideologies in planning. Some of these institutional studies have focused on the roles of international agencies in forming and implementing national plans—for example, Linda Dove's research on Universal Primary Education in Bangladesh.[18] These works challenge the field to look at institutional processes in the context of national and international politics.

While much scholarship to emerge since 1977 has called the field's attention to the institutional processes of planning, related research has emerged on how knowledge is generated and used in educational systems to make educational policy and shape society. Much of this research—but by no means, all of it—stems from world systems or conflict analysis. Some scholars have been concerned with knowledge distribution systems. Altbach's work on transnational publishing, for example, focuses on how books are produced and distributed internationally and the implications for educational and knowledge systems within specific countries.[19] Others have been concerned with knowledge generation and control. Edward Berman's research on the role of philanthropic foundations is an example of a concern with the factors that influence research and development.[20] Other scholars have been concerned with knowledge utilization. Fry, among others, studies how educational planners use research to guide policy.[21] James Coleman has considered the role of U.S.-trained political scientists in Africa and has written on the impact of foundation assistance in Asia and Africa.[22] Hans Weiler and others have written of the impact of foreign study on education and development in the Third World. This research has looked at student flows and the students' impact on host institutions and on the students' country of origin.[23] These studies, and many others, have focused on the nature of knowledge transfer and its impact on the Third World.[24]

There has also been an interest in what kind of knowledge enters the classroom and how that knowledge is communicated. Heyneman's research on the role, availability, and effectiveness of textbooks in Third World nations is an example of such scholarship. There is also a growing body of research that seeks to understand the nature of social reality conveyed in textbooks used in the Third World and the relationship of this reality to development and culture.[25]

Although comparative education has traditionally been concerned with school outcomes, there has been a new concern with the detailed study of the content of schooling and with the internal workings of the school. Some of these studies have used ethnographic and participant observation research tools to search deeply into the internal life of educational institutions. Paul Willis's study of British education is an example of this trend.[26] Other studies have looked at the interaction between the formal and the "hidden" curriculum in schools in an effort to understand school cultures.[27] Some researchers have looked at a range of variables to obtain a broad picture of the impact of education on students and on society. William Cummings's work on Japan takes such an approach.[28] Susan Shirk and Jonathan Unger analyze education in China during the Cultural Revolution from this perspective.[29] The originality of this research is its concern with the internal culture of the school, the "in-school" outcomes of education, and the effect of the relationship between these factors on society.

Another important and new stream of scholarship has been gender studies. The field in the 1980s has been challenged to look at women in the context of educational and social structures that have resulted in gender-based inequalities. This scholarship has pointed out that research can no longer assume that findings based on the study of male populations are necessarily relevant for females as well. The 1980 special issue of *Comparative Education Review* challenged the field not only to include gender as a background variable in research—something almost totally neglected in comparative education—but also to make women a central research focus.[30] The field was also challenged to ask how education changed women's lives in the family and in the work force and not confine itself to asking whether educational outcomes for males and females were the same.

We have thus far detailed currents new to the field since 1977. We have by no means represented all currents in the field. Our goal has been to call attention to innovations in the field, not to the field's mainstream. Much research in the field continues to presume the autonomous nation-state and is guided by structural functionalism and its correlates like human capital theory. Research still focuses on development and on the outcomes of schooling and, as in the past is predominantly quantitative, centered around primary through higher education.

The challenges to the field that we have outlined have, for the most part generated some debate. They have appeared in the major journals and texts in the field; they have been presented at conferences; some have been the themes of world yearbooks of education. The last part of the essay asks how the field has responded to these challenges—what kinds of debates, if any, have they generated, and how have they affected the mainstream of the field.

Response

It is always difficult to gauge the response of a field of inquiry to challenges that it reexamine its theoretical assumptions or study phenomena through the lens of theories that contradict those that the field has traditionally used. We now ask if there have been any changes in the research published in the major journals and texts in comparative education that reflect the new challenges we have outlined thus far. Is there, for example, a greater emphasis on qualitative research that seeks to understand educational processes? Are there more studies focusing on women or on education in the context of the world system or on institutional behaviors? Has there been less reliance on structural functionalism and a greater diversity of theoretical orientations?

We will show that there have been three types of responses to the new research challenges. In many instances the field has tended to ignore new challenges. Such a response, we believe, is basically a sign of weakness in comparative education. A second response has been to confront new challenges and to attempt to refute them. In some instances scholars have contested the validity of new trends and sought to end the debates that they engendered. The third response has been to co-opt the challenges. This has led to some changes in what scholars study but not necessarily in how they study it or in the theoretical assumptions that underlie inquiry. We will discuss these three types of responses separately.

Ignoring the Challenges

A common response to new trends is to ignore them. Comparative education is no different in this regard from other fields of inquiry. Many of the challenges we noted appeared in the field's major journals as "think pieces." For example, Vandra Masemann and Douglas Foley urged the field to engage in qualitative research that seeks to understand educational processes.[31] No debate followed, nor for that matter did much research of a qualitative nature on school processes. The field neither accepted nor rejected the challenge; it simply acted as if it were never made. *Comparative Education Review* continued to publish a very small number of ethnographies, but they, by and large, were in the tradition of anthropologically based works that did not seek to relate classroom phenomena to social theory. Journals in Great Britain like *Compare* carried no such material; the recent *International Encyclopedia of Education* fails to mention this work as even a part of the field, although there is substantive coverage given to ethnography and to the anthropology of education.[32]

The tendency to ignore new trends extends also to challenges to attend to gender both as a variable in research and as a focus of research. Two of the major journals in the field published special issues on women's education and sex differences in education, and the *World Yearbook of Education* in 1984 focused on women.[33] Despite this, some journals in the field have yet to run research articles on either women's education or sex differences in education. The few articles that acknowledge gender that find their way into the field's journals have women as the subject of study and are written by women as well. Very rarely does research use gender as a significant background variable, even when that research does deal with other variables like class, ethnicity, and urban/rural residence. This occurs even when scholarship focuses on inequality or the determinants of academic achievement, despite the clear-cut evidence that gender is both a basis for structural inequality and a predictor of educational outcomes. At the same time that the field has tended to ignore the sizable body of research on women and gender effects that has appeared in women's studies journals, UNESCO publications, and special issues in the field, there has also been little debate about the validity of such scholarship. Gender often becomes a nonissue, neither incorporated nor debated and then rejected.[34]

The field's reaction to the challenges to engage in the qualitative study of school processes or to make women a focus of research and gender a variable in scholarship has parallels in the case of regional analysis. A few scholars have called on the field to consider such work, and their calls so far have landed on deaf ears.

Although comparative education has ignored some new currents that have arisen since 1977, this is not the case with all new scholarship. The field has hotly debated scholarship that has directly challenged the theoretical premises underlying research. In the case of world systems analysis, the field has debated and co-opted some challenges by accepting parts of the research foci commended by such scholarship while discarding the theory that led to these very concerns. Before discussing co-optation, however, we will trace the debates that the new challenges have engendered.

Debate

Although many recent commentaries on the field have ignored the challenges posed by world systems analysis to comparative education,[35] others have attacked it on the basis of the association of world systems analysis with a Marxist problematic. Harold Noah and Max Eckstein have dubbed this approach the "new simplicitude."[36] They claim that such an approach, deriving from dependency theory and focusing on the unequal power relations between Third World and industrialized nations has tended to look on Third World nations as passive victims of the industrialized nations and to blame the current economic hardships of these Third World nations on former colonial rulers. Noah and Eckstein deny that there is any evidence of attempts on the part of Western industrialized nations to maintain economic domination that would explain either the poverty or the evolution of school systems in much of Africa, Asia, and Latin America. Rather, they attribute the problems of the Third World solely to underdevelopment, which predated colonialism and which industrialized nations are, through their aid programs, seeking to remedy. Additionally, Noah and Eckstein point out that if world systems analysis had any validity, it would be impossible to explain social revolutions in parts of the Third World or development in other parts.

Attacks on world systems analysis, similar to those initiated by Noah and Eckstein, were mounted by Keith Watson and Jon Lauglo in British journals.[37] Watson does not dispute the existence of the international ties documented by Arnove, Altbach, and others. He simply disagrees with world systems analysts' interpretation of what these ties mean. Watson, for one, sees dependency as a stage in the development of autonomous nation states.

The debates over world systems analysis do not only concern the interpretation of underdevelopment. One study has attempted to generate data to refute world systems analysis and the application of dependency theory to the evolution of schooling in the Third World. Sica and Prechel ask if there is any relation between the spread of Western-style education and economic dependency (they note the lack of relation between educational expansion and economic development).[38] They find no significant relation between measures of educational enrollments and dependency. Whether such a statistical analysis has validity is open to question—the authors themselves point out that the fact that they have found no statistically significant relation cannot be taken to mean that no relation at all exists.

The debates surrounding world systems analysis are related to those that challenges to structural functionalism have generated. Not only have scholars working in the tradition of world systems analysis questioned structural functionalism but so also have some scholars who focus their studies on education and inequality and on the role of education as an institution in maintaining existing social and political injustice. These scholars have been openly critical of structural functionalism and have applied conflict, Marxism, and/or other nonmainstream theories to the study of education. Within comparative education there have been few, if any, outright defenses of structural functionalism; rather, there have been critiques of alternative approaches, especially those identified as Marxist. Some scholars have dismissed such approaches out of hand as ideological and "biased."[39] Others, like Erwin Epstein, have tried to moderate the debate and strive for consensus in the field. In his Presidential Address to the Comparative and International Education Society, Erwin Epstein implied that the strident debates that Marxist and conflict theories had brought to the field put comparative education's future at risk.[40] He claimed that "neo-Marxism," "neo-positivism" (which he identified with functionalism), and "neo-relativism" (which he associated with Brian Holmes and his "problem approach" first articulated in the 1960s) divided the field into hostile camps. Each position generated its own data sets, none of which was comparable. Because of this, the field had reached a point where it was unable to provide "objective" evidence to guide policy. Epstein felt that comparative education would be better off if theoretical divisions were muted and attention focused on generating a knowledge base that all could use.

Epstein did not directly attack Marxian theory—his plea was one for greater consensus in the field. Paulston, in his article that outlines the divergent theories in the field, also argues for consensus.[41] He suggests that Marxian theories could be used to "diagnose" educational problems and consensual functionalist theories to arrive at reform strategies. Whether such a strategy is viable is open to question.

Not only has the application of conflict and Marxist theories been criticized for being divisive but there have also been some works that seek to disprove empirically the findings of such studies. Among these is William Cummings's *Education and Equality in Japan.* Cummings characterizes Marxist-based theories of social/cultural reproduction as refusing to posit the possibility of social transformation other than through a revolution that drastically alters the way production is organized and the ownership of the means of production. Despite a highly differentiated system of higher education and evidence that socioeconomic status closely predicts educational levels and future income, Cummings contends that the schools are making Japanese society more egalitarian than is the case in any other country, including those countries that have undergone socialist revolutions. He bases this on an analysis of attitudes of students and corporate employees, which are egalitarian. He argues that because students and corporate executives place little emphasis on social mobility and show sympathy toward income equalization, the transformation of Japanese society will soon occur. He maintains that such a change is inevitable, since individual attitudes shape social structures. He interprets his study as refuting Bowles and Gintis and other Marxist scholars of education who argue that without structural transformation there can be no social change.

Cummings's study and the other critiques of conflict and Marxist alternatives to structural functionalism represent a set of responses to the scholarship generated in recent years. Debate, however, has not been the only active response. In some instances the field has co-opted some of the recent challenges.

Co-optation

Although the field has debated and ignored many of the new currents some have been co-opted into the field. The co-optation has followed a distinct pattern. For example, world systems analysis has suggested a research agenda that includes study of international aid agencies and linkages among Third World and industrialized nations with a view toward understanding the mechanisms through which the world system is maintained. A host of studies have appeared on topics suggested by world systems analysis; most are devoid of the theoretical frames from which they initially arose. For example, the journals in the field have devoted considerable coverage to the activities of international aid agencies, most recently to the World Bank.[43] This work has, for the most part, described the policies of these agencies and changes in them over time. Some of this scholarship has not sought to explain the impact of such policies. More often than not, the assumption is that these institutions exist outside the frame of international politics and serve simply to develop Third World nations.

Another example of co-optation of world systems analysis is renewed interest in "institutional transfer." The British journal, *Compare*, for example, ran a special issue on this topic in 1980.[44] The studies that it included, aside from Robert Arnove's on the Ford Foundation, attacked the very concept of world systems analysis and focused on transfers instead. The articles, by implication, likened educational borrowing between Great Britain and the United States to that between the United States and Latin America or between Great Britain and Africa. They criticized the presumption that educational borrowing takes place within the context of either international politics or unequal relations between nation-states.

World systems analysis is not the only new challenge to be coopted in comparative education and transformed in the process. This is also the case for research emanating from scholarship on women. We pointed out earlier that the field for the most part has ignored the challenge to focus on women as a central concern and a variable in research. However, the field has begun to focus to some extent on issues raised by this challenge. Such research has not focused on women as such or on the social construction of gender. Rather, it has centered on issues presumed to be the province of women—fertility, nutrition health, and the generation of basic needs for poor families in which the male is not able to be the sole provider.[45] The focus of this research is on women in the narrowly defined roles of child bearers and child rearers in the family. Women are not the center of study or necessarily the subject of research so much as its object. In the process of co-optation the very issues initially raised about the necessity of studying women and their education have disappeared.

The ways in which the field has co-opted world systems analysis and, to an almost unrecognizable degree, the study of women stand as examples, of how the field has responded to new challenges that it has not attacked or totally ignored. These forms of co-optation exemplify the approaches that the field has taken to other issues and theoretical challenges posited over the past decade. What we have suggested about world systems analysis and the study of women's education also extends to the field's treatment of the challenge to study educational institutions and their processes.

Conclusion

We understand that our discussion of new currents and comparative education's response to them is far from complete. We have attempted in this essay to provide an overview of recent challenges and to outline the ways in which the field has responded. We hope that the reluctance with which the field has greeted many of these challenges is but a temporary phase. We do not believe it is healthy for a field of inquiry to ignore questioning about the frameworks, theories, and methods that it has used to generate research or to dismiss challenges out of hand. To do so is to consign the field to stagnation and to rehashing old questions.

Although our focus in this essay has been on new challenges, comparative education has, as a field of study, shown considerable continuity both in its approaches to research and in the theory underlying such research. Since 1977, however, this continuity has also shown some signs of change. The optimism that education could be a force for social equality, which pervaded the field in the 1960s and 1970s, has been muted by years of not always successful attempts to reform both schools and society. This sober mood has especially appeared in the scholarship on comprehensive school reforms in Western Europe, on the Chinese experiments during the Great Proletarian Cultural Revolution, and on evidence drawn from the Soviet Union, Eastern Europe, and the Third World.[46] The thought that expanded enrollments and common schooling would change social structures or the effects of parental education and income, gender, and race on children's life chances has become a subject of debate.

Much of this discussion was stimulated by a radical critique of structural functionalism that assumed that over time the transformation of society could occur without changes in social structures. The radical critique was clearly articulated, for example, by Weis in her study of Ghanaian secondary schools. Levin, in his study of Western Europe, argued that without changes in social structures the schools could only reproduce existing social relations and the inequalities currently structured into them. Others in comparative education maintained that inequality was difficult, indeed almost impossible, to eradicate, even if basic social structures were changed. Such was the argument made by Court's study of educational expansion and inequality in Kenya and Tanzania, Morrison's work on Tanzania, and Dobson's studies of the Soviet Union.[47]

Comparative educators have, to some extent, become more pessimistic—some would say, realistic—about the role of education in shaping social change and in contributing to economic development and modernization. This "new realism" has been stimulated to a considerable degree by the insights of radical critics of the past decade as well as by the failure of many of the educational efforts of the 1960s and 1970s. The fiscal crisis of the 1980s as well as the lowered expectations of the current period have stimulated further critique and analysis, this time from a more conservative stance. Scholars like Philip Coombs, George Psacharopoulos, and Mateen Thobani have questioned the viability and, to some extent even the desirability of the vision of universal, free primary education and total literacy for Third World nations.[48] Some have argued that not only is universal primary education a luxury but, in some cases, it may be harmful to economic development and to social well being, since it discourages the efficient use of resources. In the 1980s, some scholars in the field have turned increasingly to the concept of privatization as a means to improve economic efficiency in the provision of education and to enhance educational quality.[49] The recent debates on educational vouchers and on the imposition of school fees represent a return to some of the debates of the 1950s.

The field has recently reconsidered with increasing frequency the role of education of any sort—formal or non-formal, vocational or general—in development. In the 1960s and 1970s, many hoped that, given the proper form and content of education and its widespread diffusion, Third World countries would industrialize and become modern, and the poverty and accompanying ills that were associated with underdevelopment would be eradicated. The vision was development, and the field assumed that no matter how poor a country was education would lead to the creation of human capital, which in turn would develop the nation to the level of most Western countries.[50] Much empirical research has shifted its major focus from modernization to education's relation to the provision of basic needs: to crop production, small-scale technology, marketing, and family health and nutrition. Education is increasingly being looked to for survival or as a means of stemming a demographic and ecological disaster. In short, the vision of what it means to develop human capital is undergoing modification.

In this essay we have been critical of the field for the ways in which it has responded to new ways of thinking about comparative education and treated alternative theories. Unlike some who have openly attacked some of the new challenges for their divisiveness, we believe that the new strains are a sign of vitality for the field of comparative education. It strengthens the field to have more than one way of viewing the role of education in society and to debate alternatives for studying education and its context. To ignore new challenges, many of which arise from changing contexts and advances in scholarship both in comparative education and sister disciplines, is to consign the field to irrelevance in the long run. It is commendable that the field has taken time to reflect on issues that it considered in the past. Nonetheless, it is important that it explores new ones. The challenge of the next decades will be not only to explore the issues raised in the field since 1977 and to take them seriously but also to identify new areas for investigation that will bring continuing debate and vitality to research in comparative education.

Notes

[1] For a more complete discussion see Gail P. Kelly and Philip G. Altbach, "Comparative Education: A Field in Transition," in *International Bibliography of Comparative Education*, ed. P. G. Altbach, G. P. Kelly, and D. H. Kelly (New York: Praeger, 1981). See also "Comparative Education: Its Present State and Future Prospects," *Comparative Education* (June 1977): 75-150; and "The State of the Art: Twenty Years of Comparative Education" *Comparative Education Review* 21 (June/October 1977): 151-416.

[2] John W. Meyer, et al., "The World Educational Revolution, 1950-1970," *Sociology of Education* 50 (October 1971): 242-58; John Meyer and Michael T. Hannon, *National Development and the World System* (Chicago: University of Chicago Press, 1979); Robert Arnove, "Comparative Education and World Systems Analysis," *Comparative Education Review* 24 (February 1980): 48-62; Philip G. Altbach, "Servitude of the Mind: Education, Dependency and Neocolonialism,"

Teachers College Record 79 (December 1977): 188-204; Matthew Zachariah, "Comparative Educators and International Development Policy," *Comparative Education Review* 23 (October 1979): 341-54; Martin Carnoy, "Education for Alternative Development," *Comparative Education Review* 27 (June 1982): 160-77; and Martin Carnoy, *Education as Cultural Imperialism* (New York: McKay, 1974).

[3] Meyer and Hannon, op. cit.

[4] Immanuel Wallerstein, *The Modern World System* (New York: Academic Press, 1974).

[5] Philip G. Altbach, Robert F. Arnove, and Gail P. Kelly, eds. *Comparative Education* (New York: Macmillan, 1982); Carnoy, *Education as Cultural Imperialism;* Zachariah, "Comparative Educators and International Development Policy"; Edward T Silva, "Cultural Autonomy and Ideas in Transit: Notes from the Canadian Case," *Comparative Education Review 24* (February 1980): 63-72.

[6] Margaret Archer, ed., *The Sociology of Educational Expansion: Take-Off, Growth and Inflation in Educational Systems* (Beverly Hills, Calif.: Sage, 1982).

[7] See Mary Jean Bowman, "An Integrated Framework for Analysis of the Spread of Schooling in Less Developed Countries," *Comparative Education Review* 28 (November 1984): 563-83; David N. Plank "The Determinants of School Enrollment Rates in Brazil, 1940-1980" (Ph.D. diss., University of Chicago, 1983).

[8] Vandra Masemann, "Critical Ethnography in the Study of Comparative Education," *Comparative Education* 26 (February 1982): 1-15; Lois Weis, "Educational Outcomes and School Processes: Theoretical Perspectives," in Altbach, Arnove, and Kelly, eds.; Richard Heyman, "Comparative Education from an ethno-methodological Perspective," *Comparative Education* 15 (October 1979) 241-49; Richard H. Pfau, "The Comparative Study of Classroom Behaviors," *Comparative Education Review* 24 (October 1980): 400-14.

[9] Those that incorporate a Marxian approach include Paul Willis, *Learning to Labour: How Working Class Kids Get Working Class Jobs* (Westhead, England: Saxon House, 1977) and Pierre Bourdieu and Jean-Claude Passeron, *Reproduction in Education, Society and Culture* (London: Sage, 1977). Those do not include John U. Ogbu, *Minority Education and Caste: The American System in Cross-cultural Perspective* (New York: Academic Press, 1978); John U. Ogbu, "Minority Status and Schooling in Plural Societies," *Comparative Education Review* 27 (June 1983): 168-90, and Karen Coffyn Biraimah "Different Knowledge for Different Folks: Knowledge Distribution in Togolese Secondary School," in Altbach, Arnove, and Kelly, eds.

¹⁰See Andreas M. Kazamias and Karl Schwartz, "Intellectual and Ideological Perspectives in Comparative Education: An Interpretation," *Comparative Education Review* 21 (June/October 1977): 153-76; and Robert Koehl, "The Comparative Study of Education: Prescription and Practice," *Comparative Education Review* 21 (June 1977): 177-94.

¹¹John C. Bock, "Education and the Meaning of Development: A Conflict of Meaning," in Altbach, Arnove, and Kelly, eds. (n. 5 above); Rolland Paulston, "Conflicting Theories of Educational Reform," in *Better Schools: International Lessons for Reform*, ed. John Simmons (New York: Praeger, 1983).

¹²Kazamias and Schwartz.

¹³See, e. g., Carnoy, *Education as Cultural Imperialism*; Robert F. Arnove, "The Ford Foundation and 'Competence Building' Overseas: Assumptions, Approaches and Implications," *Studies in Comparative International Development* 12 (Fall 1977): 100-26; Robert F. Arnove ed., *Philanthropy and Cultural Imperialism: The Foundations at Home and Abroad* (Boston: G. K. Hall, 1980); Philip Altbach, "Servitude of the Mind" (n. 2 above); Henry M. Levin, "The Dilemma of Comprehensive Secondary School Reforms in Western Europe," *Comparative Education Review* 22 (October 1978): 434-51; Michael Apple, "Ideology, Reproduction and Educational Reform," *Comparative Education Review* 22 (October 1978): 367-87.

¹⁴Paulston.

¹⁵Bock.

¹⁶See, e. g., Hans N. Weiler, "Legalization, Expertise and Participation: Strategies of Compensatory Legitimation in Educational Policy," *Comparative Education Review* 27 (June 1983): 259-77; Hans N. Weiler, "Educational Planning and Social Change: A Critical Review of Concepts and Practices," in Altbach, Arnove, and Kelly, eds. (n. 5 above).

¹⁷See, e.g., Noel McGinn, Ernesto Schiefelbein, and Donald P. Warwick, "Educational Planning as Political Process: Two Case Studies from Latin America," *Comparative Education Review* 23 (June 1979): 218-39; James Urwick, "Politics and Professionalism in Nigerian Educational Planning," *Comparative Education Review* 23 (October 1983): 323-40; Noel McGinn and Susan Street, "The Political Rationality of Resource Allocation in Mexican Public Education," *Comparative Education Review* 26 (June 1982): 178-98; Weiler, "Legalization, Expertise, and Participation"; E. Mark Hanson, "Administrative Development in the Colombian Ministry of Education: A Case Analysis of the 1970s," *Comparative Education Review* 27 (February 1983): 89-107.

[18] McGinn, Schiefelbein, and Warwick. See also Linda Dove, "The Political Context of Education in Bangladesh, 1971-80," in *Politics and Educational Change*, ed. P. Broadfoot, C. Brock, and W. Tulasiewicz (London: Croom Helm, 1982).

[19] Philip G. Altbach, "The Distribution of Knowledge in the Third World," in *Higher Education in the Third World: Themes and Variations*, by P. G. Altbach (Singapore: Maruzen, 1982).

[20] Edward Berman, "Foundations, United States Foreign Policy and African Education, 1945-1975," *Harvard Educational Review* 49 (May 1979): 145-79.

[21] Sippandondha Ketudat and Gerald Fry, "Relations between Educational Research, Policy, Planning and Implementation: The Thai Experience," *International Review of Education* 27 (1981): 141-52.

[22] James S. Coleman, "Professional Training and Institution Building in the Third World: Two Rockefeller Foundation Experiences," *Comparative Education Review* 28 (May 1984): 180-202.

[23] Hans Weiler, "The Political Dilemma of Foreign Study," *Comparative Education Review* 28 (May 1984): 168-79. See also Philip G. Altbach and Y. G.-M. Lulat, "International Students in Comparative Perspective: Toward a Political Economy of International Study," in *Research on Foreign Students and International Study*, ed. P. G. Altbach, D. H. Kelly, and Y. G.-M. Lulat (New York: Praeger, 1985).

[24] Thomas O. Eisemon, "Scientific Life in Indian and African Universities: A Comparative Study of Peripheriality in Science," *Comparative Education Review* 25 (June 1981): 164-82; and Arnove, "The Ford Foundation and 'Competence Building' Overseas" (n. 13 above).

[25] Stephen P. Heyneman, *Textbooks and Achievement: What We Know* (Washington, D. C. World Bank, 1978). Also see Karen Coffyn Biraimah, "The Impact of Western Schools in Girls' Expectations," 24 (June 1980): 196-208.

[26] Willis (n. 9 above).

[27] See, Biraimah, "Different Knowledge for Different Folks" (n. 9 above).

[28] William Cummings, *Education and Equality in Japan* (Princeton, N.J. Princeton University Press, 1980), esp. chap. 5.

[29] Susan Shirk, *Competitive Comrades: Career Incentives and Student Strategies on China* (Berkeley and Los Angeles: University of California Press, 1982); Jonathan Unger, *Education under Mao: Class and Competition in Canton Schools, 1960-1980* (New York: Columbia University Press, 1982).

[30] See, esp., Carolyn Elliott and Gail P. Kelly, "Perspectives on Women's Education," *Comparative Education Review* 24 (June 1980): S1-S12. See also Gail Kelly, "Women's Access to Education in the Third World Myths and Realities," in *World Yearbook of Education 1984: Women in Education*, ed. S. Acker (New York: Kogan Page, 1984). For a complete bibliography of recently generated works, see David H. Kelly and Gail P. Kelly, "Women and Schooling in the Third World: A Bibliography," in *Women's Education in the Third World: Comparative Perspectives,* ed. G. P. Kelly and C. Elliott (Albany: SUNY Press, 1982).

[31] Masemann (n. 8 above). See also Douglas Foley, "Anthropological Studies of Schooling in Developing Countries: Some Recent Findings and Trends," *Comparative Education Review* 21 (June/October 1977): 311-28.

[32] Torsten Husen and T. Neville Postlethwaite, eds. *International Encyclopedia of Education* (Oxford: Pergamon, 1985), 10 vols.

[33] G. P. Kelly and Carolyn Elliott, eds., "Women and Education in the Third World," *Comparative Education Review* 24 (June 1980, part 2) S1-S266. See also Acker, ed.

[34] Husen and Postlethwaite. See also Keith Watson and Raymond Wilson, eds., *Contemporary Issues in Comparative Education: A Festschrift in Honor of Professor Emeritus Vernon Mallinson* (London: Croom Helm, 1985).

[35] Watson and Wilson.

[36] Harold Noah and Max Eckstein, "Dependency Theory in Comparative Education: The New Simplicitude," *Prospects* 15, no. 2 (1985): 213-25.

[37] Keith Watson, "Dependence or Independence in Education: Two Cases from Post-colonial Southeast Asia," *International Journal of Educational Development* 5 (1985): 85-94. See also Jon Lauglo, "Mass Schooling: A Tool of Capitalist Domination)?" *Compare* 15, no. 1. (1985): 21-27.

[38] Alan Sica and Harland Prechel, "National Political-Economic Dependency in the Global Economy and Educational Development *Comparative Education Review* 25 (October 1981): 384-402.

[39] See Brian Holmes, *Comparative Education: Some Consideration of Method* (London: Unwin Educational, 1981).

[40] Erwin Epstein, "Currents Right and Left: Ideology in Comparative Education," *Comparative Education Review* 27 (February 1983): 3-27.

[41] Paulston (n. 11 above).

[42] Cummings (n. 28 above), esp. chap. 1.

⁴³See Wadi D. Haddad, "The World Bank's Education Sector Policy Paper: A Summary," *Comparative Education* 17 (June 1981): 127-39; Milagros Fernandez, "The World Bank and the Third World: Reflections of a Skeptic," *Prospects* 11 (1981): 294-301; Martin Carnoy, "International Institutions and Educational Policy: A Review of Education-Sector Policy," *Prospects* 10 (1980); 265-83; Seth Spaulding, "The Impact of International Assistance Organizations on the Development of Education," 11 (1981): 421-33; Paul Hurst, "Aid and Educational Development: Rhetoric and Reality," *Comparative Education* 17 (June 1981): 117-25; A. R. Thompson, "How Far Free: International Networks of Constraint upon National Education Policy in the Third World," *Comparative Education* 13 (October 1977): 155-68; George Psacharopoulos, "The World Bank in the World of Education: Some Policy Changes and Some Remnants," *Comparative Education* 17 (June 1981): 141-46.

⁴⁴Ronald Goodenow, "To Build a New World: Toward Two Case Studies on Transfer in the 20th Century," *Compare* 13, no. 1 (1983): 43-60. See also "Educational Transfer" (special issue), *Compare* 13, no. 1 (1983): 1-88.

⁴⁵See, e. g., Susan Cochrane, *Education and Fertility: What Do We Really Know?*, (Baltimore: Johns Hopkins University Press, 1979).

⁴⁶Henry Levin (n. 13 above); Lois Weis, "Education and the Reproduction of Inequality: The Case of Ghana," *Comparative Education Review* 23 (February 1979): 41-50; Torsten Husen, *The School in Question* (New York: Oxford University Press, 1979); Joseph P. Farrell, "Educational Expansion and the Drive for Social Equality," in Altbach, Arnove, and Kelly, eds. (n. 8 above); Gail Lapidus, *Women in Soviet Society* (Berkeley and Los Angeles: University of California Press, 1981); Joseph R. Fiszman, "Education and Equality of Opportunity in Eastern Europe," in Altbach, Arnove, and Kelly, eds. (n. 5 above); W. D. Halls, "A Comparative Political and Sociological Analysis of Educational Opportunity in Western Europe, 1960-80," in Watson and Wilson, eds. (n. 34 above).

⁴⁷David Court, "Education as Social Control: The Response to Inequality in Kenya and Tanzania," in *Education and Politics in Tropical Africa*, ed. V. C. Uchendu (Owerri and New York: Conch, 1979); Richard Dobson and Michael Stafford, "The Educational Attainment Process in the Soviet Union: A Case Study," *Comparative Education Review* 24 (June 1980, part 1): 252-69; David Morrison, *Education and Politics in Africa: The Tanzanian Case* (Montreal: McGill-Queens University Press, 1967).

⁴⁸See George Psacharopoulos, "The Perverse Effects of Public Subsidization of Education, Or How Equal if Free Education?" *Comparative Education Review* 21 (February 1977): 69-90; Mateen

Thobani, "Charging User Fees for Social Services: Education in Malawi," *Comparative Education Review* 28 (August 1984): 402-23; Steven J. Klees, "The Need for a Political Economy of Educational Finance: A Response to Thobani," *Comparative Education Review* 28 (August 1984): 424-40; and W. Van Vliet and J. A. Smyth, "A Nineteenth Century French Proposal to Use School Vouchers," *Comparative Education Review* 26 (February 1982): 95-103.

[49] Estelle James, "Benefits and Costs of Privatized Public Services: Lessons for the Dutch Educational System," *Comparative Education Review* 28 (November 1984): 605-24. See also Thobani.

[50] See Philip H. Coombs, *The World Crisis in Education: The View from the Eighties* (New York: Oxford University Press, 1985); Irvin Sobel, "The Human Capital Revolution in Economic Development," in Altbach, Arnove, and Kelly, eds. (n. 5 above). Hans Weiler, "Educational Planning and Social Change" (n. 16 above); Hans Weiler, "Toward a Political Economy of Educational Planning," *Prospects* 8 (1978): 247-67; George Psacharopoulos, "The State of Educational Planning Revisited," *Prospects* 11 (1981): 154-58.

Dialogue:
Response to Angus's "Conflict, Class, and the Nineteenth-Century Public High School in the Cities of the Midwest, 1845-1900"[†]

It has recently become fashionable to attack social control theories applied to education. Social control theories, such as Edward Krug advanced in his study of the American high school, Michael Katz in his work on the bureaucratization of education, Michael Apple in ideology and curriculum, and Bowles and Gintis in their study of education and the class structure of the U.S., are conflicting, in some cases, Marxist theories about education.[1] These theories arose in the 1960s and 1970s to counter structural functionalism which pervaded social science educational research and the "march to democracy and equality" interpretations of American educational history. Social control theorists basically argued that the school system in the 19th century as well as today in all countries reflects the class structure of the society in which the schools are placed and serves to replicate existing social relationships. Education is not perceived as liberatory or as a vehicle for changing social relations. Rather the schools, while they may provide *individuals* a chance for upward social mobility, help maintain class relations. Bowles and Gintis argued this case based on enrollment statistics; Apple on analysis of curriculum; and Katz and Krug on policy intent.

The initial formation of the social control hypothesis has been criticized from a variety of perspectives. David Angus's article represents but one of them. Generally criticisms have focused, like his, on the following: (1) Intent—did those in power intend to use the schools to reproduce existing class relations? (2) Who supported the schools—did those who supported the schools share the views of those who ostensibly had power to make decisions about the schools? (3) Who went to school—did the schools serve an exclusive clientele, or did they recruit from a broader spectrum of the population? (4) The articulation of education to the workforce and class structure—more precisely, what happened to those who were schooled in the workforce?

[†]©1988 by The Ontario Institute for Studies in Education. *Curriculum Inquiry* 18:1 (1988). Reprinted by permission of John Wiley & Sons Inc.

I will argue in the pages that follow that critiques which focus on intent, on who supported the schools or who went to school do not necessarily address the basic premises of social control theories. Rather, they miss the point. While there may well be flaws in what Angus terms the social control hypothesis, the critiques Angus levels—namely that the hypothesis pays insufficient attention to demographics, misinterprets intent, and neglects the fact that the working class went to school—really do not basically undermine the theory. Angus merely points to phenomena to which the theory needs to attend.

What's Wrong with Angus's Critiques

Critiques of social control theorists as well as some proponents of social control theories often focus on the intent of those in power. Angus, for example, argues that social control theory is flawed because school board members in the midwestern cities he studied did not always articulate the association between education and the need to socialize working class kids into working class jobs in order to maintain the local class structure. He found this despite intense class antagonisms which at times framed educational policy making. Angus argues that many school boards in the midwest delayed the opening of secondary schools in the interests of providing mass education and thereby in the long run favored the interests of the working class and poor. He maintains that the issue school boards faced was providing enough school places to accommodate demand. Social control, he asserts, was furthest from their minds.

While what Angus describes is no doubt true, it does not constitute evidence that disproves the social control hypothesis or indeed any Marxian theories of social, cultural reproduction. Individual intent is not the issue—what many social control theorists argue is that schools *served* to maintain existing class structures through not only the distribution of educational opportunities, but also through socialization patterns embedded in the school system. The issue is how much of whose knowledge in what quality is given to whom and the effect school processes have on social class relationships.

Angus makes a good point when he states that Katz and other social control theorists tend to base their case not on what school board members said they intended to do, but rather what can be "read into" what they said or what the curriculum implied. However, having said this Angus goes ahead and derives intent from school board members' discourse on whether to open secondary schools. He commits the same mistake as do some of those he so aptly criticizes.

The problem with both Angus and those he criticizes is that guessing intent is always happenstance and leads us away from the outcomes of educational decisions. We will never know what anyone's intent truly was—and it may not matter whether we do. For example, no one has ever stated the role of schooling for women is to reinforce patriarchal relations. However, it is clear from a broad research literature that schooling as well as lack of schooling, depending on the context, has contributed to keeping women subordinate to males by socializing both males and females to sex specific roles.[2] Pedagogues often have stressed their intent to help students adjust to "life"; they have rarely stated that their goal is to oppress women. And, even if they did, it would make little difference in terms of educational practice.

I would not for a moment claim that the good schoolmen of Detroit, Cleveland, and other midwestern cities had intents other than those Angus attributes to them. The point, however, is that the test of social control theories does not rest on intent as much as on analyses of whose knowledge is taught to whom and with what effect. Dwelling on intent neither confirms nor disproves social control theory. It simply allows us to understand the terms of discourse about education in the public sphere and in the immediate consciousness of those engaging in that discourse. However, it ought to be clear by now that for every statement one can supply to bolster the intent to maintain existing social relations via schooling, one can find similar statements which view the schools as tools for change, democracy, justice or even revolution. The statements are simply part of the debate over education; they do not represent the effect of education on social relations.

Some social control theorists, like Krug, may have based their case solely on analysis of intent, but others have moved beyond to discussions of what schools taught and the outcomes of education on society which may or may not have anything to do with many of the pious and not-so-pious statements about schooling. My own work on colonial schooling in French West Africa and Indochina has demonstrated that many a schoolman's avowed statements about civilizing missions had little to do with what schools taught to whom.[3] Many pedagogues talked about assimilating Africans and Asians and making them Frenchmen. Yet, in the three Vietnamese states of Indochina the schools taught in Vietnamese, not in French, and they taught about Vietnam and not about France. While the schools of West Africa taught in French, they taught about African cultures, African history and African society and rarely about French culture and civilization.

A second criticism Angus levels at social control theories is that they ignore the possibility as well as the fact that the demand for education came not from the state but from the underclasses of society—working men's associations, for example. He questions how the social control thesis could hold when working class guilds of Detroit, Cleveland, etc., were articulate in demanding the extension of education along democratic lines and supported the decision to postpone secondary education until the demand for primary education was met. One problem with Angus's argument is not whether he is correctly stating the working-class demand for education. At issue, rather, is how such demands are interpreted in the light of social control frames. Social control frames do not deny that working classes contested social control functions of the schools or anyone's attempt to use the schools to maintain existing class relations. To the contrary, social control theorists argue that the schools served to maintain social relations *despite* individual demand for education and insistence on the part of the working class, minorities and women—both individually and as groups—to have the schools serve their needs.

Angus argues that some urban schools in the 19th century opened women's departments. Such a move does not mean that the schools changed patriarchal relations. Far from it—scholars of women's education in the U.S. are clear that the extension of education to women in the late 19th century served to allocate women into narrow occupational roles—particularly teaching and later social work.[4] For the middle class, as Mabel Newcomer pointed out in her history of women's higher education, schools like Smith were opened to provide educated mates for educated males.[5] While some women attempted and indeed succeeded in using the schools to overcome the webs of their socialization, these women were rare in comparison to the number of women left outside the schools or channeled through the schools to accepted narrowly defined and subordinate roles in production and reproduction.

In short, because the lower classes and the disenfranchised demanded education and were in some instances able to influence the course of school development, it does not necessarily follow that social control theories hold no water. All this shows is that there was and is considerable struggle over the schools. The disenfranchised have demanded in the past and continue to demand today that schools serve their interests rather than those of dominant social strata. Krug's initial statement of the social control thesis may have neglected these struggles. However, their existence does not mean that education in the long run did not serve to maintain the existing class structure.

A third critique Angus levels at social control theories is that the schools in Detroit and Cleveland enrolled appreciable numbers of working class kids. The middle-class did not, he correctly points out, dominate education entirely. This is no doubt the case, but all it indicates is that the schools enrolled working class children to a far greater extent than had been supposed. Angus's work in this regard is very much in keeping with Hogan's recent studies of Chicago and Philadelphia.[6] However, enrollment in secondary school in and of itself does not mean that schools became a means of challenging the class structure of society. Rather, enrollment patterns such as those Angus presents, indicate that working class kids went to school. It does not mean that the class structure of society or the distribution of wealth and power in society changed.

Angus assumes that enrollment in high school automatically brings into being a specific set of life chances. He assumes that white collar work and higher income immediately follow from receiving high school education. It is not all that clear that this is the case independent of social origins. Angus presents us with no evidence that the working class children who went to high school in the period he studied actually changed their life chances appreciably. All that Angus's evidence tells us is that working class kids went to high school; he assumes that this means class mobility.

Even if some working class kids used the high schools for individual advancement, which is no doubt the case for some, all this means is that the high schools provided mobility to individuals. It does not mean that the schools changed class structures or class relations. Thus, the data presented here neither proves nor disproves the theories Angus supposes he addresses.

The Use of Theory

In all fairness to Angus, he does not argue that theories of education and social control are invalid, although he implies as much. Rather, he maintains that such theories are not useful and may in fact lead the scholar to err—either by neglecting relevant data or by using today's standards to interpret the past. Angus does not directly seek to refute theories connecting education with social control, rather he dismisses them as useless and perhaps seeking to blind the scholar to historical reality.

Angus in his article, whether he meant to or not, raises the question of whether it might be wiser to do research without theory so that the scholar might avoid being misled and push a one-sided interpretation of his or her data. Such a view presumes that the "facts" speak for themselves or that contexts appropriate to explaining the phenomena under study would present themselves more readily than had the scholar come to research unencumbered by theory. Such an implication is one that seems to arise periodically in the social science literature as a way of trying to "neutralize" research and make it "objective" by resorting to positivism. This issue has long been debated in the social sciences and I cannot here hope to do justice to debates positivists stir up.[7] Others have pointed out quite eloquently that lack of explicit theory does not mean that the scholar does not use theory, it simply means that he or she uses it implicitly. What guides both the location of data as well as the interpretation of data is theory. The question really is not whether we do research guided by a theory; it is whether we are up front with the theory we use or whether we deny how we came to study what we study, how we study it and what we make of what we find. Angus presumes that theory, instead of guiding the scholar, constrains him or her.

Without theory, the scholar has little guide to how to contextualize data and interpret it. To state that social control theories are useless because the scholar ends up blind to demographics or ignores underclass demand for education is to state that a different set of theories—perhaps in this instance, free market theories of supply and demand—best guide the scholar and explain how schooling came to develop the way it did. I do not think Angus fully intends to advance supply-demand theories of educational development or to argue that theories other than those focusing on social control better explain the course of educational history. However, he ends up, through his critique, implying either that no theory or some other theory might better serve the scholar than social control theory.

It may be that social control theorists have not examined demographics or the underclass demand for education adequately. Angus's point here is well taken. However, it is not clear that social control theory cannot accommodate or account for such phenomenon. At issue perhaps is not whether social control theories are appropriate, but what directions scholars need to go to further develop the theory. Angus's seeming dismissal of social control theories evades the issue of how one uses theory in research—as a blinder or as a guide which allows the scholar to look more broadly than his or her data and to make sense of what she or he sees.

In short, Angus's article does not constitute a refutation of social control theory or any real critique of its basic assumptions. Angus's research shows us that it is important to use theory to expand rather than restrict horizons. Angus might be better off working within a tradition of debate to advance theory rather than to argue that a specific theory is useless because it hasn't yet accounted for phenomena he has located. Angus, when all is said and done, cannot argue social control theories are invalid; all he has done is to point out that social control theories have yet to adequately explain working class demand for schooling and the role of demographics in changing the development of education. With his data, these are the only claims Angus can make.

Notes

[1] See Krug, Edward A. *The Shaping of the American High School, 1880-1920.* Madison: University of Wisconsin Press, 1964; Katz, Michael. *Class, Bureaucracy and Schools: The Illusion of Educational Change in America.* New York: Praeger 1971; Carnoy, Martin. *Education as Cultural Imperialism.* New York: McKay, 1974; Bowles, Samuel, and Herbert Gintis. *Schooling in Capitalist America: Educational Reform and the Contradictions of Economic Life.* New York: Basic Books, 1976; Apple, Michael. *Ideology and Curriculum.* London: Routledge and Kegan Paul, 1979.

[2] See, for example, Graham, Patricia. "Expansion and Exclusion: A History of Women in American Education." *Signs*, 3(4) (Summer 1978): 759-737.

[3] Kelly, Gail P. "The Presentation of Indigenous Society in the Schools of French West Africa and Indochina, 1918-1938." *Comparative Studies in Society and History.* 26(3) (July 1984): 523-542; Kelly, Gail P. "Colonialism, Indigenous Society and School Practices: French West Africa and Indochina, 1918-1938." In *Education and the Colonial Experience*, edited by P. G. Altbach and G. P. Kelly: 9-32. New Brunswick: Transaction Press, 1984.

[4] See, for example, Ram, Rati. "Sex Differences in the Labor Market Outcomes of Education." In *Women's Education in the Third World: Comparative Perspectives*, edited by G. P. Kelly and C. M. Elliott: 203-227. Albany: SUNY Press, 1982.

[5] Newcomer, Mabel. *A Century of Higher Education for Women.* New York: Harper, 1959.

[6] See Hogan, David J. *Class and Reform: School and Society in Chicago, 1880-1930.* Philadelphia: University of Pennsylvania Press, 1985.

[7] See Kuhn, Thomas S. *The Structure of Scientific Revolutions.* Chicago: University of Chicago Press, 1970.

Comparative Education and the Problem of Change: An Agenda for the 1980s[†]

The 1980s have been a time of pessimism in comparative education. Earlier decades were characterized by optimism about education's ability to help eradicate poverty, contribute to the development of national economies, and assist in building national political consensus. In the 1980s, this optimism has faded. Many have begun to question education's ability to contribute to change; in some cases, scholars have argued that education has aggravated pre-existing problems rather than contributed to their solution.[1] A literature has emerged that considers countries that have yet to achieve universal primary education "overschooled" and faults education for current economic and social malaise.[2] In the 1960s, the literature in comparative education was filled with such terms as "modernization," "development," and "social transformation"; in the 1980s our parlance has shifted to such terms as "basic needs," "income generation," and "employment." This language signifies a growing disillusionment with schools as a vehicle for change. Some have questioned whether education is really a necessity. Within comparative education, some have started to ask how much education is enough and how governments might either diminish demand for education or cut back on the provision of educational services.[3]

In the 1960s, comparative education was a field that advocated the extension of education and that believed that schools were an important means of ensuring broader social goals. In the 1980s, many find themselves questioning whether this is the case. In the past two decades, the field has moved from debates about how to extend education to debates about whether and how to limit education. The general shift in thinking about change is not peculiar to our field; it now characterizes the social sciences in general. Sociologists, economists and political scientists have also increasingly questioned whether

I would like to thank Jennifer Newton, Sheila Slaughter, Lois Weis, and Manfred Weiss for their comments on an earlier draft of this article.

[†]©1987 by the Comparative and International Education Society. *Comparative Education Review*, Vol. 31. No. 4 (1987). Reprinted with permission of the University of Chicago Press.

planned social change is possible and whether institutions, including schools, can effectively promote social policy goals.[4]

Within comparative education, the questioning of education's effectiveness in bringing about change derives from a research literature that is at best ambiguous. Despite the impressive marshaling of statistical data on enrollment ratios, dropout rates, social background characteristics of students, expenditure on education, and, to a lesser extent the quality and content of education, comparative education has a problem when comes to thinking about change and education's relation to that change. Our research has been less than clear about what kind of change schools are expected to bring about and what constitutes a change worth having. I will argue in the pages that follow that, instead of abandoning the schools as a vehicle of change for the better and searching for ways to limit education, comparative education might be better off focusing its energies on clarifying what education can do rather than on what it cannot do.

I am not the first to point out that there are problems in the research literature in comparative education. Rolland Paulston, Erwin Epstein, and Steven Klees, for example, have argued that different theoretical perspectives and ideologies have led to different research strategies and interpretations of data.[5] It is not my intent here to take issue with these scholars; rather, I will argue that the problem with change that characterizes our field stems from lack of clarity about what it is we are studying and whose perspective we are studying it from and from a persistent refusal to address our study to educational processes. Some of these problems relate to theoretical approaches scholars have taken. However, they are not totally attributable to a "theory" problem. Rather, they relate to our ambiguity about what we mean by change, what we consider a change worth having, which change is seen as significant and from whose perspective it is seen as significant, and what we study about education. While my focus is on underscoring some of the problems in our research literature, my purpose in so doing is to clarify a research agenda to which the field might attend in the years to come.

Change in What?

When scholars in comparative education have talked about change, they have been less than clear about what they were looking for a change in, regardless of whether they were relating these changes to economies, politics, or social life. When it has focused on change, research in comparative education has looked at the relation of education to change in individual attitudes, individual behaviors, institutions, or those who participate in institutions, often confusing changes in one with changes in the others. This has led to a research literature that has produced contradictory results, often in the same country in about the same time span. For example, Armer and Youtz found that education brought about significant changes in attitudes, which signaled societal change for the better.[6] Their study was based in Nigeria. However, Abernethy, who studied Nigeria at the same time as did Armer and Youtz found that education undermined the progressive development of political institutions, exacerbated ethnic centrifugal tendencies, and impeded economic development.[7] Abernethy looked at education's relation to changes in institutions and individual participation in institutions; Armer and Youtz studied attitudes. Moock, again looking at Nigeria no more than 10 years after Abernethy, concluded that education was a force for change—in this case, toward economic development.[8] The changes he cited were in individual behaviors. At the same time, Nnoli claimed that education in Nigeria was related to regressive change. He found that education exacerbated ethnic and class tensions. He studied the social and ethnic background characteristics of secondary school students.[9]

These diverse and contradictory findings are not peculiar to Nigeria. They are replicated in almost every country. They cannot be explained away by time period—these Nigerian studies were conducted within a 10-year span; nor can the contradictions be attributed to ideological or theoretical perspectives taken by the researchers. In this case, all worked from what Paulston would characterize as structural functionalist perspectives.[10] What we have is a research literature that lacked any common conception of what is meant by change. One can conclude from it that education is a force for change just as easily as one can conclude that education has nothing to do with change. Such a literature raises in my mind the question of whether our current disillusionment with education's ability to promote change is warranted any more than was our optimism of the 1960s. For example, in the past, we were willing to be optimistic about education's ability to promote change because we had studies that showed us that education brought about changes in the attitudes of individuals, such as Inkeles and Smith's six-nation study and Cummings's more recent work on Japan.[11] We were quick to assume that a change in attitudes signaled changes in behaviors or institutions or in those who participated in them. In the past few years we have been less willing to make such assumptions as research has raised questions about education's relation to institutional change. We have found, for example, that education may change attitudes about family size but not necessarily fertility rates.[12] Education may change attitudes about the political system but not necessarily political behavior, the stability of the government, or its capacity to deliver services.[13]

Theories about the relations among attitudes, behaviors, institutions, and the social composition of those who participate in institutions are not fully developed, although such theory construction is necessary before we can make meaningful statements about schooling's relation to change or, more important, dismiss the schools as ineffective and urge government to curtail the extension of educational services to their citizens.

What Kind of Change Is Worthwhile?

If comparative education has been unclear about whether it expects schools to change attitudes, institutions, behaviors, or individual participation in institutions, it has not been explicit about what kind of change it thinks schools should foster. The source of the current disillusionment with schooling as an agent for change derives from a valuing of some kinds of outcomes of schools and not others.

In the 1960s, the field looked to education with great optimism to bring about two sorts of change: modification of existing class, ethnic, and regionally based inequalities and economic development (more precisely industrialization) in the Third World nations. In the 1970s and 1980s, some have argued that education is ineffective because industrialization has been stalled, economies are stagnant and unemployment is persistent and in some cases growing.[14] In addition, the expansion of education has not produced social equality. No one contests the economic stagnation of the 1980s or the inequalities that remain in most of the world. However, does the fact that schooling cannot completely eradicate inequality or necessarily stimulate economic growth mean that education changes nothing or that whatever education may do outside these two domains is not worth doing?

Schools teach people reading, writing, and numeracy skills. By and large, the expansion of education has increased literacy among the population (although perhaps in some places at rates that barely keep pace with population growth).[15] As a field that is devoted to the study of education, do we mean to imply, as some have in the 1980s, that providing literacy is not worthwhile because nations have not developed fully their economies or managed to bring about social equity? Conversely, do we want to argue that literacy is important only if it leads to economic outcomes or equalizes society? If we are disillusioned with education on these two counts, do we have reason to be disillusioned with it on all counts? Has not education brought about changes in other aspects of life? Has it had an effect on power relations in the family, on child welfare, on health and nutrition, and on the ability of women to control their life?[16] The field's exclusive focus on economic development and social equality goals has led us perilously close to concluding that, since education in the short run has fallen short of achieving these goals, education changes nothing.

Unwittingly, this has led the field to ignore what education may, indeed, change. It is somewhat indicative of the field that the vast majority of studies we have conducted in the past decades have been interested only in whether education leads to economic growth or social equality.[17] Rare are the studies that ask how education has affected the basic health or nutritional status of societies, changed child-rearing practices and power relations between men and women in the family and community, and affected the patterns of participation in political life and the redistribution of political power in society.

Comparative education neglected these issues in large part because it devalued outcomes that were not directly tied to production or to the goals of the state (often presumed the same as "societal goals"). Changes in anything else were ignored either because they raised issues relating to political power and therefore were controversial or because they related to the private, domestic domain, which was viewed as natured and therefore impervious to change. Many of these areas were part of the "women's question." It is telling that comparative education as a field ignored scholarship on these questions and any scholarship relating to women generated initially in other fields of study such as anthropology, sociology, and history. Scholarship of this sort sought to understand how women's lives in the family and in the community could be improved. It focused on the relation of reproduction and child rearing to production and economic activity.[18] Before 1980, when the *Comparative Education Review* published a special issue funded and initiated by the Ford Foundation, the field had rarely, if ever, considered women, the family, the relation between education and health and nutrition, or the role of education in mediating the effect of the family and reproduction on women's activity in the public arenas of the work force and the community. Given this "valuing"—implicit as well as explicit—the field overlooked, and continues in some instances to do so, areas in which education may make a difference. (Indeed, there is evidence that suggests that education changes child-rearing patterns and power relations in communities and in families.)[19]

Comparative education's "problem" with change extends beyond valuing solely changes in production and the class system of social stratification. Its "problem" also concerns whose perspective on change is taken.

Change for Whom and from Whose Perspective?

In the 1960s, when comparative education was optimistic about schooling's ability to improve society, most in the field shared the belief that education could be made to equalize rich and poor, male and female, urban and rural populations, and ethnic and racial minorities and majority groups. Educational expansion was seen as a major mechanism for bringing the benefits associated with schooling to those who were disadvantaged in society. Such beliefs were substantiated by a research literature generated in the 1960s on Western European, North American, and Third World nations.[20] One decade later scholars in comparative education began to argue that education, rather than bringing about social equality, was a major means for perpetuating social inequalities. Some, like Thobani, writing in the 1980s, maintained that public education served only to deepen inequalities.[21] These conclusions were drawn from those working in structural functionalist traditions, Marxist and otherwise, as well as those working on education in industrialized as well as developing societies and in socialist as well as capitalist societies. Such works were generated, for example, by Bowles and Gintis and by James S. Coleman on the United States, A. H. Halsey on Great Britain, Henry Levin on Western Europe, Josef Fitzman on Eastern Europe, Gail Lapidus and Richard Dobson on the Soviet Union, and Mateen Thobani on Malawi, although their definitions of what constitutes "success" or "failure" of the schools in relation to equality differ.[22]

Few contest the finding that the extension of education has failed to eliminate the inequalities that persist in most of the world. What is disputed is the conclusion that, because inequality persists, schooling does not benefit the poor, minorities, and women and that, therefore, extension of education to these groups changes nothing. The "low" priority on education that has resulted from such an attitude exists in the face of the strong demand for schooling that comes from the very people whom many of us in comparative education claim the schools have failed.

The persistent and strong demand for education from the poor, women, and minorities exists because, from their perspective, despite the fact that education may not provide equality, it does change the quality of their lives. The case of women provides some insight into how the perspective of the subjects of our research might inform and modify the conclusion that schools make no difference that some of us quickly draw from our research studies. The extension of education in the past 20 years has narrowed gaps between male and female enrollments at all levels, despite the fact that women's enrollments lag behind those of men.[23] More women now receive education than ever before. While their educational outcomes differ from those of men—women, for example, do not earn as much as similarly educated men—changes in women's educational pattern have resulted in changes in women's entry into the paid work force and their maintenance and status within the work force.[24] As Wainerman has shown, even if women have received only a primary education, they use education as a means to obtain gainful employment and earn income to support themselves and their children.[25] In addition, education has resulted in changes in family structures, in child-rearing patterns, and in women's participation in communities. There is evidence from Inga Elqvist-Saltzman's pioneering work on women's life histories that education is important to women—it has empowered them and effected changes in their life circumstances.[26] It is not surprising that education remains a women's demand in the face of current disillusionment on the part of governments and many scholars in the field about the ability of schools to provide them equality with men. As Schiefelbein and Farrell have shown, education provides women with the ability to earn a living despite structured discrimination against them and the burden of childbearing and child rearing.[27]

The case of women allows us to see that while many in comparative education have been concerned with education serving the poor, women, and minorities, the current disillusionment with schools does not reflect the perspectives of these populations. From their vantage point, schools are *the only* way to achieve individual and group mobility. The idea of cutting back on public education—either through privatization or through the contraction of educational services provided by the state—does not emanate from women, minorities, and the poor. Scholars may argue that the rich benefit disproportionately from education—and they are probably correct in so doing—but the educationally disadvantaged population are those who consistently demand the extension of education. They do not share our ambiguities about whether education is worthwhile and whether the changes they associate with education are big enough to warrant the extension of public schooling.

How Much Change and in How Short a Time?

Comparative education is a field that has expected education to do everything. When the schools do not do everything, we often turn around and argue that the schools have no effect at all or inhibit the resolution of the problems of development and social equity. We are, in short, a field that thinks in dichotomies. When confronted with evidence that, after 10 years of educational expansion, equality remains elusive or the economy has failed to develop or grow, we are quick to scotch the schools and recommend that governments place less of an emphasis on educational services. We begin to think of education as a "tradeable" that, like refrigerators, one could do without or might best be exchanged for something better. This tendency has often led the field to overlook changes that do occur because they are not dramatic and all encompassing. In the short run, education may not bring about development or equality, but in some instances, it has aided the poor in obtaining paid employment in the face of economies that have displaced their labor in agriculture and petty trade. Education may not bring about equality, but it is related to improvement in nutrition and the provision of basic needs.[28] Sometimes the field gets so caught up in expecting the schools to bring about the Golden Age that it neglects to ask whether, for example, the inequalities we now see might not deepen if not for the schools or whether the economic declines, caused by factors outside the school such as fluctuations in oil prices, might not be more drastic if not for the effect of the schools. Comparative education has come perilously close to valuing schools only if they bring about dramatically "big" change along only two dimensions. It becomes even easier to abandon faith in the schools to bring about change when we have not quite determined how "big" a change it is that we value in what time span.

Part of our tendency to think in extremes stems from our reliance on research methods that are sensitive only to dramatic, large-scale changes. Our use of regression analysis, for example, might help us to establish causation or "scientific law," but it might also lead us to ignore smaller, less dramatic changes that do occur.

Over the last 20 years, comparative education has become an impatient field. In the 1960s, when we believed that education could overcome underdevelopment, inequality, and poverty, we based this belief on historical research. Our belief was bolstered by scores of educational histories focusing on Japan, the Soviet Union, Great Britain, and the United States. Shipman's classic study of education and modernization spanned over 200 years. Passin's study of Japan began in 1868. Dore's study harked back to seventeenth-century Japan. Seymour Rosen's study of the Soviet Union charted reforms since Tsarist emancipation of the serfs. Theodore Schultz's positing of human capital theory was grounded in U.S. history since the Civil War.[29] In the 1960s, our faith in education was a faith that schooling over the long run—several generations, in fact—would bring about economic development. Twenty years later—in some cases, 10 years later—we begin to be disillusioned with education. For example, Morrison's pessimistic predictions about Nyerere's Arusha Declaration and subsequent policy ability to affect ethnic-and class-based inequality in Tanzania was based on research on educational expansion and reform conducted within 10 years of the date the Arusha Declaration was issued.[30] Much of the research literature that has been skeptical about schooling's ability to bring about changes in the economy and social structure is, like Morrison's work, based on evaluations of expansion and reform over less than 10 years. This is the case with literature on the comprehensive school reforms in Western Europe and postwar reforms in Eastern Europe.[31]

In the 1960s, in short, we argued that, over the long run, education contributed to economic development and to social equality. However, 10 years later, we argued that schooling did not work, often basing our disillusionment on reforms that were never enacted or on the performance of the economy in which those unaffected by schooling or the reforms in schooling expected to make a difference formed the bulk of the active work force.

My point here is not to argue that schools are either effective or ineffective in bringing about economic development or social equality. Rather, my concern is to suggest that we may be prematurely judging the effects of education and, in our haste, might ignore the long-term contribution of schooling to change. We might also undermine the school's contribution by urging continual change before we know what kind of effect a reform in education, just enacted, has had on the social structure or the economy. The history of educational reform is one in which reforms have followed one another so rapidly, often in contradictory fashion, that reforms have often been undone before they have had the chance to be effective.[32]

What Does Schooling Have to Do with Change?

Comparative education, when all is said and done, is an applied field. In the United States and, probably, elsewhere, it has sought to aid in public policy-making about education. It is full of pronouncements about how much schooling a country should have, what kind of schools best promote growth and development or equality, what kinds of structural reforms promote change, and the like. Most recently, we have a literature that tells us that schools are ineffective instruments for promoting change, that they reinforce the privileges of the already privileged, or that countries should cut back on schooling. For the most part, we have judged the schools without studying schooling. Our policy prescriptions are often based on a host of assumptions about educational processes and practices. We are a field that purports to be about education, but we rarely study education. We study, instead, presumed outcomes of education. This is the case whether study is based on liberal or on Marxist variants of structural functionalism or evolutionary, conflict or legitimation theories rooted in disciplines like sociology, economics, political science, history, and anthropology. When we have studied schooling, we have usually studied the external attributes of schools and the educational system. We have focused on what can be quantified—for example, class size, number of years a teacher has been trained, or amount of time allocated to teaching a subject (although research on even these has been quite limited). More often than not our research has focused on how many people go to school, the social background characteristics of pupils, how much money those who are educated make, individual attitudes of the schooled, the gross national product, government expenditure on education, and government policies toward the schools. Rare are the studies of what goes on in school—analyses of curriculum content, the transmission of knowledge, teacher behavior, and student learning styles and processes. So far removed are we from studying education and schools that the field has been at a loss when it comes to asking what an effective school is—since our research has focused on the outcomes of national school systems without regard to differences in educational processes and quality within those systems.[33] As a result, the field has very little to say about schooling except to suggest that the educational system be expanded or contracted, that higher education should or should not be supported relative to secondary or primary education, or that something should be done about preparing children for the world of work. Our research has yet to specify the relation between what schools teach to whom and the social, political and economic outcomes on which we have judged the schools' effectiveness. This point has been made repeatedly since 1977, but apparently has fallen on deaf ears.[34] Our pessimism about the schools in the 1980s is not grounded in any better knowledge about educational processes than was our optimism of the 1960s. Our statements in the 1980s that the schools have nothing to do with change are probably unwarranted, since the connections between educational processes, content, and quality and some rather ambiguous notions of change are yet to be made.

Comparative Education and the Problem of Change

In the preceding, I have focused on the problems our field has encountered in looking at education and change. My intent has not been to argue that school systems have been successful in solving the problems of underdevelopment, economic stagnation, and social inequality. Rather, I have pointed out that the current pessimism about education that has led our field to the brink of rejecting education as a means for change for the better is probably not warranted. Education does bring about change, but that change is not dramatic, nor is it necessarily in the specific aspects of social and economic life that we had hoped it would be in the heady days of the 1960s. Comparative education has tended to value education only for short-term dramatic changes in the economy and the opportunity structure of society. Perhaps schools are unwieldy instruments to effect these changes. In our search for dramatic, short-term changes in these two dimensions of national life, we may not have seen the very real changes education has brought about and may continue to bring about for those populations we had hoped the educational expansion of the 1960s and 1970s would serve. As a field, we were a little too fast in the 1960s to have very high expectations for education, and, in the 1980s, we have become a little too quick to abandon those expectations. Comparative education has been, perhaps, too ready to accept education as failing to contribute to change that schools may or may not have been equipped to affect or may have affected in ways we are not yet equipped to understand.

Ideology is not the issue here, as some have suggested. Rather, the field needs to sort out a series of conceptual issues that undergird research. What do we mean by change? Can we connect attitudinal, behavioral, and institutional change—and in what way? What kinds of changes other than in economies and social stratification patterns can we expect education to affect? When is a change significant? How can we link changes in educational content, quality, and processes to changes deemed significant? From whose perspective do we evaluate change? How long are we willing to wait to evaluate the effect of educational changes on different social strata as well as on the society as a whole? These issues should be on our agenda. They seem to me ones that need to be systematically addressed before we can make statements to the effect that schools make no difference or that education is a "frill." Rather than abandoning our faith in the school and focusing our energies on such questions as "How much schooling is enough?" It is high time for the field to develop a solid research base that will let us know along what dimensions schools do promote change, what kinds of changes we might expect schools to bring about within a realistic time frame, and what kind of agenda for educational reform might be warranted through the study of schooling. The field might then not find itself in its current paradox—which is being a field devoted to the study of education that neither studies education nor serves as an advocate for education.

Notes

[1] See, e. g., David Abernethy, *The Political Dilemma of Popular Education: An African Case* (Stanford, Calif.: Stanford University Press, 1969); J. P. Naik, *Equality, Quality and Quantity: The Elusive Triangle in Indian Education* (Bombay: Allied, 1975); Philip Loh, *Seeds of Separatism—Education Policy in Malaysia, 1874-1940* (Kuala Lumpur: Oxford University Press 1975).

[2] See, e. g., Marie Thourson Jones, "Educating Girls in Tunisia: Issues Generated by the Drive for Universal Enrollment," *Comparative Education Review* 24, no. 2, pt. 2 (June 1980): S106-S123; George Psacharopoulos, "The Perverse Effects of Public Subsidization of Education; or, How Equal Is Free Education?" *Comparative Education Review* 21 (February 1977): 69-90; Mateen Thobani, "Charging User Fees for Social Services: Education in Malawi," *Comparative Education Review* 28 (August 1984): 402-23.

³Thobani; Psacharopoulos; Estelle James, "Benefits and Costs of Privatized Public Services: Lessons from the Dutch Educational System," *Comparative Education Review* 28 (November 1984): 605-24.

⁴See Andre Gunder Frank, "Sociology of Development and the Underdevelopment of Sociology," in *Dependency and Underdevelopment*, ed. James D. Cockcroft, Andre Gunder Frank, and Dale L. Johnson (New York: Doubleday, 1972), pp. 321-97; Dean Tibbs, "Modernization Theory and the Study of National Societies: A Critical Perspective," *Comparative Studies in Society and History* 15 (1973): 199-226.

⁵Steven J. Klees, "Planning and Policy Analysis in Education: What Can Economics Tell Us?" *Comparative Education Review* 30 (November 1986): 574-607; Erwin Epstein, "Currents Left and Right: Ideology in Comparative Education," *Comparative Education Review* 27 (February 1983): 3-30; Rolland Paulston, "Conflicting Theories of Educational Reform," in *Better Schools*, ed. John Simmons (New York: Praeger, 1982), pp. 21-70.

⁶Michael Armer and Robert Youtz, "Formal Education and Individual Modernity in an African Society," *American Journal of Sociology* 76 (January 1971): 604-26.

⁷Abernethy, op. cit.

⁸Peter R. Moock, "Education and Technical Efficiency in Small-Farm Production," *Economic Development and Cultural Change* 29 (July 1981): 723-39.

⁹O. Nnoli, "Education and Ethnic Politics in Nigeria," in *Education and Politics in Tropical Africa*, ed. Victor Uchendu (Buffalo, N.Y.: Counch, 1979), pp. 63-81.

¹⁰Paulston, op. cit.

¹¹Alex Inkeles and David Smith, *Becoming Modern: Individual Change in Six Developing Countries* (Cambridge, Mass.: Harvard University, 1974); William K. Cummings, *Education and Equality in Japan* (Princeton, N.J.: Princeton University Press, 1980).

¹²See, e.g., Susan H. Cochrane, "Education and Fertility: An Expanded Examination of the Evidence," in *Women's Education in the Third World: Comparative Perspectives*, ed. G. P. Kelly and C. M. Elliott (Albany: State University of New York Press, 1982), pp. 331-30.

¹³John C. Bock, "Education and Development: A Conflict of Meaning," in *Comparative Education*, ed. P. G. Altbach, R. Arnove, and G. P. Kelly (New York: Macmillan, 1982), pp. 78-104; C. R. Harber, "Development and Political Attitudes: The Role of Schooling in Northern Nigeria," *Comparative Education* 2, no. 3 (1984): 442-69;

Mark Bray, Peter B. Clarke, and David Stephens, *Education and Society in Africa* (London: Edward Arnold, 1986), pp. 23-35.

[14]Bray, et al. See also Philip Coombs, *The World Crisis in Education: The View from the Eighties* (New York: Oxford University Press, 1985).

[15]Coombs, op. cit.

[16]See, esp., Robert A. LeVine, "Influences of Women's Schooling on Maternal Behavior in the Third World," *Comparative Education Review* 24, no. 2, pt. 2 (June 1980): S78-S105. See also Barbara K. Larson, "The Status of Women in a Tunisian Village: Limits to Autonomy, Influence, and Power," *Signs* 9, no. 3 (Spring 1984): 417-33; and Margaret Strobel, "African Women," *Signs* 8, no. 1 (Autumn 1982):109-31.

[17]See Gail P. Kelly and P.G. Altbach, "Comparative Education: Change and Response," *Comparative Education Review* 30 (February 1986): 89-107.

[18]Kelly and Altbach. See also Ellen C. DuBois et al., *Feminist Scholarship: Kindling in the Groves of Academe* (Urbana: University of Illinois Press, 1985), esp. chaps. 1-3.

[19]LeVine; Larson; Oya Culpan and Toni Mazotto, "Changing Attitudes toward Work and Marriage: Turkey in Transition," *Signs* 8 (Winter 1982): 337-51.

[20]See, e. g., George Z. F. Bereday, "Social Stratification and Education in Industrial Countries," *Comparative Education Review* 21 (June/October 1977): 195-210; Robert Havinghurst, "Education, Social Mobility and Social Change in Four Societies: A Comparative Study," *International Review of Education* 4, no. 2 (1958): 167-85; Philip Foster, *Education and Social Change in Ghana* (Chicago: University of Chicago Press, 1965); Remi Clignet and Philip Foster, *The Fortunate Few: A Study of Secondary School and Other Students in the Ivory Coast* (Evanston, Ill.: Northwestern University Press, 1966).

[21]Thobani (n. 2 above); Psacharopoulos (n. 2 above).

[22]Samuel Bowles and Herbert Gintis, *Schooling in Capitalist America* (New York: Basic, 1976); James Coleman et al., *Equality of Educational Opportunity* (Washington, D.C.: Government Printing Office, 1966); A. H. Halsey, "Towards Meritocracy? The Case of Britain," in *Power and Ideology in Education,* ed. J. Karabel and A. H. Halsey (New York: Oxford University Press, 1977): pp. 173-86; Henry M. Levin, "The Dilemma of Comprehensive Secondary School Reforms in Western Europe," *Comparative Education Review* 22 (October 1978): 434-51; Josef Fitzman, "Education and Equality of Opportunity in Eastern Europe," in Altbach et al., pp. 381-410; Gail W. Lapidus, *Women in Soviet Society* (Berkeley: University of

California Press, 1978); Richard Dobson, "Social Status and Inequality of Access to Higher Education in the USSR," in Karabel and Halsey, eds., pp. 254-75; Thobani, op. cit.

[23] See e. g. Isobel Deble, *The School Education of Girls* (Paris: UNESCO, 1980); Gail P. Kelly, "Setting State Policy for Women's Education in the Third World," *Comparative Education* (in press).

[24] See Audrey Smock, *Women's Education in Developing Countries: Opportunities and Outcomes* (New York: Praeger, 1981); Lapidus; Rati Ram, "Sex Differences in the Labor Market Outcomes of Education," *Comparative Education Review* 24, no. 2, pt. 2 (June 1980): S53-S78; Ernesto Schiefelbein and Joseph P. Farrell, "Women, Schooling and Work in Chile: Evidence from a Longitudinal Study," *Comparative Education Review* 24, no. 2, pt. 2 (June 1980): S160-S179; Kathleen Howard-Merriam, "Women, Education and the Professions in Egypt," *Comparative Education Review* 23, no. 2 (June 1980): 256-70.

[25] Catalina H. Wainerman, "The Impact of Education on the Female Labor Force in Argentina and Paraguay," *Comparative Education Review* 23, no. 2, pt. 2 (June 1980): S180-S195.

[26] Inga Elqvist-Saltzman, "The Life History Approach—A Tool in Establishing North-South Educational Research Cooperation?" Working Paper no. 7 (Umeå: Universitet Pedagogiska Institutionen, Weed-projecktet, 1986).

[27] Schiefelbein and Farrell, op. cit.

[28] LeVine; James Sheffield, "Basic Education for the Rural Poor: The Tanzanian Case," *Journal of Developing Areas* 14, no. 1 (October 1979): 99-110; Moock (n. 8 above); W. H. M. L. Hoppers, "Youth, Apprenticeship and Petty Production in Lusaka," *International Journal of Educational Development* 3, no. 2 (1983): 113-28; Claire Robertson, "Formal or Nonformal Education? Entrepreneurial Women in Ghana," *Comparative Education Review* 28 (November 1984): 639-58; Barbara C. Lewis, "Economic Activity and Marriage among Ivorian Urban Women," in *Sexual Stratification: A Cross-cultural View*, ed. Alice Schlegal (New York: Columbia University Press, 1977): pp. 161-91; D.A. Mitchnik, *Improving Ways of Skill Acquisition of Women for Rural Employment in Some African Countries* (Geneva: International Labor Organization, 1977); J. C. Caldwell, "Education as a Factor in Mortality Decline: An Examination of Nigerian Data," *Population Studies* 33 (November 1979): 395-413; D. F. S. Fernando, "Female Educational Attainment and Fertility," *Journal of Biosocial Science* 9, no. 3 (July 1977): 339-51.

[29] M. D. Shipman, *Education and Modernization* (London: Faber & Faber, 1971); Ronald Dore, *Education in Tokugawa Japan*

(Berkeley: University of California Press, 1965); Herbert Passin, *Society and Education in Japan* (New York: Teachers College Press, 1965); Seymour Rosen, *Education and Modernization in the USSR* (Reading, Mass.: Addison-Wesley, 1963); T. W. Schultz, *The Economic Value of Education* (New York: Columbia University Press, 1963).

[30] David Morrison, *Education and Politics in Africa: The Tanzanian Case* (Montreal: McGill Queens University Press, 1976).

[31] See, e. g., Levin; and Fitzman, op. cit.

[32] See, e. g., Gail P. Kelly and Maxine S. Seller, "Considerations: Historical Perspectives on Reform in New York State," in *Excellence in Education: Perspectives on Policy and Practice*, ed. P. G. Altbach, G.P. Kelly, and L. Weis (Buffalo, N.Y.: Prometheus 1985), pp. 253-74. See also Kathleen B. Fischer, *Political Ideology and Educational Reform in Chile, 1964-1976* (Los Angeles: University of California, Los Angeles, Latin American Studies Center, 1979).

[33] Gary L. Theisen, Paul P. W. Achola, and Francis Musa Boakari, "The Underachievement of Cross-national Studies of Achievement," in *New Approaches to Comparative Education*, ed. P. G. Altbach and G.P. Kelly (Chicago: University of Chicago Press, 1985), pp. 27-50.

[34] See Andreas M. Kazamias and Karl Schwartz, "Intellectual and Ideological Perspectives in Comparative Education: An Interpretation," *Comparative Education Review* 21 (June/October 1977): 153-76; Robert Koehl, " The Comparative Study of Education: Prescription and Practice," *Comparative Education Review* 21 (June/October 1977): 177-94; Lois Weis, "Educational Outcomes and School Processes: Theoretical Perspectives," in Altbach et al., eds. (n. 13 above), pp. 484-504.

Vietnam[†]

Vietnam, a country of over 63 million people, has only recently emerged from centuries of foreign domination and warfare. Standing at the intersection of Southeast Asia and China, this Southeast Asian nation was invaded and ruled by China for over 1,000 years. Chinese influence sustained itself long after the Chinese were driven out. Until the twentieth century the Vietnamese language was written in Chinese characters; Vietnamese traditional architecture is fashioned on the Chinese, and the Citadel in Hue, the Imperial City, mirrors the Forbidden City in Peking.

While Vietnam was set apart from Southeast Asia by China, French colonial rule further deflected the country from other Southeast Asian countries. France dominated the country for nearly 100 years, irrevocably changing the economy and social structure. French rule reoriented Vietnamese intellectual and cultural life away from China toward Western models. The French built Western cities, notably Hanoi and Saigon, instituted a plantation agriculture, and introduced capitalism.[1] France also established schools based on Western models. These schools became the basis for the educational system of contemporary Vietnam.

French rule ended only after years of protracted war. The "first" Indochina war left the country divided just north of the city of Hue. The North underwent major social change, becoming a communist state with ties to the Soviet Union and Eastern Europe. The South was initially ruled by Ngo Dinh Diem, a southern intellectual with ties to the Catholic Church and to Vietnam's former monarchy. The South became a state run by the military and bolstered by increasing amounts of U.S. aid and, by the late 1960s, U.S. military forces. In 1975, the government of South Vietnam collapsed after decades of fighting the "second" Indochina war. The North Vietnamese Army occupied Saigon and the South and brought about reunification.

This chapter focuses on the changing roles and status of women in Vietnam through these turbulent times of foreign rule, civil war, and revolution. It will discuss how changes in women's education relate to

---

[†]Reprinted with permission from *International Handbook of Women's Education*, Gail Kelly, ed. Greenwood, 1988, an imprint of Greenwood Publishing Group, Inc., Westport CT.

dramatic changes in women's social, political, and economic roles and status. Over the years women have achieved major advances, gaining access to education, entering economic and political life, and developing basic rights in marriage and the family. Today, more than in Vietnam's feudal past under French colonialism, or the southern regime, women are better educated; they are in the workforce in unprecedented numbers, and they hold more political power than ever before. However, this does not mean that they have achieved equality. The real commitment of the Vietnamese government to women's liberation has brought about many of these changes, but the problems of poverty—which are very real to Vietnam—and the current economic crisis in which Vietnam finds itself, has created policies which at best will delay further progress for women and at worse will threaten to undermine the progress women have made. The government has made economic development its top priority and, while gender equality remains one of its goals, the government has adopted policies aimed at stimulating economic growth. These policies—privatization, decentralization, and the development of a market based economy— may put a country long committed to gender-based equality on the road to developing inequalities characteristic of other Third World nations and the industrialized capitalist countries.

Our discussion starts with a consideration of women before and under French colonialism and ends with a look at education in Vietnam during the period of the two Vietnams and after reunification in 1975. It will look at educational policies and enrollment patterns as well as their workforce and political outcomes. The discussion of education in contemporary Vietnam is based largely on interview data collected in January 1988. Other kinds of data on contemporary Vietnam, which are also cited here, are not all that common or comprehensive. The use of interview data may involve some bias since the individuals interviewed were members of Vietnamese governmental and quasi-governmental agencies. Even so, their bias tends to be on the optimistic rather than pessimistic side. Some of the literature on Vietnam is avowedly anticommunist and begrudges any positive changes that may have occurred since 1945.

From Tradition to the French Colonial Order

Even though Vietnam was ruled by China for over 1,000 years, gender relations in Vietnam did not mirror those of Confucian China. Vietnamese traditions were different. Footbinding, for example, was never practiced, and the Vietnamese family, while patriarchal, did not make the father all powerful. Girls did not take their father's names, and they were free to choose their own husbands. Females even became folk heroines. The Trung sisters, who led armies to rid the country of foreign invaders, have few parallels in other Asian societies. In the very distant past Vietnamese women were thought to be the equal of men; some even insist that, before the Chinese invasion, Vietnam was a matriarchy in which women held power and authority.[2] Despite such traditions, in the 1,000 years of Chinese domination (to A.D. 939) and a succession of post-Chinese Vietnamese monarchs, efforts were made to rigidly circumscribe women's roles and reinforce women's subordination to men. From the time of Chinese domination, Confucianism was the official ideology. Confucianism was characterized by an age/gender hierarchy wherein women could gain a modicum of power only through their sons. The dominant ideology held that "One hundred women are not worth a single testicle."[3] Most Vietnamese women were peasant women who toiled in the fields. The ideology that confirmed women's inferiority to men did not preclude a woman's labor in her husband's or her father's fields.

In the fifteenth century, the Le Dynasty Legal Code gave women the right to own property and stated that parents should divide their land equally among sons and daughters. This provision was rescinded by the Gia-Long Code of the early nineteenth century. The Le Dynasty Code also stated that women's property, once hers, remained hers whether she was married or divorced and that she had the right to will her property to whomever she designated. She was entitled not only to her own property, but upon her husband's death, also to half of his.[4]

Despite women's right to hold property and a tradition of contributing to the economy (in the past women formed the bulk of the agricultural labor force, as they do today), they rarely had access to power. In Confucian Vietnam, the route to power was state service, and that was obtained solely through education. Education was for men alone. Vietnam was governed through a highly centralized bureaucracy. Examinations administered every three years were key to obtaining work in the bureaucracy. Throughout the country males attended Confucian schools of characters, memorized the Four Books and Five Classics, and spent their lives taking examinations.[5] Women worked the land to support their sons and husbands who aspired to high office. Women of the landed gentry became traders and the backbone of Vietnam's exchange economy. Many a Vietnamese folk saying warned women against marrying those who aspired to the bureaucracy. One went: "Girls, heed the advice and don't marry a scholar. His back is long. It takes lots of material for his gown. And after he stuffs himself, he goes to sleep."[6]

The Confucian hierarchy depended on women's labor to survive but devalued that labor. The hierarchy accorded merchants and traders the lowest place in social rank and the scholar/bureaucrat the highest. The state could always usurp money. Only males and scholar/bureaucrats had power and status.

The French invasion of Vietnam, which began in the 1850s, profoundly changed Vietnamese society. The advent of French rule meant the alienation of land. Cochinchina (South Vietnam) was the scene of a fruitless "scholars' resistance." Large tracts of land were abandoned as Vietnamese fled to fight against the French further north. This land was redistributed to Frenchmen who often sold it to Vietnamese entrepreneurs, or it was given to Vietnamese collaborators as a reward for their services to the new colonial state.[7] Landlordism became the rule in Cochinchina through the years of French rule—75 percent of the rural population became landless laborers. In Annam and Tonkin, over half the peasants were landless, and about 90 percent of those who held land had such small holdings that they sold their labor to maintain subsistence.[8]

The alienation of land changed women's economic position. Rural women no longer worked their own land; rather, they became wage labor in the rural economy. By the 1920s, the French abolished the Vietnamese monarchy's civil service, recruited via the triennial examinations, and established their own age-specific educational system which led to salaried employment in the colonial regime. Men who had at one time spent their days studying Chinese classics in the hopes of landing a position in the administration now entered the rural workforce. The impoverishment of the Vietnamese peasantry intensified under French colonialism. With the famines of the 1930s thousands died on the roads of Annam. The Nghe-An-Ha-Tinh uprisings of 1930-1931 took the form of long marches to the cities and towns in search of food and the raiding of local granaries.[9]

Peasants who worked as sharecroppers and tenants were, of course, the most disadvantaged. The sex-role division of labor meant that women not only transplanted rice and weeded it, but also pulled the plow in lieu of water buffaloes. Women agricultural workers were given only half the pay males received and were hired solely for planting and harvesting.[10]

Although rural peasants suffered under colonial rule and women's economic position deteriorated along with men's, the impact of colonialism was not the same on elite women from families in which male heads of household had attended French colonial schools or were from the French-created landlord class. These women tended to manage the family's landed wealth whereas the men focused their efforts on business or on work for the French colonial administration. These women were often educated in Catholic or private schools under the French colonial regime.

Colonial rule brought with it a new set of schools. As early as the 1880s, the French established a number of institutions to train administrators and interpreters. By the twentieth century, a new school system controlled from Hanoi by the French was created. It provided the gamut of elementary through higher education and became the basis for the modern schools of Vietnam. They were predominantly schools for boys, for while France may have had a different sex-role division of labor than precolonial Vietnam, France was a patriarchal society. In France gender based inequality in education and throughout society generally was all pervasive. Perhaps thinking it was upholding local traditions, France reproduced and even exaggerated these traditions in the colonies.

Colonial Schools

Schooling in colonial Vietnam was limited to a very small proportion of the population. Even by the rosiest of French estimates, by 1939 less than 10 percent of the age cohort attended schools.[11] A literacy survey, conducted by P. Chesneau in 1938 and published in the government-sponsored pedagogical journals, the *Bulletin of Public Instruction,* found high illiteracy rates in Thanh Hoa Province (in Northcentral Vietnam) which had 200 schools.[12] In the provincial capital of Phu Quang, 19.5 percent of the men over sixty years of age were literate in Chinese characters whereas no women in that age range could claim any degree of literacy in either Chinese, Vietnamese written in roman script, or French. However, 2 percent of males over sixty years of age were literate in French, and 3 percent could read Vietnamese written in roman script. Among the fifty-one to sixty-year-olds, the inequality intensified—1.2 percent of the men were literate in French, 12.1 percent in Vietnamese written in the roman script, and 31.7 percent in Chinese. All the women in this age group were illiterate in any language. This held for the forty-one to fifty-year-olds as well. In the younger age cohorts Chesneau interviewed, literacy rates among males were higher, as were those of females, but gender differences persisted. Among ten to twenty-year-olds, 26 percent of the males were literate in French, 55.4 percent could read and write Vietnamese written in roman script, whereas 1.2 percent of females ten to twenty years old could read and write French and 5.8 percent could read and write Vietnamese written in the roman script. In short, in thirty years of French school construction Phu Quang City went from total illiteracy, except in Chinese, to a city where half the men were literate in Vietnamese written in roman script and one quarter of the men were literate in French, whereas most of the women remained illiterate in any language. In the rural areas of Thanh Hoa Province, the pattern of male literacy and female illiteracy remained, although men were less likely to be literate than their peers in the provincial capital. Being in the

Table 9.1
School Enrollment, by Gender and Region, 1939

	Education Level					
	Elementary (Govt. funded)	Elementary (Commune funded)	All Elementary	Primary (Govt. funded only)	Primary Superior	Secondary (Includes Normal Courses)	Total Enrollment (all levels)
Tonkin							
Males							
Number	70,282	64,438	134,720	18,054	1,849	176	154,799
Percent	88.35	73.07	90.54	88.54	90.06	93.62	90.30
Females							
Number	9,268	4,801	14,069	2,336	204	12	16,621
Percent	11.6	6.93	9.46	11.46	9.94	6.38	9.69
Cochinchina							
Males							
Number	92,460	8,760	101,220	17,673	1,346	152	120,391
Percent	70.3	87.0	71.5	75.95	80.36	87.36	72.22
Females							
Number	39,044	1,306	40,350	5,596	329	22	46,297
Percent	29.7	12.97	28.5	24.05	19.64	12.64	27.8

Annam					
Males					
Number	19,801	62,330	82,131	15,030	892	97	98,150
Percent	83.09	93.05	90.44	89.84	84.23	94.17	90.29
Females					
Number	4,030	4,654	8,684	1,699	167	6	10,556
Percent	16.91	6.95	9.57	10.16	15.77	5.83	9.71
All Vietnam					
Males					
Number	182,543	135,528	318,071	50,757	4,087	425	373,340
Percent	77.72	92.6	83.4	84.05	85.38	91.4	83.5
Females					
Number	52,342	10,761	63,103	9,631	700	40	73,474
Percent	22.28	7.36	16.55	15.95	14.62	8.6	16.45

Source: Government General de l'Indochine francaise, *Rapports...1939, Deuxieme Partie*, Tableau VI

capital made a greater difference for male literacy rates than female literacy rates.

The gap in male and female literacy rates was unquestionably the result of government policies which emphasized the construction of boys' schools. Whether girls attended school was in large part a result of government decisions to build a girls' school or to make a local school coeducational. Public school enrollments, broken down by gender for 1939, are presented in Table 9.1. Girls overall accounted for 16.45 percent of all students. Of the 446,814 who went to any public school, 73,474 were female. Most of the girls in school were in the first three years of schooling where girls comprised 16.55 percent of enrollments. Table 9.1 does not provide dropout rates. In Cochinchina, which enrolled 39,044 girls in official elementary schools, 18,039 girls were in the first year, whereas 7,825 were in the third and last year. The dropout rates were considerable for males as well: there were 36,437 boys in the first grade and 22,535 in the third grade. Girls made up 25.77 percent of the last-year class and 33.11 percent of the first-year class.[13]

In Tonkin (northern Vietnam) half the girls dropped out between first and third grades. In Annam (central Vietnam) girls in government-funded schools tended to remain through the elementary course, whereas boys tended not only to remain but also to repeat grades. In 1939, the third grade class was close to 600 students larger than the first-year class. In Annam, the central provinces which were a protectorate where the Vietnamese monarchy still maintained a presence in governance, the dropout rates were high in the schools funded by local villages—which were the mainstream of education. In 1939, 80 percent of the girls and about 65 percent of the boys dropped out in the first three years of schooling.

Girls' chances of obtaining primary education (Grades 4, 5, and 6) were quite low. Girls accounted for about 16 percent of primary school students in 1939. Again, most were clustered in the fourth grade. In Tonkin, of the 2,336 girls in primary school, 1,042 were in the fourth grade and 562 were in the sixth grade (versus 7,520 males in the fourth grade and 4,897 in the fifth). In Annam, 759 girls were in the fourth grade and 445 in the sixth. In the south, Cochinchina, female enrollment in the primary grades was the highest but here too of the 5,596 girls, 2,382 were in the fourth grade.

As Table 9.1 shows, very few Vietnamese went beyond the primary grades, and girls remained a minority here as well: 14.62 percent of postprimary students were girls. Again, most were in the first year or two of the course of study. In Annam, 71 were in the first year and 27 in the fourth year; in Cochinchina 118 were in the first year and 47 in the fourth and last year, whereas in Tonkin 69 girls were in the first year and 43 in the last year. Girls did not go to secondary school. In 1939, 40 girls were enrolled (versus 425 boys). The Indochinese University was a male institution. Only the Midwifery School took in girls.

As Table 9.1 shows, there was considerable regional variation in the extent to which government schools were made available to girls. Girls accounted for 27.8 percent of all students in southern Vietnam (Cochinchina), 9.71 percent in central Vietnam (Annam) and 9.69 percent in the north (Tonkin). In the south, the female enrollment share was twice that of the rest of the country.

Girls' access to schooling was a class phenomenon, and it also related to the extent to which Vietnamese traditional structures were replaced by France. The north and the center were French protectorates in which a Vietnamese administration remained in place, albeit directed by Frenchmen who served as advisers. In Annam, the center, the Vietnamese monarchy ruled for the French. It attempted to undermine French efforts to erode the little power it retained, and it sought to prevent the development of new social strata via French-created schools. In Annam, elite girls' schools were opened in the capital, Hue, to serve the daughters of the Vietnamese monarchy and its bureaucrats. The College Dong Khanh was founded in 1922 as the female counterpart to the College Quoc Hoc (literally National Learning), which was an elite all-male *lycée* situated directly across the Perfume River from the Citadel, the Vietnamese equivalent of the Chinese forbidden City. In Annam, these girls remained in schools through the primary and postprimary grades. It was in the rural commune-funded elementary schools where education was offered for the most part to boys only and where the few girls who managed to enter school left quickly. In 1939, a total of 2,833 girls were attending the first grade in rural schools and 393 were in the third grade. The same trend of high female attrition rates among the rural poor held in Tonkin in "unofficial" commune-funded schools. Parental social class was the major factor determining access to schools; for girls it was the only factor, but for boys it was one of several factors.

The public sector formed the major educational route during the French colonial period. However, substantial numbers of children were schooled in private institutions. In 1933, a total of 29,781 students were enrolled in Catholic diocesan elementary schools; another 4,554 attended diocesan primary schools. Most of these Catholic schools were in Cochinchina where over half the elementary Catholic school enrollments were concentrated. The church ran five postprimary schools. On the postprimary level the private secular schools were far more important than the church-run schools. There were 17 private secular postprimary schools serving 2,429 children in 1933. About 5 percent of the students were girls.[14]

Girls who were educated in the colonial period were rare, and these women constituted an elite. Girls educated in the prestigious private Ecole des Jeunes Filles Indigènes of Saigon, or the government-run Collège Dong Khanh in Hue, or the private Ecole Brieux in Hanoi were taught a curriculum similar to that of their male peers, although they were also instructed in domestic science and in needlework for two to three hours a week in place of the despised manual labor instruction given boys. The school curriculum focused on teaching to males and females alike Vietnamese written in the Roman script, French, mathematics, history, geography, moral education, and general science. The moral education curriculum was adapted from what the French thought was Vietnamese traditional moral codes and expurgated of any seemingly anti-French content. This part of the curriculum explicitly emphasized women's subjugation to men. Several moral education texts were developed specifically for girls because Vietnamese neo-traditionalists, in the face of new values and competing social visions, feared that women might abandon their roles long defined in the Confucian texts.[15] The moral education texts approved by the government for school use focused on the cardinal relations and obligations befitting the virtuous. Central was the gender-age hierarchy pointing to the king as the Son of Heaven (and Heaven was male) who was to be obeyed as the son obeys his father and the wife her husband. David Marr, in his study of the women's rights debates in Vietnam in the 1920s, points out that some of the moral education texts put even greater emphasis on the role of woman as docile housewife, loyal and obedient to her husband and ever sensitive to her family's needs, including those of a second wife and servants. Private entrepreneurs produced these texts in large quantities for home study.[16] Like the school texts, they provided a view of women, particularly upper class women who had servants to supervise, which at that point in time was being disputed among Vietnamese intellectuals.

Without doubt, both the informal and formal curriculum of the schools emphasized woman's roles as mother and housewife. In the French-language curriculum, the Ecole Brieux in Hanoi assigned essays on hygiene and health as well as on how mothers should discipline their children and the qualities of a good housewife. In boys' schools, the French composition topics focused on describing objects, on writing letters to the French local administrator, on occupations students might assume after graduation, on the work of the peasant, and on the benefits of France.[17]

Girls did not always easily accept the narrow roles the schools proposed for them. When assigned a composition topic in French, "Describe the Qualities of a Good Housewife," Vu-Thi-Tin, a student in the sixth grade of the Ecole Brieux in Hanoi, wrote of the housewife's work in language befitting a general directing an army or the governor general leading his staff in running Indochina. She wrote: "It is not easy to direct a domestic government with order, economy, and cleanliness. The first method of directing the work well is to have a woman who has all the good qualities [of leadership]."[18] Vu-Thi-Tin continued her essay by describing a division of labor within the household promoted by the school. Her choice of words changed as she repeated the school's teaching, moving from administrative language to domestic language: "The man earns a living, the woman spends, each has his own role. The good housewife does not buy superfluous goods which spendthrift women buy. She knows how to keep to her budget—that is why her money is carefully counted out and allocated for each purchase. But after all [is bought] she puts some of her husband's wages aside to save for days of [his] sickness and unemployment."[19]

While girls may have been asked to write about future roles as housewives, schoolgirls were sometimes embroiled in anticolonial struggles that reemerged in Vietnam in the 1920s. Girls at the Ecole des Jeunes Filles Indigènes in Saigon repeatedly walked out of school in protest over the ways in which they, as Vietnamese elites, were treated by their French teachers. The girls at this particular school went out on strike over racism at least twice in the 1920s. One incident that occurred in the early 1920s involved a dispute over whether Vietnamese girls had to give up seats in front of the classroom to French girls. When Phan Boi Chau, a prominent Vietnamese nationalist died in 1924, these girls collected money for memorial wreaths, wore arm bands denoting personal as well as national mourning (which was forbidden by the schools), and joined street demonstrations.[20] The girls at the elite Collège Dong Khanh in Hue led the school walkouts in 1926 after a male student, related to the Vietnamese Royal Family, was slapped by a French teacher who accused him of cheating.

Girls educated in colonial Vietnam were schooled in the context of intellectual and social ferment in Vietnamese society. Vietnamese elites of the 1920s and 1930s debated a range of questions, many of which centered on the relevance of Vietnamese traditions and whether those traditions have been responsible for the loss of nationhood and French colonialism. The role of women was one issue hotly debated.[21] Vietnamese traditionalists, like Pham Quynh who wrote a number of tracts on Confucianism and modern moral values, upheld a traditional role for women based on Confucian values. (Pham Quynh later became minister of education in Annam, the central provinces administered by the monarchy under French tutelage.) Pham Quynh argued that Vietnamese culture could be revived if it returned to its Confucian roots—and this included the subordination of women.[22] Not all Vietnamese shared such views. Nationalists like Phan Boi Chau saw women assuming major roles in liberating the country from colonialism as the Trung sisters in the past had led Vietnamese in the struggle against China. A number of women's groups arose like the Women's Labor Study Association which was established in 1926. The association published the journal *Women's Review*, which asserted new roles for women and rejected those embedded in neotraditionalist Confucian ideology. More radical and overtly feminist groups also arose among educated women. The Communist party and the Vietnam Women's Union, both founded in 1930, advocated full equality between men and women and sought to mobilize women, particularly peasant women, in the struggle against colonialism and for a socialist revolution. The Communist party organized women into the Women's Union and into workers' associations. In the 1930s, the party passed a number of resolutions calling for the full emancipation of women from the tyranny of Confucian hierarchy and feudalism.[23] As in China and the USSR, women became an important part of the communist movement, and the liberation of women was an avowedly important goal of that movement.

Independence and the Period of the Two Vietnams: War and Revolution

Toward the end of World War II, Japan occupied French Indochina, wresting power from the Vichy generals who had cooperated with Japan throughout the war. With Japan's collapse, the Vietnamese Communist party marched into Hanoi and declared itself the legal government of Vietnam. Soon thereafter, Allied troops dislodged Ho Chi Minh's government and reclaimed Indochina for France, setting off the first Indochina war.

After the defeat of France at Dien-Bien-Phu, the Geneva Accords were signed dividing the country in two. North Vietnam, the Socialist Republic of Vietnam, was a communist state; the South emerged as the Republic of Vietnam, led by Ngo Dinh Diem, a Vietnamese Catholic who had served in the short-lived Japanese puppet government. Elections provided for by the 1954 Geneva Agreements were never held, and Diem established a military government that was backed by the United States. Not until 1975, after years of bloody warfare, was Vietnam reunited as the Saigon government fell, defeated on the battlefield.

The period 1954 to 1975 was a time of separate development for the two Vietnams. North Vietnam shared the ideology, common to most communist states, of equality between social classes and between the sexes. Commitment to women's liberation was a strong element of government policy. The 1946 constitution granted women the same political, economic, cultural, social, and family rights as men. The constitution openly set forth the principle of equal pay and guaranteed women the right to vote and to hold public office. The marriage laws provided women with the right of free choice in marriage; they outlawed polygamy and legalized divorce. They also established women's right to children, to property, and to the land.[24]

The North set women's liberation, at least on paper as a national goal. The southern government, dominated as it was by conservative Catholics, many of whom had fled from the North to avoid living under a communist government and many of whom were neotraditionalists, moved to reinforce the family and personal morality, reminiscent of neo-Confucianism but called "personalism."[25] Diem's sister-in-law, Madame Nhu, formed a Women's Solidarity league, which was a paramilitary organization dedicated to supporting personalism as an ideology and fighting against communism. The Solidarity league was an urban organization that reached women of urban, elite families. The southern government did not set forth policies that focused on improving the lives of rural women who formed the vast majority of women in South Vietnam. Madame Nhu's league campaigned against prostitution—an occupation that grew greatly, especially among poor women who had taken refuge in urban areas as the war was waged in the countryside. American soldiers meant big business for bar girls and prostitutes. The women's league also sought to maintain Vietnamese traditional dress codes and inveighed against mini-skirts and Western-style dancing.

The civil war which raged in the South between 1954 and 1975 destroyed much of the fabric of rural life and profoundly affected women's roles. Much of the male population disappeared from the countryside. Men were drafted into the South Vietnamese Army or the National Liberation front, or were dragged away as suspected Viet Cong. Women became much of the rural population, and they were disproportionately victimized by the bombings, strafings, and search and destroy missions. In many areas women took over the rural economy, and as the war dragged on, large numbers of them joined the Frontline National Liberation Front (NLF) troops.[26] Women also became leaders: the vice commander-in-chief of the NLF troops in the South was a woman.

Education, Reconstruction, and the Contradictory Impact of Socialism and Poverty

Literacy campaigns have historically come to be associated with communist revolution. In the USSR, Cuba, and China, literacy campaigns and the spread of mass education were initiated as communist governments came to power. Vietnam, like these countries, made literacy and the spread of mass education a priority. In 1946, when Ho Chi Minh flew the National Liberation Front flag over the governor general's palace in Hanoi, over 90 percent of all women were illiterate. The NLF, after it was driven from Hanoi by the Allies, initiated literacy campaigns in the zones it controlled. In 1946, the literacy campaigns reached over 2 million adults. By 1948, 4 million women in the liberated zones had moved from illiteracy to being able to read and write in the Vietnamese language. By 1958, all illiteracy was eliminated in North Vietnam.[27]

In 1954, when the first Vietnam War ended, the government in Hanoi set about reforming the school system much in the image of the schools of the Soviet Union. In 1956, private schools were abolished, and public education came to consist of four years of elementary education, three years of junior secondary education, and three years of senior secondary education. University education was also provided. In the South, the school system retained the French colonial form of five years of primary education, four years of junior secondary, and three years of secondary school. Higher education was provided in a number of institutions. Unlike the North where the emphasis in higher education was on specialized technical instruction tied to economic development, in the South the university emphasized the liberal arts. In the early 1970s, 60 percent of all enrollments in the South were in literature and law, and only 10 percent studied medicine, engineering, and agriculture. In the South, over 30 percent of the population was illiterate.[28]

When the country was reunited, the schools underwent reform, harmonizing the northern and southern systems. In January 1979 the Politburo of the Vietnamese Communist party created an educational structure that consisted of nine years of general education, three years of secondary education, specialized secondary-level technical/trade schools, and universities. Although general education in Vietnam is in theory universal, male/female enrollments are not equal at any level. As of 1982, females constituted 42.8 percent of the students in the four years of general education, 45.8 percent of those in secondary education, and 28.4 percent in higher education.[29] This is more unequal than it seems—about 52 percent of the Vietnamese population is female. The sexual imbalance of the population is due to the years of bloody warfare, and it is greatest among those in the age cohorts currently in higher education.[30] The gap in male/female enrollments seems to be lessening somewhat. In 1988, women made up 37 percent of enrollments in higher education. The prospects for educational equality are somewhat dismal since many "key" schools—those schools that are funded out of provincial versus municipal budgets and that recruit from a wide geographical area—tend to have more boys than girls. The Quoc Hoc School in Hue is one such school. It prides itself on being an elite institution, and it was founded by the French early in the twentieth century to serve Annam's male elite. Today it is a coeducational school and accommodates 1,600 students in the three-year secondary course.[31] (Twenty percent of the students go on to higher education; the national average is somewhere under 10 percent of all secondary school graduates.) The students have won prizes in mathematics in international competitions in London and France. In 1988, the Quoc Hoc school enrolled 921 males and 737 females. In Grade 10 there were 275 girls and 333 boys; in Grade 12 there were 213 girls and 257 boys.

Part of the reason for the gender imbalance at Quoc Hoc School has to do with fees, which officially do not exist in Vietnam (except in universities). At Quoc Hoc, parents donate 70 dong a month. They are less willing to invest in girls who ultimately will be paid wages lower than men's and who upon marriage, are thought to join their husband's family.[32]

The pattern of women's education is quite similar to that of many other countries in that not only are there fewer women than men the higher one goes in education, but also in that the fields of study are segregated by sex. This extends to experimental schools on the primary level like the May the 15th School in Ho-Chi-Minh City which provides working children with basic literacy skills and job training as well as university-level studies. At the May the 15th School, boys are taught carpentry whereas girls are taught sewing, embroidery, and basket weaving.[33]

In higher education women constitute a minority. Women represent a very small proportion of Vietnamese holding the doctorate, the proportions ranging from 21.2 percent (medicine and pharmacy) to 4 percent (technology).[34] Women tend to concentrate not only in the lower levels of higher education, but also in certain fields—the natural sciences and social sciences in specialized secondary colleges where they earn half the degrees. At the university, women hold 46.4 percent of first degrees in medicine and pharmacy, 35.3 percent of first degrees in the social sciences, and 35.6 percent of first degrees in natural sciences. In contrast, they hold only 16.5 percent of first degrees in science and technology.

Equality in higher education seems a long way off as Table 9.2 indicates. As a percentage of students enrolled in university-level courses, women accounted for 4.8 percent of students in technology, 17.7 percent in agriculture and forestry, and 15.4 percent in social sciences. Women did constitute 32.2 percent of students enrolled in the natural sciences and 24.5 percent of students in medicine and pharmacy at the university level. The pattern only partly approximates that of other socialist countries. In Poland, the USSR, and East Germany, women outnumber men.[35] However the clustering of

Table 9.2
Women as a Percentage of Those Possessing Degrees and Enrolled in Higher Education, by Field, 1982

Field	Specialized Secondary (College)	University (First Degree)	Graduate Student (Currently Enrolled)	Ph.D.
Natural Sciences	51.1% (n=14,711)	35.6% (n=13,744)	32.2% (n=287)	7.6% (n=94)
Technology	30.0% (n=1,109)	16.5% (n=8,284)	4.8% (n=15)	4% (n=40)
Medicine and Pharmacy	39.1% (n=824)	46.4% (n=7,156)	24.5% (n=98)	21.2% (n=35)
Agriculture and Forestry	30.4% (n=530)	30.7% (n=5,422)	17.7% (n=21)	6.6% (n=9)
Social Science	50.5% (n=15,833)	35.3% (n=20,934)	15.4% (n=176)	10.6% (n=60)

Source: Hoang Xuan Sinh, "Participation of Women and Their Emancipation Through the Development of Education and Science in Vietnam" in *Proceedings of the Southeast Asian Seminar on Women and Science in Developing Countries*. Hanoi, Vietnam, 8-10 January 1987, p. 8.

women in the natural sciences and medicine and pharmacy is reminiscent of other European socialist countries.

The lack of parity in education is partly responsible for the persisting inequalities in the workforce.

The Socialist Workforce in Vietnam

The Vietnamese socialist revolution, like other socialist revolutions, sought to resolve the problem of women's oppression, as well as the problems of underdevelopment, via the workforce.[36] The assumption was, as in Marxist ideology worldwide, that gender-based inequality was due to women's lack of participation in productive labor. Socialist Vietnam focused on getting women into the workforce. By 1988, the government had succeeded in getting women into wage labor where their rate of participation is close to that of men, but their remuneration for their work is quite different from that of men. In 1988, women made up 46 percent of public sector (state) employees and 60 percent of cooperative employees. Women formed 65 percent of the agricultural workforce and 64 percent of the light industry workforce. They accounted for only 29 percent of workers in heavy industry.[37] The segregation of women into agricultural employment and work in light industry means that women are paid less than men because their work is different, as are their employers. They, like their sisters elsewhere, earn on an average 60 percent of men's wages, despite legislation that on paper guarantees women wages equal to those of men.

The workforce in Vietnam is segregated not only by industry and productive sector, but also within sectors. Teaching, for example, is a feminized profession: 72 percent of all those working as teachers are women. In 1982, in the universities women accounted for 3.4 percent of all professors, 26.6 percent of junior faculty, and 36 percent of the university support staff.[38] Medicine is another "female" field with 68 percent of all workers being women. However, women constitute most of the nurses and few of the hospital administrators.

The entry of women into the workforce did not mean economic equality in the past nor will it in the future for a number of reasons. Vietnam is an impoverished nation that has been hard pressed to provide more than rudimentary subsistence, albeit with a modicum of equality not found in other Third World nations. Feeding the growing population has been an easy task, and it is likely to get more difficult as the population continues to grow but food production continues to stagnate.[39] Basic child care services are lacking, and women work at jobs that can be combined with family and childbearing and rearing. While the old and new marriage laws call for sharing housework and child care responsibilities between spouses, enforcement is not easy.[40]

Women will continue to work at jobs where they can juggle home and family in a society that calls for the sharing of and socialization of housework but cannot come up with adequate funding for such programs.

Another reason for the present workforce position of women relates to protective labor legislation introduced in the 1950s and strengthened, in large part, at the instigation of the Vietnam Women's Union. Such legislation has made firms involved with heavy industry reluctant to hire women. Women workers are entitled to six months of paid maternity leave, and there are workplace environment laws relating to having pregnant and nursing women on the job. These laws are typical of other socialist countries, and in Vietnam, like the Soviet Union and many Eastern European countries, industrial firms, pressed to meet production quotas and reinvest profits in new industry, have been reluctant to bring women into their workforce.

Yet another reason for the workforce pattern is the fact that Vietnam is an underdeveloped country strained to provide employment to its growing population. Unemployment has been exacerbated by the demobilization of the army which has flooded the workforce with men seeking employment. This occurred at precisely the time when capital fled the South as the Saigon regime fell and as markets for Vietnamese goods outside the Soviet bloc crumbled. The Vietnamese invasion of Cambodia made a bad situation worse. It is indeed ironic that the invasion of Cambodia has become a way to provide Vietnamese males a job as the Soviet Union has borne the costs of the military outside the country.[41] The government has ended up giving men greater opportunity to find work, although this is not stated policy. The army, heavily female in the war of national liberation against the southern regime and the United States, has become a male army over the past ten years. Policies instituted in the 1960s and 1970s to give priority in industrial and government employment to combat veterans have come to mean preferential hiring of men. Women, who are no longer combat soldiers, have been pushed into agriculture and less desirable forms of work unless they possess educational credentials. The Vietnamese Women's Union, mindful of such trends, has sought to increase female school enrollment, particularly in science and technology. The assumption is that Vietnam will eventually industrialize and that skills will overcome the current policies militating against female employment in industry and government.[42]

The problem with such a strategy is that it neglects the fact that most Vietnamese are employed in agriculture and that the reforms in agriculture over the past decade have served to reinforce gender-based inequalities. Vietnam went through numerous agricultural reforms after the 1954 revolution, including, over time, land redistribution, collectivization, the development of cooperatives, and finally the privatization of production. Under the cooperative system, part of which is still in effect, individuals are allocated points for the work they perform for the cooperative. The model Yen-So Cooperative outside of Hanoi, which is shown to foreign visitors, is involved in brickmaking, rug manufacturing, and embroidery as well as fish culture, hog and poultry raising, and rice and other food crop production. At Yen-So, women's work receives fewer points than men's work—weeding and hoeing simply count for less than plowing; brickmaking more than embroidery or rugmaking (which consists of handlooming and hand-knotting carpets). Until all work receives equal points, women's work will have less value.[43]

Under the economic reforms of the Sixth Congress of the Communist party, the work point system is being abolished. Cooperatives lease land to families. Each family is free to produce and market as well as reinvest its profits as it sees fit. The family is therefore free to exploit female labor. More often than not, land is put under the control of males who are heads of household. The Yen-So Cooperative distributes land to male heads of households. Sons receive land from the cooperative upon marriage. In an interview in 1988, the chief of planning of Yen-So Cooperative explained that women did not need land since they would work on their husbands' land. Most women in the cooperatives worked in crafts and teaching which, she pointed out, was less difficult work than work in brickmaking and plowing and therefore was paid less.[44] Such a policy distorts the intent of Vietnamese marriage and family laws which give women equal right to property. When the chief of the Planning Committee of Yen-So Cooperative was asked about this matter, she thought it was not a problem since after all, all girls marry and, if they do not, they can always work at the cooperative in the rugmaking shop, embroidery factory, the nursery, or, with some education, in the kindergarten or school.

Women and Political Power in Revolutionary Vietnam

Women were an important part of the Vietnamese Revolution. The Vietnam Women's Union was formed in 1930 to fight for women's emancipation and to struggle against French colonialism. Over the years it was an integral part of the war for national liberation, mobilizing women to fight in the National Liberation Front forces as well as in the North in the Vietnamese Army. After 1954, the women's union was instrumental in the literacy campaigns and in the development of night and part-time education.[45] The union has also struggled for and gained protective labor legislation, monogamy, free consent in marriage, equality between husband and wife, obligations of husbands to support children, and the right to inherit and own property.

The union through its branches throughout the country has the task of controlling and enforcing implementation of laws concerning women and children. The Vietnamese Women's Union is a quasi-official nongovernmental agency.[46]

Women in Vietnam today have greater access to political power than prior to and after French domination. Progressively, since 1954 in the North, women have risen to positions of national leadership, and women's concerns have been brought to the fore by the Vietnam Women's Union. Despite these very real gains, women's access to political power remains limited and certainly has never been the same as men's. Women are still a small minority in positions of leadership in the government. In 1988, only 17.7 percent of the elected representatives to the Vietnamese National Assembly were women; in 1986, 21.7 percent were.[47] The representation of women may have declined, but the number of women who headed government legislative committees rose from none before 1986 to three (out of seven committee chairs) after 1986. Currently, a woman is vice-president of the government's cultural affairs committee. Clearly, a generation of women did rise to national leadership. They were a small minority, but they were able to gain access to political power through the Communist party and the army. In part, their power in the party was the result of the need to mobilize women to work and sacrifice in wartime—which characterized Vietnam until 1975. The problem, as Duong Thi Duyen of the Vietnam Women's Union pointed out, is that the younger generation of women, coming to adulthood after the war, is less involved in politics and more involved in the day-to-day business of earning a living and raising children. In addition, women have lost some of the traditional pathways to national political leadership. In the past, the army was one such route. After 1975, the Vietnamese Army became a male army. Conscription is restricted to men; women can "volunteer" for the army, but, unlike the past, when they served in combat troops and in positions of leadership and authority, today women are assigned support work in communications, logistics, and medical services. Women are trained in local militias where they form half the forces. The militia training comes in addition to work and family.

The Vietnam Women's Union itself has turned some of its concerns away from attempts to gain representation in the national political arena to support of the contemporary Vietnamese government's family planning programs. In the past the Union focused on promoting women's rights; today many of its energies are focused on controlling women's reproduction.

The Future

Without question, over the past 100 years gender relations in Vietnam have changed markedly, and much progress for women has occurred. Before the onset of French colonialism, women were denied the most basic rights, and, while peasant women toiled in the fields alongside men, their economic contribution meant little in terms of giving them power over their lives. Colonialism did not introduce patriarchal relations to Vietnam; it extended them.

French rule did bring lasting changes to Vietnam. With France came the intensification of production for export and the development of a tax system that forced much of the Vietnamese peasantry, male and female, into wage labor. The French built a new bureaucratic and political patriarchal infrastructure. New Vietnamese social classes arose, and the colonial period saw the development of a small urban middle class of entrepreneurs, teachers, medical and technical personnel, and bureaucrats in the service of the French state. A group of intellectuals arose who questioned the political and cultural institutions that had brought Vietnam under Western domination. These intellectuals focused on modernizing the country and searching for new cultural forms that would bring Vietnam into the twentieth century. The intellectual ferment involved the questioning of women's traditional roles and the development of women's organizations among the tiny urban, Westernized elites.

The French did introduce education for women. This education was confined to the urban elites and strove to prepare women to be the wives of urban elites. However much French school authorities may have wanted schools to train women for the role of bourgeois housewife, such roles were not easily assimilated by women who saw education as a route to national renewal in much the same way as did many Vietnamese men caught up in the Vietnam nationalist movement. It is not surprising that a good number of educated women ended up forming the Vietnam Women's Union and its precursors.

In the long run changes for Vietnamese women came less as a result of education, which few women had either before or during the colonial period, and more as a result of protracted armed struggles against foreign domination for nearly three decades. The wars mobilized women for new roles—as producers in wartime economics, as frontline soldiers, and as revolutionaries. As a result, in 1954 and throughout the years to reunification, major changes occurred in the North. The government of socialist Vietnam provided greater access to education, and growing numbers of women have managed to obtain education. Despite the enormous gains women have experienced, equality has remained elusive and is likely to remain so. Although the Vietnamese Women's Union sees education as the means by which women will gain equality, educational enrollments have fallen off in the past five years.[48] In large part, this is due to the economic crisis in which families cannot afford "donations" to keep their children in schools and girls are more frequently withdrawn from school than are boys. Higher education, strapped for funds, has begun admitting fee-paying students. At the University of Dalat, which is a technical university, half of the students in the 1987/1988 school year paid for their own room, board, and tuition; the other half held state scholarships. Not surprisingly, only one-third of the university's students were female.[49]

School fees are new to socialist Vietnam. They were instituted by new party policies that made economic development the top priority in socialist Vietnam and focused on privatization, decentralization, the development of salary differentials and incentive plans in the hopes they would boost productivity, and the opening of the free market. Such programs are not peculiar to Vietnam; they characterize the four modernizations policy in China and Gorbachev's liberalization policies in the Soviet Union. In each, as in Vietnam, the stress on economic development has shifted to the generation of laissez-faire attitudes that put sex and social equality on the backburner. The new policies are also an admission that the government finds the demands of women's liberation and economic development contradictory and has postponed one in the hopes that the other via education or through economic development will resolve itself. Unfortunately, Vietnam has not learned from the experience of other Third World countries or from the industrialized West: namely, that increasing women's education does not resolve persisting gender-based inequalities in income, power, and the family and that economic development does little to change them either.

Notes

[1] For a discussion of changes in intellectual life, see David Marr, *Vietnamese Tradition on Trial* (Berkeley: University of California Press, 1980); Martin J. Murray, *The Development of Capitalism in Colonial Vietnam (1870-1940)* (Berkeley: University of California Press, 1980); Milton Osborne, *The French Presence in Cambodia and Cochinchina: Rule and Response (1859-1905)* (Ithaca, N.Y.: Cornell University Press, 1969).

[2] Mai Thi Tu and Le Thi Nham Tuyet, *La Femme au Viet Nam*, 10th ed. (Hanoi Editions en Langues Etrangeres, 1978).

[3] Arlene Eisen Bergman, *Women of Viet Nam* (San Francisco: Peoples' Press, 1974), p. 19.

[4] For a discussion of the Le Code, see Mai Thi Tu and Le Thi Nham Tuyet, *La Femme au Viet Nam*, and Ngo Vinh Long, *Vietnamese Women in Society and Revolution. I. The French Colonial Period* (Cambridge, Mass.: Vietnam Resource Center, 1974), pp. 8-11.

[5] For a description of the pre-French examination system, see Alexander Woodside, *Vietnam and the Chinese Model: A Comparative Study of the Vietnamese and Chinese Government in the First Half of the Nineteenth Century* (Cambridge, Mass.: Harvard University Press, 1971); Ngo Vinh Long, *Vietnamese Women in Society and Revolution*, op. cit.; Pierre Pasquier, *L'Annam d'autrefois* (Paris: Challamel, 1907).

[6] Cited in Ngo Vinh Long, *Vietnamese Women in Society and Revolution*, p. 12.

[7] For a discussion of the land alienation, see Pierre Broheux, "L'Economie et la société dans l'Ouest de la Cochinchine pendant la période coloniale, 1898-1940" (Université de Paris, Faculté des Lettres, Thèse 3è cycle, 1969); see also Murray, *Development of Capitalism in Colonial Indochina*.

[8] Ngo Vinh Long, *Vietnamese Women in Society and Revolution*.

[9] See James Scott, *The Moral Economy of the Peasant: Rebellion and Subsistence in Southeast Asia* (New Haven, Conn., and London: Yale University Press, 1976).

[10] Ngo Vinh Long, *Vietnamese Women in Society and Revolution*.

[11] For school enrollment figures, see Gail P. Kelly, "Schooling and National Integration: The Case of Interwar Vietnam," *Comparative Education* 18 (1982): 175-195.

[12] P. Chesneau, "Enquête sur l'analphabetisme en milieu rural dans une province du Nord-Annam,"*Bulletin général de l'instruction publique, partie générale*, 17e Année, No. 8 (April 1938): 267-278. Many of the statistics cited here are from page 268.

[13] Gouvernement Général de l'Indochine Française, *Rapports au Grand conseil des intérêts economiques et financiers et au Conseil du gouvernement, deuxième partie*, Tableau VI. Effectifs par cours dans l'enseignement public primaire élémentaire et primaire complementaire Indochinois (Hanoi: Imprimerie d'Extrême Orient, 1939).

[14] Gouvernement Général de l'Indochine Française, *Rapports au Grand conseil des intérêts economiques et financiers et au Conseil de gouvernement, deuxième partie: Fonctionement des divers services Indochinois* (Hanoi: Imprimerie d'Extrême Orient, 1933), Tableau, "Enseignement privé en Indochine" (no page number given).

[15] For a discussion of these texts, see David Marr, "The 1920s Women's Rights Debates in Vietnam," *Journal of Asia Studies* 35 (1976): 371-390.

[16] Ibid.

[17] A number of student composition books and class notebooks (cahiers de roulement) are available for the schools of Tonkin for the 1929-1930 and 1930-1931 school year. See Archives de France, Section d'Outre Mer, 46 PA. The differences in student composition topics between girls' schools like the Ecole Brieux and boys' schools like the Lycée of the Protectorate are striking.

[18] Cahiers de composition Française, Cours superier A, Ecole Brieux, Archives de France, Section d'outre mer, 46 PA, Carton 9, Dossier 89, entry dated October 19, 1929.

[19] Ibid.

[20] For a discussion of the school strikes of the 1920s, see Gail P. Kelly, "Conflict in the Classroom: Case Study of Colonial Vietnam," *British Journal of Sociology of Education* 8 (1987): 191-212.

[21] See David Marr, *Vietnamese Anti-Colonialism, 1885-1925* (Berkeley: University of California Press, 1971); David Marr, *Vietnamese Tradition*; and Marr, "The 1920s Women's Rights Debate."

[22] See, for example, Pham Quynh, *L'Evolution intellectuelle et morale des Annamites depuis l'establissement du protectorat Français. Conference faite a l'Ecole coloniale le 31 mai 1922* (Valence Impr. df Ch. Legrand et M. Granger, 1922); Pham Quynh, *Les Etudes classiques sino-annamites* (Hanoi: Impr. Tonkinoise, 1924); Pham Quynh, *Nouveaux essais franco-annamites* (Hue: Bui-Huy-Tin, 1938); Pham Quynh, *Un Problème d'education des races. Comment doit être faite des Annamites par la France* (Paris: Alcan, 1923).

[23] See Marr, "The 1920s Women's Rights Debate"; on the Communist party, see Mai Thi Tu and Le Thi Nham Tuyet, *La Femme au Viet Nam.*

[24] For a full discussion of the marriage laws, see Mai Thi Tu and Le Thi Nham Tuyet, *La Femme au Viet Nam*; and Bergman, *Women of Vietnam.*

[25] See also Douglas Warner, *The Last Confucian: Vietnam, Southeast Asia and the West* (Baltimore: Penguin, 1964), especially Chapter 13.

[26] Interview with Nguyen Van Luong, President, People's Committee, Binh Tri Thien Province, Hue, January 8, 1988. (Nguyen Van Luong was a colonel in the NLF fighting forces in the Hue District for much of the second Indochina war); Interview with Duong Thi Duyen, Vietnam Women's Union, Hanoi, January 4, 1988. In addition,

Tom Mangold and John Penycate's book *The Tunnels of Cu Chi* (New York: Random House, 1985) discusses women fighters in the Vietnamese NLF in the Iron Triangle.

[27] For discussions of the literacy campaigns, see *The Struggle Against Illiteracy: Vietnamese Experience* (Hanoi: Foriegn Language Publishing House, 1983); Le Thanh Khoi, *Socialisme et developement au Viet Nam* (Paris: Presses Universitaires de France, 1978); *Etudes vietnamiennes*, No. 5 (1965), No. 30 (1971), No. 49 (1977), No. 52 (1978) (entire issues); Ngo Vinh Long, *Vietnamese Women in Society and Revolution*, pp. 137-138.

[28] See Le Thanh Khoi, "Vietnam: System of Education," *International Encyclopedia of Education*, Vol. 9, pp. 5449-5451. See also P. W. Naughton, "Some Comparisons of Higher Education in Vietnam, 1954-1976," *Canadian and International Education* 8 (1979): 100-116.

[29] Le Thanh Khoi, "Vietnam System of Education," p. 5450.

[30] Interview with Duong Thi Duyen, Vietnam Women's Union, Hanoi, January 4, 1988.

[31] Interview with Duong Xuan Trinh, Director, Quoc Hoc School, Hue, January 8, 1988.

[32] Interview with Duong Thi Duyen, Vietnam Women's Union, Hanoi, January 4, 1988.

[33] Visit to May the 15th School, Ho-Chi-Minh City, January 16, 1988.

[34] Huang Xuan Sinh, "Participation of Women and Their Emancipation Through the Development of Education and Science in Vietnam," *Proceedings of the Southeast Asian Seminar on Women and Science in Developing Countries*, Hanoi, Vietnam: January 8-10, 1987, p. 8.

[35] See Chapters 14 and 16 on Poland and the Soviet Union, respectively, in Gail P. Kelly, ed. *International Handbook of Women's Education* (New York, Greenwood Press, 1989).

[36] See, for example, Margery Wolf, *Revolution Postponed: Women in Contemporary China* (Stanford, Calif.: Stanford University Press, 1985).

[37] Interview with Duong Thi Duyen, Vietnam Women's Union, Hanoi, January 4, 1988. These statistics may be unreliable, but if anything they may present a more optimistic picture of women's workforce participation patterns.

[38] See Huang Xuan Sinh, "Participation of Women and Their Emancipation." See also David Marr, "Tertiary Education, Research,

and the Information Sciences in Vietnam," Unpublished manuscript, 1987, pp. 5-6.

[39] Interview with Director, Viet-My, Hanoi, January 3, 1988; interview with Mr. Lindblad, Swedish Ambassador to Vietnam, Hanoi, January 3, 1988.

[40] See "La Nouvelle loi sur le marriage et la famille," *Bulletin de Droit* No. 1, 1987 (Numero Special), Association des Juristes de la Republique Socialiste du Vietnam et Union des Femmes de la Republique Socialiste du Vietnam. Interview with Duong Thi Duyen, Vietnam Women's Union, Hanoi, January 4, 1988.

[41] Interview with Mr. Lindblad, Swedish Ambassador to Vietnam, Hanoi, January 3, 1988; Interview with Philip Mayhew, Consul for Political Affairs, U.S. Embassy, Bangkok, Thailand, December 29, 1987.

[42] Interview with Duong Thi Duyen, Vietnam Women's Union, Hanoi, January 4, 1988.

[43] Interview with Chu-Chuc, Chief, Planning Committee, Yen-So Cooperative, Hanoi, January 3, 1988; Interview with Nguyen Van Luong, President, People's Committee, Binh-Tri-Thein Province, Hue, January 8, 1988.

[44] Interview with Chu-Chuc, Chief, Planning Committee, Yen-So Cooperative, Hanoi, January 3, 1988.

[45] For some of the history of the Vietnamese Women's Union, see Ngo Vinh Long, *Vietnamese Women in Society and Revolution*.

[46] Interview with Duong Thi Duyen, Vietnam Women's Union, Hanoi, January 4, 1988.

[47] Interview with Duong Thi Duyen, Vietnam Women's Union, Hanoi, January 4, 1988.

[48] See Marr, "Tertiary Education, Research and the Information Sciences in Vietnam."

[49] Interview with Chair, Teaching Department, Dalat Technical University, Dalat, January 12, 1988.

Education, Women and Change[†]

Since the 1960s women's educational enrollments have grown considerably at the primary, secondary and tertiary levels. More women than ever before have had an opportunity to attend and stay in school. Paradoxically, while schooling at all levels has become more accessible to women, the number of women illiterates has been growing as has the number of females left unschooled or semi-schooled.[1] This chapter focuses on changes in women's educational enrollments worldwide since the 1960s. It will show that, while female educational enrollments have dramatically increased in most countries, these increases have occurred in the absence of specific policies focused on bringing greater educational equity to women. Second, changes in enrollment, which in many countries have closed the gap between male and females in education, even at the tertiary level, have had little effect on women's income or their participation in the paid labor force. More women than ever before have had access to education. Despite this the economic outcomes of education have not been the same for women as they have for men. Why this is the case is explored in this chapter.

Changes in Women's Education: Expansion since the 1960s

Women's educational enrollments at all levels have grown spectacularly since the 1970s. The numerical rise in female enrollment in some countries has been impressive, growing threefold or more. In Ethiopia, for example, the number of females in primary school went from 349,000 in 1975 to 1,097,000 in 1987;[2] in Nigeria they rose from

---

[†]This article combines two versions of one of Gail Kelly's articles. Reprinted from "Education, Women and Change" in R. Arnove, P. G. Altbach, and G. Kelly, eds. *Emergent Issues in Education.* By permission of the State University of New York Press. And reprinted from *International Journal of Educational Development,* Vol. 10, Gail Kelly, "Education and Equality: Comparative Perspectives on the Expansion of Education and Women in the Post-War Period," pp.136-140 (1990) with kind permission from Elsevier Science Ltd., The Boulevard, Langford Lane, Kidlington OX5 1GB, UK

2,625,061 to 6,331,658 between 1975 and 1983. The doubling of the number of females attending primary school is common throughout the Third World in the decade or so since 1975.

Primary Education

While in most of the Third World the number of females attending primary school rose markedly, in most of Eastern and Western Europe, North America, and a few Asian countries, the number of girls studying at this level declined. In Canada, for example, 1,190,489 girls were in primary school in 1975; in 1987 1,104,550 girls were enrolled. Corresponding numerical declines for the United States were 14,820,000 in 1975 versus 13,127,000 in 1986. These declines, for the most part, are a function of zero population growth in systems where, with the exception of China, universal primary education had been long achieved.

While the numerical increases in female enrollment at the primary level are dramatic, particularly in the Third World, male enrollment rose as rapidly, if not more than that of females, leaving the gap between male and female enrollments scarcely touched. For example, females were 31% of all students in Benin primary schools in 1975; after their number doubled between 1975 and 1987, they were 34% of all enrollments. In most of Africa the female share of primary school enrollment grew one percentage point in nine countries and by between two and four percentage points in sixteen countries. They stagnated or declined in another twelve countries including Burkina Faso where girls are still 37% of primary enrollments.

In Central America, South America and the Caribbean the female share of primary school enrollments have more or less stagnated at between 48% and 50%, particularly in those countries which have universal primary education.

In Asia, only in Afghanistan and Nepal were female increases in the share of primary enrollments dramatic, going from 15% in 1975 to 29% in Nepal and from 15% in 1975 to 33% in Afghanistan in 1987. Elsewhere, except for Bangladesh where female enrollment rose to 44% of the total in 1987 versus 34% in 1975, female shares of primary school enrollment stagnated. In some twelve countries they remained between 47% and 49% of all enrollments from 1975 to 1987.

In the Middle East, female shares of primary enrollment climbed in most countries. For example, in Algeria they rose from 40% in 1975 to 45% in 1987.

Females' share of primary school enrollment remained stagnate, at about 49% to 50%, in Europe and North America between 1975 and 1986, despite numerical decline of the female enrollment in the time period.

The data clearly indicate that since 1975 worldwide there has been an equalization in male/female enrollments at the primary level. Table 17.1, which presents enrollment ratios for males and females at the primary, secondary, and tertiary levels, underscores this movement to equality. It also indicates that the greatest increases in female enrollment on the primary level occurred between 1960 and 1975. In that period, female ratios jumped from 72.9 worldwide to 86.7—a leap of 13.8 points. Between 1975 and 1987 the increase was slightly smaller. In Sub-Saharan Africa female enrollment ratios almost doubled between 1960 and 1975 going to 53.9 from 29.6. Their increase halved in the 1975 to 1987 period, going from 53.9 to 68.2. Similarly in Asia, the increase in the enrollment ratios of females grew from 68.5 in 1960 to 88.5 in 1975 while the increase between 1975 and 1987 was from 88.5 to 95.8 or less than half the gain in an earlier period. A similar phenomenon holds for the Middle East. In Latin America and the Caribbean also the greatest gains were between 1960 and 1975. By 1980 universal primary education was reported throughout the region. The gains in female enrollment ratios have been consistent everywhere but in sub-Saharan Africa. Here, female enrollment ratios reached 70.9 in 1980 to plummet to 66.5 in 1985. By 1987 they had risen to 68.2.

Secondary Education

Women's access to secondary education has grown every bit as dramatically, if not more so, than has their access to primary schooling, but there are greater inequalities between males and females in the secondary sector. The numerical increases in female enrollment are startling. In many countries female enrollments tripled between 1975 and 1987. In other countries, particularly in the Third World, the increases were substantial but less dramatic.

In North America, Japan, and much of Europe, the numbers of females in secondary schools either declined or registered small gains in the period. In these countries secondary education tended to be universal, female enrollments had been equal to those of males on the secondary level, and population growth was quite low. In these countries, while the numbers of females in secondary education declined the female share of enrollments did not.

While the numerical increases in secondary education are dramatic, changes in the female share of secondary enrollments have been slow to increase. In most of the Third World women are a minority in secondary schools. In many countries of Africa for which data are available, female share of secondary school enrollments has remained the same between 1975 and 1987. In fourteen countries girls' share of enrollment has risen, but only by a few percentage points while in three

Table 17.1
Enrollment Ratios for Primary, Secondary, and Higher Education 1960-1987

Regions	Year	Primary Education			Secondary Education			Higher Education		
		Total	Male	Female	Total	Male	Female	Total	Male	Female
World Total	1960	84.1	94.8	72.9	27.6	31.3	23.7	5.3	7.1	3.5
	1970	88.5	95.8	80.8	36.2	40.7	31.5	8.5	10.4	6.5
	1975	94.5	102.0	86.7	42.7	47.8	37.4	10.6	12.4	8.7
	1980	96.1	103.5	88.3	44.6	49.6	39.4	11.5	12.9	9.9
	1985	98.8	105.7	91.6	46.1	51.4	40.5	12.1	13.4	10.7
	1986	99.6	106.3	92.6	47.3	52.6	41.7	12.3	13.6	10.9
	1987	99.6	106.1	92.8	48.6	54.1	42.9	12.6	14.0	11.1
Sub-Saharan Africa[1]	1960	40.4	51.2	29.6	3.5	4.9	2.2	0.3	0.5	0.1
	1970	52.0	61.6	42.5	7.9	10.5	5.3	0.8	1.2	0.3
	1975	63.1	72.2	53.9	11.0	14.3	7.7	1.1	1.7	0.4
	1980	80.4	89.9	70.9	18.7	24.0	13.5	1.6	2.6	0.6
	1985	80.4	82.2	66.5	22.7	29.5	15.8	2.1	3.4	0.9
	1986	74.4	81.5	67.3	24.1	31.6	16.6	2.2	3.4	0.9
	1987	75.3	82.3	68.2	25.9	34.0	17.8	2.2	3.5	0.9
Asia[2]	1960	85.6	101.7	68.5	20.9	26.1	15.5	2.6	3.9	1.2
	1970	89.8	99.9	79.1	28.0	34.2	21.4	3.5	5.0	2.0
	1975	98.9	108.5	88.5	34.9	41.9	27.4	4.7	6.4	2.8
	1980	97.0	106.6	86.7	37.8	44.7	30.5	5.6	7.5	3.5
	1985	103.4	112.4	93.8	39.0	45.9	31.8	6.5	8.3	4.5
	1986	104.9	113.6	95.7	40.4	47.2	33.2	6.8	8.7	4.8
	1987	104.7	113.2	95.8	41.8	48.7	34.4	7.2	9.2	5.1
Arab States of Africa and Asia	1960	48.3	63.0	33.2	10.2	15.0	5.3	2.0	3.2	0.7
	1970	62.5	77.9	46.4	20.4	28.1	12.5	4.1	6.3	2.0
	1975	73.1	88.9	56.5	28.3	36.4	19.8	6.9	9.6	4.0
	1980	79.9	92.5	66.8	38.0	46.7	29.0	9.5	12.8	6.0
	1985	81.8	92.6	70.6	47.1	55.5	38.4	10.8	14.2	7.2
	1986	82.3	92.5	71.6	48.4	56.7	39.8	11.2	14.3	7.8
	1987	83.1	93.3	72.4	49.3	57.2	41.0	11.3	14.5	8.1

Region	Year									
Latin America and the Caribbean	1960	72.7	74.7	70.7	14.6	15.2	14.0	3.0	4.2	1.8
	1970	90.7	91.9	89.4	25.5	26.3	24.6	6.3	8.0	4.5
	1975	97.0	98.5	95.5	36.6	37.4	35.7	11.7	13.5	9.9
	1980	104.8	106.4	103.3	44.9	44.4	45.4	13.5	15.3	11.7
	1985	106.4	108.7	104.1	50.7	49.0	52.4	15.9	17.3	14.4
	1986	107.2	109.5	104.8	51.7	49.9	53.5	16.2	17.2	15.1
	1987	107.9	110.1	105.5	53.7	51.7	55.6	16.9	18.0	15.7
Europe (including USSR)	1960	106.7	107.7	105.8	54.5	56.2	52.7	10.3	12.9	7.6
	1970	105.1	105.6	104.5	72.7	73.8	71.6	17.3	19.4	15.0
	1975	101.9	102.0	101.9	81.6	81.9	81.3	20.3	21.8	18.8
	1980	103.0	103.3	102.8	83.6	82.4	84.9	22.1	23.0	21.1
	1985	103.1	103.6	102.7	86.4	86.3	86.6	24.3	24.6	24.1
	1986	103.3	103.7	102.8	87.8	87.8	87.7	24.5	24.6	24.4
	1987	103.0	103.5	102.6	89.4	89.3	89.5	25.2	25.6	24.7
North America	1960	105.8	107.0	104.6	87.4	87.2	87.6	28.9	36.2	21.5
	1970	103.2	103.5	102.8	93.1	92.6	93.6	45.4	52.8	37.8
	1975	99.2	99.8	98.6	99.8	101.0	98.6	53.2	57.9	48.5
	1980	99.4	99.7	99.0	89.4	88.2	90.7	54.3	52.1	56.5
	1985	99.9	99.8	100.1	98.1	98.4	97.7	60.4	56.6	64.3
	1986	100.7	101.5	99.9	99.0	98.5	99.5	62.6	58.1	67.3
	1987	101.1	101.9	100.3	101.2	100.8	101.7	63.8	60.0	67.7
Oceania	1960	109.1	110.0	108.0	54.2	55.5	52.8	9.9	14.0	5.7
	1970	111.7	113.8	109.6	70.8	72.3	69.2	14.2	18.3	9.9
	1975	108.8	111.2	106.4	76.0	76.2	75.8	20.4	24.2	16.4
	1980	110.2	111.8	108.5	74.6	73.2	76.1	22.1	24.3	19.9
	1985	108.3	109.6	106.9	79.9	78.9	81.0	24.4	25.3	23.3
	1986	108.8	110.0	107.5	80.5	79.5	81.5	25.3	25.8	24.9
	1987	109.4	110.7	108.1	81.0	80.0	81.9	26.0	26.4	25.6

1. Excludes Arab States of the Middle East
2. Excludes Arab States of Asia

Source: Derived from *UNESCO Statistical Yearbook*, 1989, Table 2.10, pp. 2.31–2.32.

countries females' share of secondary enrollments declined. A similar picture emerges in the Caribbean, Central America, and South America.

In Asia females' share of secondary enrollments grew, except in Japan, where women's share approached equality. In some countries, the increases were great. For example, in Pakistan, females went from 23% of all secondary enrollments in 1975 to 28% in 1987; in Nepal they climbed from 17% to 23% in the same time period while in Bangladesh they went from 11% to 33% in 1986 and in Korea they rose from 41% in 1975 to 47% in 1987. In China, Hong Kong, Malaysia, and Singapore, females' share of secondary school enrollments rose between one and two percentage points between 1975 and 1988. In the Philippines it fell by one percentage point.

In the Middle East, females' share of secondary enrollment grew the most. In Algeria, between 1975 and 1986 the percentage rose from 34% to 41%; the same increase characterized Libya and Tunisia. In Iraq females' share of enrollment went from 29% to 37% between 1975 and 1987; in Jordan the increase was from 41% to 48% while in the United Arab Emirates females went from 38% to 50% of secondary school enrollments.

Females' share of secondary enrollment stagnated in most of Europe and North America. In these countries universal secondary education had long been attained. In some countries, like Finland, Czechoslovakia, and France, the percentage of the secondary school female population exceeded that of males.

The gains in females' access to secondary education are quite real worldwide and outpace those females have made in primary schooling. Worldwide, as Table 17.1 shows, in 1987, 42.9% of girls ages twelve to seventeen, went to secondary school (as opposed to 54.1% of boys). Worldwide the gap between males and females at the secondary level has been closing, but these gaps are still, as Table 17.1 indicates, very great in Africa, where the enrollment rates for boys were twice as high as for girls in 1987.

The trend toward equalization solely concerns access to secondary education, but females do not receive the same kind of secondary education as do males. In most countries, secondary education is highly diversified and consists of not only academic secondary education but also teacher training and vocational education.[3] A few examples will illustrate the differences between males and females' educational routes at the secondary level. In Botswana, where females were 52% of all secondary enrollments in 1986, they were 84% of students in teacher training courses and 31% of vocational school students. Fifty-three percent of students in academic secondary schools were girls. In Tunisia, where girls were 42% of all secondary students in 1987, they were 43% of those in academic secondary education programs, 71% of enrollments in teacher training courses and 34% of vocational school students; in Zimbabwe where females were 40% of secondary students in 1988, they were 13% of vocational school students. In Cuba where 51% of secondary school students were female in 1987, females were 52% of the students in academic courses, 77% of those enrolled in teacher training classes and 46% of vocational school students. These patterns hold through most of the Third World, regardless of the female proportion of secondary students. Women are disproportionately enrolled in general academic courses which tend to ill prepare them for the workforce that most will enter upon completing secondary school. Most women will not go on to the university. Females are also disproportionately represented in secondary programs designed to prepare elementary school teachers. Overall females' secondary school enrollment patterns presage the sex segregated workforce in which women become unemployed or primary school teachers and clerks. Women are underrepresented in vocational and technical schools preparing skilled workers. The extent of that underrepresentation varies from country to country. In the 1980s there has been a tendency to increase female access to vocational schooling. In China, for example, women went from 34% to 43% of vocational students between 1975 and 1987; in Indonesia their share grew from 29% to 36% of vocational school students. Despite this, the largest increases in female secondary school attendance between 1975 and 1987 in the Third World appear to be in teacher training, except in a number of countries which have relegated all teacher preparation to tertiary level institutions.

Female enrollment patterns in Europe and North America replicate those found in Third World countries. In Austria, for example, females were 50% of all secondary school students in 1987 and 64% of all students in teacher preparation courses and 53% of vocational school students. They were 48% of students in academic programs. In the German Democratic Republic in 1987 females were 48% of all students in 1987 and 43% of vocational school students while in Greece females were 48% of secondary students and 29% of vocational school students.

Statistics are not available as to the type of gender differentiation that exists among vocational school students. For the most part, girls, even when they gain access to vocational training, which seems to be increasingly the case, receive preparation in different kinds of skills than do boys. They tend to be shunted off to secretarial and clerical preparation, and to other programs training students for "female" occupations. Women do not enter programs that prepare students for traditionally male occupations in the skilled trades—carpentry, masonry, electronics, mechanics, and so forth. Increasing preoccupation with the articulation between secondary schooling and employment has meant greater gender segregation within the secondary sector, paralleling the sex segregation of the modern workforce. The change, in short, in secondary education has meant females everywhere have greater opportunity to study, but they do not have the opportunity to pursue the same kind of secondary education as do males.

In addition, many of the gains females have made in secondary education since 1960 were greatest before 1980. Between 1975 and 1980, female secondary school enrollments grew 3.5%; after 1980 they grew 2.3%. In Sub-Saharan Africa these rates more than halved in the two periods—the rate of growth was 15.8% between 1975 and 1980; it slowed to 4.9% between 1980 and 1987.[4] While the rates of increases in female enrollment in secondary education in the Third World slowed most in Sub-Saharan Africa, they also fell in Latin America and the Caribbean and in Asia.

Higher Education

Inequality in educational enrollments between males and females is greater in higher education than it is at the primary and secondary levels. In most countries of the world, women are in the minority. In only twenty-four countries as of 1986 did the proportion of female students equal or exceed those of men.[5] In sixteen nations, on the other hand, women constituted less than 20% of all tertiary level students and in an additional sixteen women were between 20% and 29% of all students. These inequalities in enrollment persist despite the fact that the rate of expansion of higher education has been far greater than that of either primary or secondary education and the increases in female enrollment have been greater proportionately than at other levels.

The changes in the number of women enrolled in higher education are dramatic. But still the absolute number of females in higher education in many countries is low.[6] In most of Sub-Saharan Africa the number of women students in higher education grew tenfold since 1965. For example, in Ethiopia there were 152 female students in higher education as of 1965; by 1981 their number reached 4,881. In Ghana in 1965 there were 346 women pursuing higher education studies; by 1981 there were 3,326. In Asia the increases were about fivefold or more. In India 200,480 females were enrolled in the tertiary sector in 1965; by 1986 the figure had risen to 1,396,466. In the Philippines the increase was from 282,266 in 1965 to 1,070,045 in 1985. Similar increases can be charted for the countries of the Middle East and Latin America and the Caribbean. The number of women enrolled in higher education in Europe and North America grew between three and tenfold between 1965 and 1986. In Belgium, for example, female enrollments expanded from 27,523 to 118,491 in this time period while in France they went from 167,810 to 653,330. The increases in the Federal Republic of Germany were even greater. In the former Soviet bloc nations of Eastern Europe the changes in female enrollment are nowhere near as dramatic as they were in the rest of the world, with the exception of the German Democratic Republic where the number of women students rose from 24,186 in 1965 to 236,383 in 1986. More characteristic of these countries is Bulgaria, where the number of women students increased from 43,427 in 1965 to 69,498 in 1986 or Czechoslovakia, where the corresponding growth was from 54,049 in 1965 to 71,664 in 1986.

Not only did the numbers of women entering higher education grow, their proportion also grew (except in a few countries like Angola, Congo-Brazzaville, Togo, Mozambique, Afghanistan, Hong Kong, and Fiji). For example, in Ethiopia, women's share of higher education enrollment rose from 7% to 29% between 1965 and 1985; in Ghana it went from 8% to 21%; in Rwanda the corresponding increase was from 1% to 14%. Similar gains characterize Asia, Latin America and the Caribbean and the Middle East.

In Europe and North America the gains in the proportion of female students in higher education were less spectacular but nevertheless substantial, especially given the numerical stagnation, or even decline of enrollment at the primary and secondary levels. In most of these countries women became 40% or more of all students in higher education. In Finland the number of women tripled, while their proportional representation in higher education remained static at 53%. In France, however, women's share went from 30% to 51% between 1965 and 1986; in Greece it rose from 32% to 48%. In the United Kingdom the percent of students who were female rose from 30% to 45%; in the United States it went from 39% to 53%.

Table 17.1, which charts enrollment ratios on the primary, secondary, and tertiary levels for males and females, indicates that worldwide female enrollment ratios in higher education still lag behind those of males, although the gap between the two has consistently narrowed since 1960. The table also shows the gaps are greatest in sub-Saharan Africa, the Middle East, and Asia. In sub-Saharan Africa the gap between male and female enrollment ratios never narrowed between 1960 and 1987; rather it widened considerably. This is also the case in Asia and the Middle East although on a less exaggerated scale. Only in Latin America and the Caribbean, Europe, and North America have gaps really closed. In North America female enrollment ratios in tertiary education actually came to exceed males' by far by 1987.

While the number and in most countries the proportion of women enrolled in tertiary education have grown, so also has gender stratification in higher education. Females tend more than men to receive their higher education outside of the university—in teacher training institutions, colleges of nursing, or "distance" or correspondence courses. Fragmentary as they may be, UNESCO data indicate that as of 1986 women tend to disproportionately enroll in nonuniversity based tertiary institutions.[7] In some countries females are 85% of all enrollments in nonuniversity higher education. In a number of nations female enrollments in tertiary education outside of university settings exceed their enrollment in universities. In some countries the number of females enrolled in nonuniversity based higher education is four times greater than the number of females attending universities.

In the majority of countries, one-third to one-half of all women in higher education attend nonuniversity based tertiary institutions. This is the case in countries as diverse as Poland, Israel, Sweden, Syria, Switzerland, Gabon, Afghanistan, and the United States.

Within universities, women are usually segregated from men by field of study.[8] In most nations, 40% or more of all female students specialize in Education, the Humanities, and the Social and Behavioral Sciences. In Lesotho 83% of all women were enrolled in these fields by 1985; the corresponding figure for Nepal was 72%; Israel, 68%; the Sudan, 62%; Iran, 49%; Turkey, 48%; the Republic of Germany, 47%; Italy, 46%; Spain, 45%; the United Kingdom, 44%; and Nicaragua, 42%. The sex segregation is so great in some countries, like Argentina, that women are 92% of all education students. In Poland 80% of all education students were female as of 1985.

Women are excluded in most countries from a number of specializations. They are noticeably absent from Engineering, Mathematics, and Computer Science programs. In 1985 only three countries—namely the former German Democratic Republic, Israel, and Turkey—did as many as 10% of all women specialize in Engineering. In most countries less than 5% of all women study Engineering. Less than 3% of all women in the vast majority of countries studied Mathematics or Computer Science by 1985. Women also tend not to be enrolled in the Natural Sciences. In no country in 1985 did more 10% of all women in higher education study Natural Sciences.

There are a number of fields in which women's share of enrollment varies considerably by nation. In 1986 women formed a disproportionately high percentage of Law students in fifteen countries, while they were a disproportionately low percent of students enrolled in that field in thirty countries. In another twenty-one countries the percent of women studying Law was equivalent to their share of enrollment in higher education as a whole. Women's enrollment in Social and Behavioral Sciences follows a similar pattern.

Sex segregation in higher education has increased, rather than decreased, as more women have entered universities. Women tend to enter fields which already have substantial numbers of women enrolled in them. Thus, Humanities and Education, which always had female students, as higher education expanded, became female ghettos in much of the world.

Expansion of female enrollments has also meant increasing sex segregation by level of study in most of the world. The greatest gains in female higher education have been on the undergraduate level. In Sweden, for example, in the mid-1980s women were 60% of all undergraduates and 30% of students pursuing post-baccalaureate degrees.[9] In Australia women received only one-third of all graduate degrees in the 1980s.[10] Only in the United States did women constitute half of master's degree recipients; most of these were in Education.[11] In Norway of 6,632 women enrolled in the Humanities in the 1983-84 academic year, only 168 were in graduate programs.[12] Similar patterns exist worldwide, as Kathryn Moore's and Margaret Sutherland's respective works have amply pointed out.[13]

Thus, while women's gains in higher education have been substantial, they have, as in the secondary sector, been accompanied by increasing differentiation between courses of study females versus males pursue. The type of programs in which women enroll at both of these levels accounts in large part for the patterns of occupational segregation in the contemporary workforce.

The Workforce and Political Outcomes of Women's Education

The rapid expansion of educational opportunity for women worldwide demonstrated in the preceding pages has had precious little impact on the workforce outcomes of female education, women's wages, and women's access to power and authority in society. In the pages that follow I will turn first to a discussion of the workforce outcomes in women's education since 1960 and then to a consideration of the political outcomes of changes in female education.

The Workforce

Worldwide women's workforce participation rates have stagnated since the 1960s despite improvements in women's educational access; there are however, differences between industrialized versus developing countries. In 28 industrialized nations including the United States, Canada, Great Britain, the USSR and Poland, women's paid labor force participation rates rose from 52% in 1960 to 57% in 1980. In Third World countries of Africa, Asia, Latin America, and the Middle East, where increases in women's access to education at all levels were the most dramatic, the rates of women's participation in the paid labor force declined from 45% to 42% between 1960 and 1980

(Cebotarev, 1986). In countries like Kenya, India, Iran, Nigeria, Zaire, Peru, Chile, Mexico, and Bangladesh, increases in the number of women being educated have been accompanied by erosion in the proportion of women working for a wage.

The jobs women hold have at the same time changed as a result of their changing educational levels. In developing as well as industrialized countries the structure of employment has changed. As this structure has changed, so too have the educational levels of those who obtain employment in the emergent industrial and service sectors of the economy. In industrialized nations like Sweden, the United States, the USSR, the German Democratic Republic, Canada, and Great Britain, women have increasingly moved into occupations which demand a secondary or better education (Jones, 1984; Bernard et al., 1982; Lloyd, 1975). Many of these occupations, like primary and secondary school teaching and nursing, have been traditionally female occupations. However, increasingly, women have begun to enter lower level white collar occupations, technical employment and employment in social services and health-related professions. Without education many women would be unemployed. In some of these countries, women stay in school longer than do men to qualify for new jobs that have emerged in post-industrial society. This trend has been accentuated in countries like the United States, Canada, and France, where jobs women have traditionally held have either ceased expanding or have been obliterated by the emergence of new technologies. A number of studies conducted in the Third World context suggest similarly that women have begun to remain in school longer because the only paid employment open to them is that which requires secondary or higher education (Jones, 1984). However, these occupations are highly segregated by sex, so much so that it has been estimated that in countries as diverse as Canada and the Soviet Union three quarters of the workforce would need to change their occupations in order to eliminate sex segregation in the workforce (Lapidus, 1980; Almquist, 1977; Blau and Jusenius, 1976; Smock, 1981). The sex segregation of the workforce by occupation not surprisingly parallels the types of preparation females versus males receive in secondary and post-secondary education.

In the developing nations of Africa, Asia, Latin America, and, to some extent, the Middle East, the pattern of changes in women's employment is different. The labor force in developing countries is segmented by sex in the context of a dual economy, one of which is traditional and involves subsistence farming and petty trade, the other of which is an urban industrial economy. In many of these countries women's labor force participation has been traditionally quite high, but women have been heavily concentrated in the non-waged sector of the economy. In the process of modernization, women's work has been increasingly displaced by mechanization and by the extension of corporate retailing (Smock, 1981; Boserup, 1970; Robertson, 1984). Women in greater numbers have sought employment into the modern, urban paid labor force and their entry into this labor market has become dependent on education. The relation between women's education and employment for a wage in many of these countries tends to be J-shaped (Jones, 1984). Poor uneducated women enter the paid workforce out of necessity and work in low wage jobs as domestic servants and in trade (more women are employed as domestics in Latin America and Southeast Asia than in any other occupations). Women with primary education tend to withdraw from the paid workforce and women with secondary or better schooling tend to enter the modern sector of the workforce in clerical, semi-professional and professional occupations. In countries like Turkey and Egypt the number of women in the professions has risen while the overall workforce participation rates of women have stagnated or experienced a decline (Sullivan, 1981; Abadan-Unat, 1986).

While increasing women's educational levels does not seem to significantly change women's rate of entry into the paid labor market, it does seem to affect how long women remain in the paid workforce once they enter it. A number of studies conducted in Canada, the United States, Argentina, and Paraguay, for example, suggest that educated women do not leave the workforce through marriage, child bearing and child rearing at as high rates as do women with lesser levels of education (Wainerman, 1980; Paukert, 1982). The number of years of education that produce such an effect varies by country: in Paraguay primary education has such an impact; in Canada, however, secondary and higher education has such an influence. Research has yet to explain why it is that education seems to affect the continuity of women's employment or disentangle the effect of social class background from education.

Increasing women's education has on the other hand had precious little effect on the wages women earn relative to those men earn. Despite the changes in women's employment and the educational levels required for that employment, women worldwide earn 75% of men's wages (Cebotarev, 1986). There are national variations: wage disparities appear greatest in countries where women's educational levels overall are higher as are their rates of participation in the wage earning labor force. These disparities have increased rather than declined over time (Vander Voet, 1986).

While it may appear that in countries where there are fewer educated women, income disparities between men and women in the paid labor force decline, the disparities are in all likelihood much greater than they appear. Women tend to work without wages in farming and petty trade. In Egypt, for example, while the 5.7% of women who are in the paid labor force earn 93.7% the wages of males, most women work as wageless laborers in agriculture (Vander Voet, 1986).

Data suggest that increasing educational opportunities for women and equalizing women's access to schooling do not necessarily equalize the labor force outcomes of education. Education may serve to put women into wage labor and sustain them in the workforce, but it does not provide them with equal work or equal pay. Women's work, particularly in highly industrialized nations, remains as underpaid, relative to work men perform, as the work women did for a wage twenty years ago which required lower levels of skill and education. This pattern holds even in countries like the USSR, Poland, and France where women remain in school longer than men do.

The Political System

Most research on the outcomes of education has focused on the labor force. However, the labor force is not the only outcome within the public sphere of education. Scholars have tended to look at the labor force because they presumed that working for a wage is the major indicator of changes in power relations in society. Such an assumption has been increasingly called into question. The pages which follow ask whether changing and equalizing women's educational opportunities relate to providing women with access to power in national political systems. Research on this topic is fragmentary and just beginning, since most scholars and policy makers in the past have seemed uninterested in questions of women's access to power in society. Rather, given the dominance of economic development paradigms, the focus has been on enhancing women's role in production.

In spite of the lack of solid research, it is quite clear that nowhere have women obtained access to political power and full representation in national political decision-making. Over time, there has been very little change in women's participation in politics or their roles in governing society. In many countries—namely in Vietnam, China, Poland, Algeria, and Iran, for example—increasing women's education appears to be associated with progressive political disenfranchisement of women (Lapidus, 1980; Vandervelde-Dailliere, 1980; Delcroix, 1986; Knauss, 1987; Kelly, 1989b).

Why increasing women's education seems to have coincided with regression in women's access to political power is not easily understood. Scholarship on China, the USSR, and Algeria suggests that during revolutions, women become very active in politics, but that in post-revolution society particularly in developing countries, increasing women's role in production rather than their role in the state, becomes the government's overriding concern. In China, the USSR,

Vietnam, and elsewhere, revolutionary governments used education as a means of facilitating women's entry into the workforce, often bringing the control of women's labor out of the family and placing it under the control of the state. Education may have the effect in some instances of bringing women into production, but little has been done to change women's unpaid work in the family and household. One result is that women became saddled with two jobs—one paid, the other unpaid. With the double shifts, women simply have no time for politics. In countries like China and the USSR women, once actively involved in politics, have become less visible in both national and local government and in the Communist Party. In Algeria and Iran, women who were prominent and active in revolutionary politics decades ago, have become progressively less so as Islamic fundamentalism has replaced other ideologies guiding revolution, allocating women to separate and unequal spheres (Knauss, 1987).

Entry and sustenance within the labor force, which relate loosely to changes in women's educational pattern, appear overall to have had the effect of limiting women's roles in national politics. Despite this, in some countries the increasing number of women being educated for longer periods of time has paralleled the re-emergence of the women's movement. This has particularly been the case in the United States, Australia, Canada, Great Britain, India, France, and the Scandinavian countries (Kelly, 1989). Increasing educational levels have not provided women in these nations with access to political power, but education appears to have changed women's consciousness of oppression and has provided a means for women to organize to put women's issues on national political agendas. Such developments suggest that education may serve in the long run to empower women to struggle against persistent gender-based inequalities in society. How education does this, however, is not at all clear.

Concluding Remarks

This article has shown that over the past decades educational expansion worldwide has provided women with greater opportunities to go to school and remain in school longer than ever before. Many nations have achieved equality of access to primary school: inequalities based on gender often appear more pronounced on the secondary and tertiary levels of education. Such inequalities in many Third World contexts are in educational access, as well as in process and outcome. Industrialized nations may provide women with the opportunity to enter primary, secondary, and higher education at rates equal to or even greater than men, but women do not have the opportunity to receive the same quality and type of education. With equality of access has come greater sexual differentiation in curriculum on the secondary and tertiary levels.

Inequality in educational processes has, in turn, maintained inequality in educational outcomes and in the economic and political outcomes of schooling. Increasing women's educational levels has simply increased the educational levels of women in the workforce; it has not meant increasing female participation rates in paid labor, nor has it equalized male/female wages. Equality of access to schooling, achieved in much of the world, has very little influence on the workforce outcomes of education for women relative to those of men. The influence of increasing education on women's access to power and authority in the political sphere seems similarly minimal.

Why has the expansion of women's schooling failed to eradicate persistent inequalities in the public spheres of work and politics? The answer to such a question is complex. First, equality of access to education is only part of the issue. Rarely have the issues of equality of educational processes been addressed. The exclusive focus on access issues has deflected policy makers away from issues about what kind and type of education females relative to males receive and the impact of educational differentiation on the generation of sex differences in the cognitive as well as economic and political outcomes of education.

It would, however, be a mistake to assume that gender-based inequalities in educational processes and outcomes are the only reason why inequalities between males and females have persisted and in some cases widened in the workforce, in income, and in the political sphere. The conception of education as an enabling condition of equality is premised on the assumption that gender-based inequality in society is somehow based on rationality and stemmed from women's lack of qualifications equivalent to those possessed by men. Women are presumed to have little power or authority because they are not engaged as men in waged labor since, in theory, with wages came power, authority, and autonomy. Thus, education was seen as integrating women into male-dominated social structures on much the same terms as men. The sex role division of labor in the family, the impact of marriage, child bearing and child rearing on women versus men were deemed irrelevant. Thus, education was seen as a means of enabling women to work like men at a job for a wage and, unlike men, in the household bearing and rearing children. Reforms in education have not been accompanied with changes in women's roles in the household, the structure of occupations, workforce segregation, discrimination against women in employment, and in remuneration. Education, in short, can only provide knowledge, skills, and credentials, but the extent to which these translate into equality in society depends on whether the structures which keep women subservient to men are changed. This extends not only to the work place but also to the sex role division of labor in the family. As long as the domestic sphere remains women's domain women are unlikely, unless in poverty, to work at jobs, no matter how educated they are, that do not allow them to combine their double shift of work without a wage at home and work outside of the home for a wage. Employers will continue to discriminate against women who they consider "bad" workers because their work is divided between wage earning employment and non-wage earning employment in the family and because, as has been the case in the USSR, Vietnam, China and Sweden, profits decline when employers are mandated to provide maternity benefits. Under the double shift women will continue to remain outside positions of power and authority in society because they lack the time to participate in politics. Achieving equality in access to education is quite possible, as the data in this paper indicate; achieving equality in society, however takes more than opening schools to women.

Notes

[1] See, for example, Nelly Stromquist, "Women and Illiteracy: The Interplay of Gender Subordination and Poverty," *Comparative Education Review* 34 (no. 1, 1990): pp. 95-111.

[2] All the enrollment statistics cited here are from UNESCO, *UNESCO Statistical Yearbook* (Paris: UNESCO, 1988).

[3] Ibid., table 3.7.

[4] Ibid., table 2.4, pp. 2-17.

[5] See Gail P. Kelly, "Women and Higher Education," in Philip G. Altbach, ed., *International Encyclopedia of Higher Education* (New York: Garland, 1991).

[6] Statistics on women in higher education here are taken from *UNESCO Statistical Yearbook,* 1988.

[7] Ibid.

[8] Ibid.

[9] Inga Elqvist-Saltzman, "Educational Reforms—Women's Life Patterns: A Swedish Case," *Higher Education* 17 (no. 5, 1988): pp. 479-490.

[10] Lyn Yates, "Australia" in Gail P. Kelly, ed., *International Handbook of Women's Education* (Westport, CT: Greenwood Press, 1989), pp. 213-242.

[11] Maxine S. Seller, "The United States," in Gail P. Kelly, ed., *International Handbook of Women's Education* (Westport, CT: Greenwood Press, 1989), pp. 515-546.

[12] Hildur Ve and Nina Fjelde, "Public-Private Tendencies within Higher Education in Norway from a Woman's Perspective" in Gail P. Kelly and Sheila S. Slaughter, eds., *Women's Higher Education in Comparative Perspective* (Amsterdam: Kluwer Academic Publishers, 1990).

[13] Margaret Sutherland, "Women in Higher Education: Effects of Crises and Change," *Higher Education* 17 (no. 5, 1988): pp. 479-490; Kathryn M. Moore, "Women's Access and Opportunity in Higher Education Toward the Twenty-First Century," *Comparative Education* 23 (no. 1, 1987): pp. 23-34.

References

Abadan-Unat, N. (1986) *Women in the Developing World: Evidence from Turkey.* University of Denver School of International Studies, Monograph Series in World Affairs, No. 22.

Almquist, E. M. (1977) Women in the Labor Force. *Signs* 1.

Bernard, C. (1982) *La Politique de l'Emploi Formation au Maghreb* (1970-1980). Editions du Centre National de la Recherche Scientifique, Paris.

Blau, F.D., and Jusenius, C. L. (1976) Economic Approaches to Sex Segregation in the Labor Market: An Appraisal. *Signs* 1, 181-199.

Boserup, E. (1970) *Women's Role in Economic Development.* St. Martin's, New York.

Cebotarev, E. A. (1986) Women, Work and Employment: Some Attainments of the International Women's Decade. In *The Decade for Women: Special Report* (edited by Thomson, Aisla). Canada Congress for Learning Opportunities for Women, Toronto.

Delcroix, C. (1986) *Espoirs et Realities de la Femme Arabe? Algerie-Egypte.* Editions l'Harmattan, Paris.

Jones, C.W. (ed.) (1984) *Economic Growth and Changing Female Employment Structure in the Cities of Southeast and East Asia.* Development Centre Monograph, No. 33, Australian National University.

Kelly, G. (ed.) (1989) *International Handbook of Women's Education.* Greenwood Press, Westport, CT.

Kelly, G. P. (1989b) Women and Education in Vietnam: The Dilemmas of Socialism and Development. *International Handbook of Women's Education.* Greenwood Press, Westport, CT.

Knauss, P. R. (1987) *The Persistence of Patriarchy: Class, Gender and Ideology in Twentieth Century Algeria.* Praeger, New York.

Lapidus, G. (1980) *Women in Soviet Society.* University of California Press.

Lloyd, C. B. (ed.) (1975) *Sex Discrimination and the Division of Labor.* Columbia University Press, New York.

Paukert, L. (1982) Personal Preference, Social Change or Economic Necessity: Why Women Work. *Labour and Society* 7, 311-331.

Smock, A.C. (1981) *Women's Education in Developing Countries: Opportunities and Outcomes.* Praeger, New York.

Sullivan E. L. (1981) Women and Work in Egypt. Cairo Papers in Social Science, Monograph No. 4, pp. 1-44.

Vandervelde-Dailliere, H. (1980) *Femmes Algeriennes a Travers la Condition dans Le Constantinois Depuis l'Independence.* Office des Publications Universitaires, Algiers.

Vander Voet, S. M. (1986) The United Nations Decade for Women: The Search for Women's Equality in Education and Employment. In *The Decade for Women: Special Report* (edited by Thomson, Aisla), pp. 78-79. Canadian Congress for Learning Opportunities, Toronto.

Wainerman, C. (1980) Impact of Education on the Female Labor Force in Argentina and Paraguay. *Comparative Education Review* 24, S180-S195.

Setting the Boundaries of Debate about Education[†]

In 1983 and 1984 over a dozen major reports on the state of the nation's schools appeared.[1] Each was critical in varying extremes of current practices; each suggested a myriad of changes in school curriculum, standards, instructional methods, the teaching profession, and school administration. All stressed the need for "excellence" in education. The reports emanated from diverse sources:[2] the federal government and its agencies (notably the National Science Foundation and the Terrance Bell-appointed National Commission on Excellence); state governments and their agencies like the Education Commission of the States; diverse private philanthropic organizations like the Carnegie Fund for the Advancement of Teaching and the Twentieth Century Fund; business interests like Dow Chemical Company, AT&T, and Texas Instruments; testing organizations like the College Board; and individuals, like Theodore Sizer and John Goodlad, who were funded by public and private philanthropic foundations and educational organizations like the Association of Secondary School Principals to study American schools. There is much overlap among individuals sitting on the many commissions that produced these reports—for example, Patricia Graham and John Goodlad sat on several. Despite this, there is considerable diversity among the reports about the nature and degree of crisis in America's schools, what reforms are necessary, and how "excellence in education" relates to the country's political, social, and economic life.

This chapter discusses the differences among the reports: their analyses of current educational practices; their prescriptions for change; and what agencies they believe should be responsible for bringing about reform. My purpose here is to show that not only is there little consensus about what reforms are needed to improve the schools, but also that the various reports do not provide a consistent plan for change. Rather, they provide a context for discussing reform and rethinking

[†]From: Philip G. Altbach, Gail Kelly, and Lois Weis, *Excellence in Education* (Buffalo, N. Y.: Prometheus Books). ©1985 by Philip G. Altbach, Gail P. Kelly, and Lois Weis. Reprinted by permission of the publisher.

both the direction of education and the role of government and the courts in this process. The reports reorient policy away from social justice goals that had dominated education in the 1960s and 1970s to new goals of employment, productivity, national defense, and "excellence." They not only focus debate about the role of the courts in educational policy formation, but they also open to question which level of government—federal, state, or local—has responsibility for the schools. The reports discuss whether government should play a major role in education at all, or whether the business market and individual parental demand should determine who goes to what school, for how long, and what kind of education schools should make available.

What's Wrong with the Schools?

The federal government's Commission on Excellence labeled the primary and secondary schools of the United States a state of disaster that put the "nation at risk." Another federal agency, the National Science Foundation, decried science and mathematics instruction in the secondary schools. The Education Commission of the States, which was funded by a multitude of industrial and business concerns, faulted the primary and secondary schools for teaching students too little about anything. The College Board blamed the high schools for inadequately preparing youth for college. The Business Higher Education Forum saw higher education as unable to train skilled managers and technicians that they believed industry needed. These reports claim, in short, that student achievement has declined because schools do not demand enough of their students, do not apply stiff criteria for promotion, do not test students enough, and particularly in high school, provide students with too many choices about what subjects they study. Students do not, according to these reports take enough courses in mathematics, science, and technology; nor, in the case of the Paideia Proposal and the College Board Reports, do they study enough foreign languages, English, or social studies. The latter two reports claim that colleges have slackened their admissions requirements, letting in a larger proportion of unqualified youth. Many of the reports claim high school and college graduates are at best mediocre—Americans don't know as much as their Japanese peers—and the mediocrity (which is directly produced by the schools) is, according to several reports, responsible for high unemployment rates and America's decline in defense and in world trade.

This condemnation of the secondary schools, and to a lesser extent primary and college education, is by no means unanimous. While all the reports believe the time has come to reform the schools, a decline in student test scores and achievement in general is not the major impetus for all reform. The reports of the Carnegie Foundation for the

Advancement of Teaching, the Twentieth Century Fund, John Goodlad's study, *A Place Called School* funded by Ford, the NIE, and various other agencies) and Theodore Sizer's study, *Horace's Compromise* (which was prepared for the National Association of Secondary School Principals and The Commission on Educational Issues of the National Association of Secondary Schools), have little nostalgia for the supposed "good old days" when SAT scores were high, America's high school students excellent, and the American economy strong. Ernest Boyer, who wrote the Carnegie report and Paul E. Peterson, who authored the background paper accompanying the Twentieth Century Fund report, *Making the Grade*, both point out that if there is a decline in achievement, it is not all that dramatic if measured by SAT scores, since the population base sitting for the SATs has broadened considerably. Boyer argues that other measures of student achievement do not show a decline over time at all. The real decline, he emphasizes, is in support for the public schools among the aging white middle class.

In his study Peterson agrees with Boyer that the crisis in American education cannot be attributed to overall decline in student achievement, so much as to the fact that the differences in achievement scores between black and whites and between males and females have decreased. Drop-out rates among black males have declined while they have risen among white males. Schools have moved toward equalizing educational disparities borne of gender, ethnicity, and race. This trend toward equalization, or fear of it, has contributed to an erosion of total middle class support for public education.

Where there is disagreement among the various commissions about whether student achievement, particularly that of white males, signals mediocrity in education, most reports contend that schools do not teach what they ought to teach. Herein lies the crisis of the schools. The National Science Board report for example, faults the high school for not teaching enough science, mathematics, and technology; so does the Carnegie report, and those of the National Commission on Excellence, the Business-Higher Education Forum, and the Twentieth Century Fund, to name a few. Not only do schools fail to offer an adequate number of courses in these subjects; but students, when given a choice, do not enroll in them. The National Science Board report clearly documents the leveling-off in the number of high school students taking biology, chemistry, and physics and taking advanced placement courses in the hard sciences as well as mathematics. The report claims diffusion of such knowledge in the secondary school is tied directly to America's "competitive edge," currently under challenge by the Japanese in world trade and technology. The association between the American economic recession and secondary school instruction in science, mathematics, technology, and computers characterizes the reports generated by the federal government and the business community.³

Not all the reports agree that the secondary school curriculum ought to stress science, mathematics, and technology; rather, the Paideia Proposal which was funded by the John D. and Catherine T. MacArthur Foundation as well as the College Board report and Sizer's and Goodlad's studies, which were sponsored by private philanthropic foundations and professional educators' associations, see high schools as places where all students ought to receive a general education reminiscent of the University of Chicago's undergraduate curriculum of the 1950s under Robert Hutchins. The problem, according to these reports, is that American schools do not teach students how to learn or think critically. Rather, American schools have engaged in filling students' heads with fragmented bits of information and have failed to make students conversant with all aspects of knowledge and the interrelationships between knowledge generated by different disciplines. While they agree that the teaching of sciences, mathematics, and technology could be strengthened, the central concern is strengthening the entire curriculum to produce a truly educated person. Specialization, Boyer argues in the Carnegie Report, is for higher education, not the high school. Sizer maintains the schools do not need to introduce more and more courses and greater specialization; they need, rather, to teach the full range of knowledge, including the language arts and social sciences in greater depth. The issue is not whether the schools help the United States compete in a world market, but whether students graduate from high school with a strong general education.

Many of the reports bemoan the fact that students in the secondary school have a range of options available to them. They are critical of the schools for tracking and for giving students choice over what they will learn. Most, but not all of the reports, urge that students be given less latitude and control over their own education. Goodlad's report is an exception. Goodlad sees student alienation as a key reason for mediocrity and faults the schools for giving students too little power over what they will learn and how they will learn it. Goodlad is critical of the "sameness" in American high schools throughout the country.

The considerable disparity in the reports on how far secondary education has degenerated, if at all, is not surprising, given the lack of common criteria for assessing the schools. Some reports used the American economy as the standard (this is the case, for example, in the American Business-Higher Education Forum report); some attempt to use student performance on standardized tests (for example, the Carnegie report) others, like the report from the Paideia group, start from some idealized conception of what a truly educated person is while still others, like Goodlad, judge the schools on the basis of whether students, parents, teachers, or the community are "satisfied" with the schools. The National Science Board evaluates the schools by the demand for scientific research and development. As Goodlad aptly pointed out in his report, *A Place Called School*, American society "wants it all"; there are no clearly articulated, agreed-upon goals for American schools; rather, a host of different constituencies make conflicting demands on the schools, leaving no clear direction for schools and providing little consensus for how schools ought to be assessed, much less reformed.[4] As several reports stated, we just don't know how good or bad the schools are; all we really know at this point is that, for a diversity of reasons, most Americans seem to be dissatisfied with the schools and that, in and of itself, makes educational reform a priority.[5]

Prescriptions for Reform

The reports all call for changes in school practices, but they vary as to which practices they believe are the key to bringing about "excellence" in education. Many of the reports insist upon changes in curriculum and in the teaching profession—how it is recruited, trained, and rewarded. Several reports stress greater cooperation with industry and business. Few of the reports suggest changes in the ways schools are organized, changes in the way in which knowledge is distributed within them, or changes in the conditions of teaching and learning. Most of the reports, in short, propose reform of content without necessarily proposing reform in the way in which knowledge is presented in schools and the ways schools are organized.

The Curriculum

The reports stand in agreement that the curriculum of the schools needs revision; most insist that "more" be taught. Almost all the reports agree that students should have fewer choices in what they study and that there should be less curricular differentiation between college and non-college-bound students. However, there is little consensus among the reports as to what should be "added" to the curriculum and in what doses. The National Science Board calls for greater emphasis on mathematics, science, and technology, beginning in the kindergarten and extending through the primary and secondary grades. The board specifically calls for one hour a day devoted to mathematics and one half-hour per day devoted to science in kindergarten through sixth grade and full-year courses in mathematics and science in the middle school. It also proposes all high-school students take three years of mathematics and science and one semester of computer science, while the college-bound student should be required to study mathematics and sciences for four years. The National Science Board also recommends that probability and statistics be included in the curriculum.

The National Science Board recommendations, which are mirrored only in part in the other reports, do represent much of the approach the various reports take to curriculum reform: namely, limiting students' options by requiring that more of certain subjects be taken by all; insisting on less differentiation between courses taken by college-bound and noncollege-bound students; and introducing computer science into the high school. While the National Science Board recommends that mathematics and science be given more space in the primary and secondary curriculum, not all of the reports urge that curricular reforms be limited solely to science, mathematics, and technology. Many of the reports urge "more" of all basic subjects—reading, social studies, the arts, communication skills, and writing—as well as mathematics and science. Some urge that more foreign-language instruction be added; others were mute on the question. The Twentieth Century Fund called for the end of all bilingual programs.[6]

The "add-on" approach to curriculum reform does not characterize all reports; the recommendations generated by Sizer, Goodlad, and the Paideia group call for a radical restructuring of curriculum that places less emphasis on the disciplinary, topical division of knowledge embedded in "add-on" approaches and more on the interconnections of inquiry grounded in diverse subjects. The Paideia group and the Sizer study both propose that schools reorganize knowledge into three areas: (1) language, literature, and the arts; (2) mathematics and science; (3) history and social sciences. The curriculum, they contend, should not focus as much on basic skills as enlargement of understanding. They make no distinction whatsoever between secondary education for college- and non-college-bound students. All should receive a general liberal arts education in high school that will help to develop individual creativity. Not only do they call for a restructuring of the knowledge schools teach, but they also urge that teaching methods be altered drastically. Instead of teacher-centered learning, they recommend greater individualization, where coaching becomes the norm rather than the exception in the classroom.[7]

It is interesting to note that only three of the reports see instructional methods related to curricular reform. Most of the reports presume that more knowledge can be imparted through the same methods. They assume higher standards for matriculation and greater emphasis on testing will ensure excellence if taught, as will be explained shortly, by more intelligent teachers. Only the reports written by Mortimer Adler, Theodore Sizer, and John Goodlad associate changes in the knowledge schools teach with how school knowledge is taught.

Setting the Boundaries of Debate

While the various reports urge the schools to teach "more," new, and perhaps reorganized curricula, few directly address the question to how such new curricula will be generated. Most implicitly place the burden of excellence on the individual teacher. Only the National Science Board dealt specifically with this issue and concluded that the infusion of $1.51 billion would be necessary to develop a first-rate science and technology curriculum for primary and secondary schools.[8] For the board, school reform is not simply a question of urging teachers and schools to teach more.

The question of curriculum development in most of the reports is not touched; nor do most call for greater investment in education. Several commissions believe that business and industry miraculously would come to the rescue, donating their expertise to teach the new curriculum without generating greater costs. The business community, in reports they generated, volunteered little in the way of expertise and assistance: the Business-Higher Education Forum and the Panel on Secondary School Education for the Changing Workplace simply called upon the schools to train skilled labor.

Since most of the reports did not directly deal with how to develop the curriculum they propose, it comes as little surprise to find that the reports tend to focus on individual teachers who, to most of the commissions' way of thinking, were primarily to blame for the perceived crisis in the schools. Reforming teachers is, in many of the reports, the way to revise curriculum, and one that certainly would not entail the expenditure of $1.5 billion that the National Science Board proposes.

Teachers

With rare exceptions, most reports on the schools take an extremely dim view of the nation's primary and secondary teachers and see them, rather than the conditions under which they work, as key to educational quality. Many of the reports have little sympathy for teachers. The Twentieth Century Fund goes as far as to blame teachers' unions for education decline.

The reports all allege that the teaching profession has gone downhill—apparently oblivious to the many reports from the past that have spoken equally as dismally about teachers.[9] The Education Commission for the States claims that those going into teaching are the least intelligent of their collegiate peers. Except for Goodlad's and Sizer's studies, few take issue with this condemnation. The reports further assert that good teachers abandon the profession because of unionization, which prevents school districts from rewarding merit and from firing the incompetent. Teachers' pay, they recognize, is low and there is little wage/status hierarchy in the profession. Excellence in teaching, the Education Commission of the States, the National Commission on Excellence, and the Twentieth Century Fund assert is a question solely of salary—if teachers are paid better, they will perform better; if there are salary and rank incentives attached to performance, then teachers will strive to improve their instructional behaviors. Without the incentive of merit pay and rank, teachers will be mediocre at best. With the possibility of higher salaries, these reports claim, more intelligent individuals will be attracted to the profession, and the problem of excellence will thereby be resolved.[10]

Out of the reports that recommend salary incentives as a way of bringing excellence to education, only a few deal with teacher training. Those that do enter into an age-old debate on whether teachers should be trained in instructional methods or in subject areas; by schools of education or on the job; by professors of education or by fellow teachers. The reports add little to that debate. The bias of the few reports that deal with teacher education is decidedly against the schools of education that have trained teachers; the tendency is to favor subject area, disciplinary training, although the Carnegie report does point out that currently teachers are trained more in subject areas than in methods and that further grounding in the subject areas may not provide the hoped-for panacea. Only Goodlad's study recommends intensified training of teachers in methods.

While many of the reports roundly condemn the teaching profession for its mediocrity, beyond proposing salary incentives tied to performance and a few changes in their pre-service training, they rarely touch upon changes in the conditions under which teachers work. Only three reports even consider work conditions, and all argue that effective teaching is well-nigh impossible in secondary classrooms. Teachers, Sizer's study points out, have an extremely heavy teaching load. They lack control over their own classrooms: instruction they give is continually interrupted, and they are overburdened with administrative tasks.[11] No provision is made for their keeping current in their teaching fields; often they are assigned classes they are not trained to teach. The reports that consider the conditions of work focus less on creating hierarchy and salary incentives tied to performance than on the ways in which teacher autonomy and professionalism can be restored. For the Goodlad and Sizer studies as well as the Carnegie Commission report, excellence in teaching cannot be brought about solely by material incentives; rather, it depends on restoring to the teacher control over what is taught and how it is taught.

Most reports, however, do not perceive teacher autonomy as particularly important. Like the Education Commission for the States, the emphasis is on evaluating teacher performance. In large part this is because many of the reports do not appear to perceive teachers as a distinct professional group with special training needs, or with needs relating to their work conditions that go beyond those affecting a technician in an industrial plant. In fact, several of the reports, in waxing eloquent about the necessity for a school-business alliance, recommend that technicians from private industry and government be loaned out to the schools to teach a range of courses, from science, technology, and mathematics to social studies.[12] They also recommend that teachers work in industry as a way of improving their teaching skills. By making such recommendations, the reports blur the boundaries of the profession, further proletarianizing teacher labor. In the same way, performance-based material incentives, so prominent in several reports, are seen as a way to get teachers to improve their work, just as cash bonuses serve to improve production in a factory.

If the various reports on excellence are by no means unanimous in their prescriptions for reforming curricula and improving teaching, there is even less unanimity over who should take responsibility for bringing about excellence in education—parents, teachers, school administrators, the states, or the Federal government.

Who Is Responsible for Reform

It is indeed telling that the National Commission on Excellence appointed by Ronald Reagan's secretary of education addressed its findings to parents and individual citizens and not to the Congress or the federal government and its agencies. The National Commission on Excellence, if anything, absolved the federal government of any responsibility, beyond a moral one, for educating the nation's young people. Rather, it shifted the responsibility to parents, business, and the local community. In a similar vein, the Twentieth Century Fund questioned federal responsibility for reform. Peterson's lengthy essay accompanying the report addressed but one question: had the federal government's intervention in education caused current mediocrity? The answer was neither yes nor no; what the report opened up was the possibility that the government's shouldering responsibility for excellence was harmful and should be avoided at all costs. These reports rejected a rethinking of not only the federal role in education, but also the role of *any level* of government in education.

The federal government, in the form of the National Commission on Excellence, seemed willing to divest itself of responsibility for reforming the schools. The National Science Board, also addressing its report to "parents" and the population as a whole, made no attempt to remove the federal government from setting policy for education. The National Science Board recommended that the president appoint a national education council to establish national educational policy. It envisioned the federal role as setting educational standards, developing national testing programs, initiating model programs, running summer teacher institutes, etc. In short, the National Science Board suggested that the federal government expand its role in education and significantly increase its funding of primary and secondary schooling.

The Twentieth Century Fund, while insinuating that the federal government's intervention in education had been innocuous at best and destructive at worst, was not as willing as the Reagan-appointed National Commission on Excellence to withdraw the responsibility for changing the schools from the federal government. Yet, the commission did not foresee the same role for the federal government as did the National Science Board. The Twentieth Century Fund report saw the federal government intervening only to provide equality in education, not to assure quality or excellence or take active leadership in educational policy, which the fund believed was the province of local communities.

The reports not only vary in their perception of the federal government's role in bringing excellence to the schools; they also are less than clear as to what part state government should play. The National Science Board scarcely mentions the states at all in allocating responsibility for educational reform; the Twentieth Century Fund omits the states entirely, as do the Paideia group and Sizer in writing for the National Association of Secondary Principals and the Commission on Educational Issues of the National Association of Secondary Schools. Goodlad calls upon state government to set educational goals much like the National Science Board called upon the federal government, but Goodlad clearly argues for decentralization, vesting responsibility in the local district and individual school. Only the governor-chaired Education Commission of the States in its report, *Action for Excellence: Task Force on Education for Economic Growth*, put the responsibility for national school reform in the hands of state government. The states were to marshal resources for educational reform, foresee links between business and the schools and set standards for students, teachers, and principals.

Many of the reports put the responsibility for reform on individual schools, teachers, or parents, and not on government at any level. Assuring excellence almost seems a question to be resolved at the classroom or individual school level: teachers are to strive to improve education, or local principals and/or superintendents are to provide necessary leadership for reform while garnering assistance from friendly local business and community leaders. Sizer, for one, in the report of the National Association of Secondary School Principals and the Committee on Educational Issues of the National Association of Secondary Schools puts the onus of reform on the teacher; Boyer, in the Carnegie report sees it as the province of the principal; while Goodlad places the responsibility on the district superintendent. Other reports, like that of the Twentieth Century Fund, see parents as key to reform. The fund recommends giving parents greater control over their children's education through a system of educational vouchers. The vouchers would give parents free reign in choosing their child's schooling; the marketplace of parental demand would, therefore, ensure quality in education, since schools would have to compete for students much in the same way as supermarkets for customers.

Where the reports spend much time urging a business-school partnership, none of the reports, even those deriving from the business community, recommend that business be responsible for or take a leadership role in heralding an era of excellence in the schools. Rather, the role of business appears to be one that sets the goals for the schools, since the schools are to train a capable workforce for companies.[13] But business is not expected to directly contribute to education in exchange. School reform is, in many of the national reports, a matter for individual schools, and not a matter for any level of government or the business community.

The Ideological Role of the Reports

The preceding pages have demonstrated that there is much disagreement among the many reports on education that have appeared in 1983 and 1984. There is no agreed-upon analysis of what is wrong with American schools, and no clear-cut agenda for reform has emerged beyond numerous exhortations to give students fewer choices in their own education and to provide the secondary schools with a more stringent curriculum. No other clear-cut mandate has arisen from the many commission reports other than that someone should take the initiative for reform and something should be done about teachers. Contrary to what is suggested in the written homilies that purport to interpret the reports for practitioners, the reports do not provide an agreed-upon prescription for reform; rather, they set the terms of a national debate about how we go about defining excellence in education, criteria that might be used to assess the schools, and ways of thinking about reform.[14] The reports raise the question of whether schools should be evaluated in terms of the vagaries of the economy and the job market, or America's position in the world market; by cognitive outcomes like academic achievement, or social outcomes like equality, personal alienation, or creativity.

These reports serve to take discussions about education policymaking out of the arena of the courts and to reopen a debate about the role of government in schooling that had been dormant since the 1960s. In the past two decades, educational goals were defined largely in social justice terms and the courts, by virtue of numerous lawsuits, were charged with the responsibility for the nations schools in that direction. The emphasis had been on equality of educational opportunity for minorities, women, and the handicapped. The current reports, issued within the first two years of the conservative Reagan administration, have reoriented educational policy away from issues focusing on social justice. Instead, the reports have directed educational policymaking to questions of national defense and the economy, and have reopened discussion regarding the proper role of government in education in relation to that of teachers, parents, and school administrators. The reports have not provided a clear agenda for reform; rather, they question the government's role in reforming schools and open for debate the responsibilities of parents, teachers, business, and the state in bringing about "excellence."

Notes

[1] The reports discussed in this paper include: Education Commission of the States, *Action for Excellence: Task Force on Education for Economic Growth* (June 1983); *Making the Grade: Report of the Twentieth Century Fund Task Force on Federal Elementary and Secondary Policy* (New York: Twentieth Century Fund, 1983); John Goodlad, *A Place Called School: Prospects for the Future* (New York: McGraw-Hill, 1984); National Science Board, Commission on Precollege Education in Mathematics, Science and Technology, *Educating Americans for the 21st Century: A Plan of Action for Improving Mathematics, Science and Technology Education for All American Elementary and Secondary Students So That Their Achievement Is the Best in the World by 1995* (Washington, D.C.: National Science Foundation, September 1983); Theodore Sizer, *Horace's Compromise: The Dilemma of the American High School* (Boston: Houghton Mifflin, 1984); National Academy of Sciences, National Academy of Engineering, Institute of Medicine, Committee on Science, Engineering and Public Policy, *High Schools and the Changing Workplace: The Employer's View* (Washington: National Academy Press, 1984); The College Board, *Academic Preparation for College: What Students Need to Know and Be Able to Do* (New York: The College Board, 1983); Ernest Boyer, *High School: A Report on Secondary Education in America: The Carnegie Foundation for the Advancement of Teaching* (New York: Harper and Row, 1983); *America's Competitive Challenge: The Need for a National Response: A Report to the President of the United States from the Business-Higher Education Forum* (Washington, D.C., April 1983); National Commission on Excellence in Education, *A Nation at Risk: The Imperative for Educational Reform* (Washington: U.S. Government

Printing Office, 1983); Mortimer J. Adler, *The Paideia Proposal: An Educational Manifesto* (New York: Macmillan, 1982).

[2] A useful discussion of the differing groups sponsoring the reports may be found in Sheila S. Slaughter, "The Pedagogy of Profit: National Commissions Report on Education." See also, Frances Kemmerer and Alan Wagner, comps., "Summaries of 'Recommendations for the Improvement of School Quality and the Costs of Recommendations for Improving School Quality,'" Center for Educational Research and Policy Studies, State University of New York at Albany, Fall 1983, mimeo.

[3] The reports generated by the federal government include the National Science Board report, *Educating Americans for the 21st Century*; the National Commission on Excellence in Education, *A Nation at Risk*; The National Academy of Sciences report, *High Schools and the Changing Workforce*. Those generated by the business community include the Education Commission of the States, *Action for Excellence*; the Business-Higher Education Forum, *America's Competitive Challenge*.

[4] Goodlad, *A Place Called School*, 33.

[5] See Goodlad, *A Place Called School*; Boyer, *High School*, and Paul E. Peterson, background paper in *Making the Grade: Report of the Twentieth Century Fund Task Force*.

[6] Boyer, *High School*; Adler, *Paideia Proposal*; College Board, *Academic Preparation for College*, all called for foreign-language instruction and stressed general education rather than simply science, technology, and mathematics. Sizer and Goodlad emphasized general education as well but did not specifically call for greater foreign-language instruction.

[7] This is the case as well in Goodlad's report, *A Place Called School*.

[8] National Science Board, *Educating Americans for the 21st Century*, p. xiii.

[9] See, for example, David Tyack, *The One Best System: A History of American Urban Education* (Cambridge, Mass.: Harvard University Press, 1974).

[10] Reports that dwell specifically on hierarchy, career ladders, and merit pay include the National Science Board, *Educating Americans for the 21st Century*; National Commission on Excellence, *A Nation at Risk*; Education Commission of the States, *Action for Excellence*; Twentieth Century Fund, *Making the Grade*. Other reports place less stress upon creating material incentives for teachers, but do urge salary increases as well as greater autonomy and changes in the conditions of work—which are missing in the above-mentioned reports.

[11] Sizzer, *Horace's Compromise*; Boyer, *High School*; Goodlad, *A Place Called School*.

[12] Education Commission of the States, *Action for Excellence*; National Science Board, *Educating Americans for the 21st Century*; National Academy of Sciences, *High Schools and the Changing Workplace*.

[13] See note 1.

[14] See, for example, J. Lynn Griesemer et al., *Education Excellence under Study: Implications of Recent Major Reports* (Chelmsford, Mass.: Northeast Regional Exchange, 1983); A. Harry Passow, *Reforming Schools in the 1980s: A Critical Review of the National Reports* (New York: ERIC Clearinghouse on Urban Education, 1984); U.S. Department of Education, *The Nation Responds: Recent Efforts to Improve Education* (Washington: U.S. Government Printing Office, 1984); Frances Kemmerer and Alan Wagner, "Summaries of Recommendations for the Improvement of School Quality and the Costs of Recommendations for Improving Schools Quality," Albany: Center for Educational Research and Policy Studies, SUNY/Albany, 1983, mimeo.

Center on Education in the Inner Cities[†]

Gail P. Kelly and Maxine S. Seller

Mission and Conceptual Framework

The mission of the proposed Office of Educational Research and Improvement National Center Education in the Inner Cities is as follows:

1) to develop a knowledge base on educational practices in the inner cities which can serve as a foundation for setting policy and improving practice.

2) to generate and disseminate research on schooling in the inner city. Such research will focus on current and past practices as well as projected reforms aimed at improving:
    a. educational processes for inner city children at the primary and secondary levels;
    b. the delivery of educational services in the inner city;
    c. educational outcomes for inner city children.

3) to involve the constituencies of inner city schools in the research and its dissemination. These constituencies include but are not limited to parents and students within the diverse ethnic and racial communities inner city schools serve, teachers, administrators, local policy makers, and businesses as well as university-based researchers.

Conceptual Framework

There is little doubt that outcomes among schools in the major inner cities in this country generally represent the greatest failure of the American educational system (Carnegie Foundation for the Advancement of Teaching, 1988). Irrespective of whether the indicator selected for measuring success is dropout rates, academic achievement on standardized tests, continuation to college, or rates of employment on leaving school, students from inner city schools consistently do

---

[†] Gail P. Kelly and Maxine Seller had many collaborators in this project. Robert Stevenson and Hugh Petrie share equal responsibility for the conceptual framework. Maxine Seller co-authored the two projects included and has given me permission to include them.

more poorly than their suburban and rural counterparts. Furthermore, students in inner city schools are disproportionately confronted with social problems stemming from poverty as well as from drug abuse and alcoholism, teenage pregnancy, and violent crime. It is not surprising, therefore, that confidence in inner city schools is on the wane among policy makers, local politicians, businesses and industry, teachers, individual parents, and community organizations.

While there is considerable disillusionment with inner city schools, many of the minorities and the poor, who constitute the major populations these schools serve, still view education as the most likely means of achieving upward social mobility. Despite dissonance between the cultures of inner city schools and the cultures of many families and children the schools serve, high educational expectations remain. The schools are the locus of both the hopes and frustrations of American society. The challenge of inner city schools is to provide quality education to linguistically, culturally, and racially diverse populations many of whom live on the margins of American economic life.

A number of reports have called attention to the failure of the massive educational reforms of the 1980s to have a significant impact on educational outcomes in inner city schools (Carnegie Foundation for the Advancement of Teaching, 1988; MBC, Inc. for the Charles Stewart Mott Foundation, 1988; Committee on Policy for Racial Justice, 1989). There is now greater recognition that improvement of inner city schools should be at the top of the nation's agenda. Over the years various reforms have been attempted. They have included a focus on student readiness for school, imparting basic literacy and numeracy skills, recruiting and retaining talented teachers to work in inner city schools, providing cultural diversity, and offering greater choice for parents and students (Oakes, 1987).

The initiatives of the past decades have been instructive. They have demonstrated that there is no panacea for solving the multiple problems confronting inner city schools. Indeed, we have learned that there is tremendous diversity among inner cities as well as in the problems their schools face. The schools of mid-size urban areas such as Buffalo and Pittsburgh do not necessarily confront the same challenges as do schools in megacities like New York, Chicago, or Los Angeles. The populations served are different and the complexities in bringing about reform are magnified in cities with large populations and with school systems that often have more students than many European nations. Relations with the surrounding community, the extent of bureaucratization, and student achievement and failure rates vary among cities. Therefore, our assumption is that reforming and improving inner city schools is not a question of developing one strategy; instead, the process will entail developing a range of strategies that are appropriate to specific inner city contexts.

Many of the initiatives undertaken thus far in inner city schools are a cause for optimism and show us that inner city schools can be reformed and become effective educational institutions which actively engage students. In some of our largest cities today can be found educational innovations that hold great promise, such as Central Park East in Harlem (Corcoran, Walker and White, 1988; Wilson and Corcoran, 1988). Such schools recognize that the problems encountered by their students are symptoms, not causes, of more fundamental social problems underlying education in the inner cities. This perspective has enabled them to look beyond models of cultural deficiency to models of responsiveness to cultural diversity.

A second assumption of the proposed Center on Education in the Inner Cities is that problems of education in inner cities stem from diversity and poverty and not from deficiency. The linguistic, cultural, social, and economic circumstances of students in inner city communities pose a number of challenges for schools. Some of these challenges derive from the poverty of many inner city neighborhoods and the cultures of the street that are antithetical to education.

Past experience has shown us that reforms in the schools are ineffective unless they deal with the broader social context in which the schools function (Ogbu, 1974). In the inner city that context is one of diversity, poverty, and high unemployment. Health and social services are overstrained in striving to serve a population with pressing health and material needs. The inner city is also characterized by high crime rates and drug trafficking. No programs aimed at improving inner city schools can possibly succeed unless they deal with the environment in which the schools are placed. They must seek to overcome the destructive elements that lead to high dropout rates, juvenile crime, and drug and alcohol abuse. Our assumption is that improving education in inner cities is related to improving the environment in which the schools are situated.

Just as the schools of the inner city cannot be fully reformed without attention to their social and economic ecology, equally important is the need to develop support and to marshall resources of the entire community in improving schools. Teachers and administrators on their own cannot hope to mobilize the necessary resources to bring about meaningful educational improvement. They need the support and cooperation of business, of industry, of civic organizations, local political and cultural leaders, and of universities and colleges (Oakes, 1987). How such support might best be organized and for what specific purposes are questions we will explore in the proposed Center projects. We underscore a key assumption underlying our effort: improvement in inner city schools necessarily entails the direct involvement of all elements of the local political, social, and economic constituencies with an interest in rebuilding the inner city and its educational institutions.

Reforms in inner city schools do not only need to involve community and business leaders, they also need to take cognizance of and work with the diverse ethnic communities inner city schools serve. These communities, made up of African Americans, Hispanic Americans, recent immigrants, and lower income white ethnic as well as a small white middle class community, often have conflicting views of the schools (Seller, 1988; Ogbu, 1987). For some the schools are alien institutions of little value to their children; most, however, see the schools as the key to social mobility and success in the United States and strive to supplement public education with tutoring and community-based academic and cultural enrichment programs.

A fifth assumption underlying the OERI Center we propose is that there are diversities in the cultures of the home that influence student engagement in the schools. We view an understanding of the culture of the home of diverse ethnic communities as a key element in understanding how inner city schools can be made more effective. Understanding the nature of home culture, parental expectations of the schools, and political conditions such as how parental and community groups support the schools or develop alternatives to them, is key to involving these communities in the educational enterprise, bringing them into the process of educational improvement, and providing a basis for curricular reform.

Students and their engagement in their own education must constitute the major focus of reform in inner city schools. Too often reform initiatives have concentrated on resource allocation and adult governance issues to the virtual exclusion of students' understandings of, responses to, and resistances to schools. Student peer group cultures and their relation to engagement in schooling is an area in need of further investigation. We need to understand how student cultural forms emerge and the extent to which they militate against or foster engagement in the schools and why (see Weis, 1990). The elements of schooling that inner city students perceive as irrelevant and the ways that changes in curriculum, school organization, and teaching could enhance student involvement in learning are issues the Center proposes to address.

Student engagement, while necessary, is not a sufficient condition for quality education. Students must be engaged in educationally worthwhile work that challenges them to use their minds. Given the emphasis in many urban schools on lower order cognitive processes (such as the memorization of fragmented and mindless information), we will be concerned about forms of curriculum, teaching, and school organization that promote not only cultural relevance, but also intellectual challenge.

The extent to which students become involved in their own education may well be a function of how teachers perceive and interact with them. Increasingly inner city teachers come from white middle class suburban backgrounds. Their preparation programs, for the most part, stress instructional methods and do not in any way introduce them to the realities of the inner cities, its cultural diversity, or different learning styles of inner city students. The Center proposes to investigate how inner city teachers' beliefs concerning their students' capabilities, cultures, and families shape their teaching behavior.

Through the Center projects we will unravel the complex interactions among the three distinct cultures of the home, the students, and the teachers. To date we have little knowledge about how the interactions among these often competing cultures are played out in inner city schools.

While our emphasis is on the social, economic, and cultural milieu of the schools and the culture of students and teachers, we remain acutely aware that the economics of inner city schools profoundly affect teaching and learning. Most schools in the inner city are resource poor in relation to schools located in the more affluent suburbs. Many, as in New York City, Buffalo, and Los Angeles, have deteriorating physical plants. Classrooms are grossly overcrowded and in some cities classes are held in auditoriums or hallways for lack of classroom space. A number of schools lack basic equipment; computers are a rarity and are often confined to a few select schools. Many schools use outdated texts. The teaching staff in inner cities is often young and inexperienced, an appreciable number lack certification, and turnover rates tend to be higher than elsewhere (Bruno, 1981, 1986; Mark and Anderson, 1978).

Inner city school districts have been characterized, in the main, by centralized bureaucracies which more often than not support standardization and the maintenance of existing practices. The bureaucratization of the schools has made it difficult for many inner city schools to respond to the different communities that individual schools in the system serve and to the specific learning needs of individual students, and has inhibited initiatives on the part of parents, teachers, and building administrators to innovate and improve daily practice. Current reform proposals emphasize the restructuring of inner city schools so that people working directly with students have more autonomy and authority to respond to the specific and diverse needs of their constituencies. The proposed National Center on Education in the Inner Cities will be committed to investigating the efficacy of a range of educational alternatives and their impact on student engagement. We propose to investigate and compare choice plans, movements

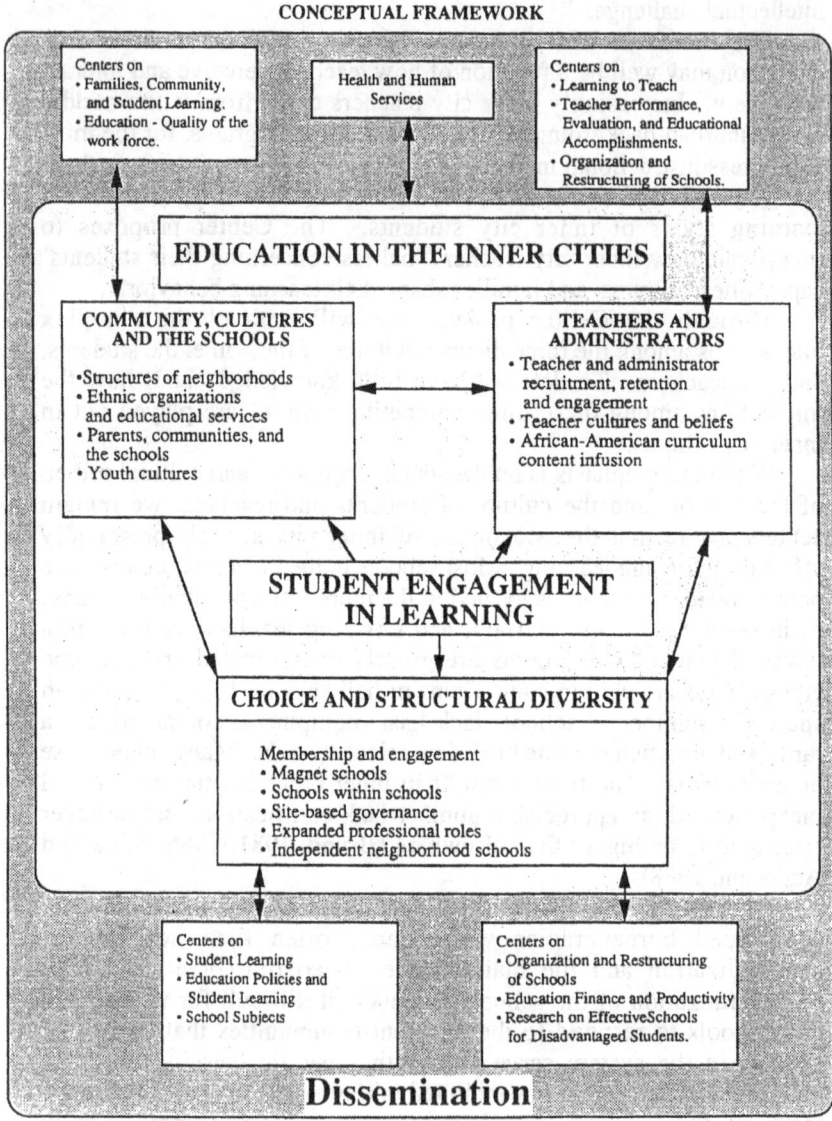

Figure 1

toward decentralization and school-based decision-making, expanded professional roles within schools that alter the relations between teachers and administrators, and the development of independent neighborhood schools. Structural reforms like these may be key elements to improving inner city schools.

In summary, the proposed Center on Education in the Inner Cities will be informed by several perspectives. In focusing on the social and economic ecology in which inner city schools operate, our research will be informed by a perspective which emphasizes the interaction between the diverse cultures of the communities the schools serve and teacher and organizational cultures within schools, and the active roles of those communities, student peer cultures, and teacher cultures in shaping inner city education. Our research agenda also incorporates structural models in order to address issues of resource allocation, organizational structures, and the recruitment, retention and engagement of teachers and administrators. Finally, given the dynamics of inner city government and the large centralized bureaucracy of many inner city school districts, a political perspective is essential to developing a comprehensive understanding of urban schools and the challenges of reform.

Research Projects

Overview of Projects

The goal of the proposed Center for Education in the Inner Cities is to identify the conditions whereby people of diverse cultural and ethnic communities living in the inner cities of the United States actively engage in their own educational futures. The projects we initially propose are unified by a concern for understanding how all students in the inner city can become engaged in learning. We also recognize that teacher engagement and parental involvement in schools are necessary antecedents for promoting such engagement. We define student engagement in learning as the student's psychological investment and exertion of a serious or committed effort in understanding or mastering the worthwhile knowledge, skills, and dispositions intended to be developed by academic work (Stevenson, in press).

As indicated in Figure 1, we view the engagement of inner city students in learning resulting from the interaction of contextual factors within the urban and school environment and school processes. Our first assumption is that student engagement is influenced by a student's ethnic and cultural community and that community's perceptions of the schools, the demands it places on schools, and the alternatives it creates. Similarly, the knowledge students gain in and through their families, as well as through the youth cultures of the street and the mass media, profoundly affects their patterns of school learning and their subsequent academic success. Circumscribing and mediating these cultural influences are the social and economic conditions of the inner city, as demonstrated, for example by Ogbu's (1974) work on the impact of students' perceptions of future economic opportunities on their school success. Through projects on families/communities and student cultures we seek to understand the range of cultural forms extant in the inner cities.

In addition to this urban ecological context, the school context is reflected in teacher and student cultures and the organizational structure of inner city schooling. Thus, projects will examine teachers' beliefs about their students, parents, and their ethnic communities; and the expectations and values of the peer subcultures within inner city schools. These projects will also address the relation between teacher and student cultural forms. We will also investigate curriculum innovation and its relationship to student engagement. In particular, attention will be given to the inclusion of African and African American content as one means of providing cultural diversity. In addition to studying administrator and teacher attitudes toward such curriculum innovation, we will consider student engagement by examining the extent to which students find curriculum and teaching practices interesting, intellectually challenging, and relevant to their cultural and lived experiences.

Other projects will focus on the impact of organizational structures on student and teacher engagement and community involvement in inner city schools. For example, certain workplace conditions can impinge on teacher engagement. Recent reforms, such as merit pay plans and career ladders, are intended to provide extrinsic rewards for enhancing such engagement. Since different structural forms also affect the conditions under which schools are able to respond to the personal, family, and cultural circumstances of their students, we will seek to understand how these various reforms may or may not provide the enabling conditions for students' active participation in their schooling.

The projects we propose are multidisciplinary and are informed by perspectives originating in a number of disciplines both within and outside of educational studies. Many of our projects are situated firmly in ethnographic and survey research techniques characterizing anthropology and sociology. Others rely on demographics and social psychology. The research teams we have assembled consist of historians, linguists, sociologists, political scientists, anthropologists, demographers, business management specialists, and psychologists, as well as specialists in policy studies, educational administration, curriculum studies, and comparative education.

We initially propose eight center projects over the five years of the National Center for Education in the Inner Cities. It is anticipated that projects focusing on resource allocation, on school/business partnerships, integrated health and social services, and other issues will be added in the third year of the Center's existence. Such projects will be planned in conjunction with OERI Centers on School Finance, on Families and Communities, on the Disadvantaged, and on School Restructuring.

In addition, it is expected that new research questions will arise from the initial projects we propose. Annually we will review our research program and seek to develop further, in conjunction with the National Advisory Committee, the Center's research agendas.

The Center's projects are divided into three program areas; the first focuses on Communities, Cultures, and Schools of the Inner Cities; the second is on Teachers and Administrators in Inner Cities; while the third investigates Choice and Structural Diversity in inner city schools. The three project areas are not discrete; we see them as interconnected and building on one another. For example, our proposed project on ethnic associations and their educational programs is related to our projects on structural reforms and alternative educational models for inner city schools. Similarly, our project on parental trust in inner city schools, while it focuses on identifying parental perceptions of and involvement in public education, forms a cornerstone for our projects on reforming the structure and organization of urban schools. The projects we propose on teachers and administrators also relate to the other project areas. In the course of our research we plan to draw linkages between teacher recruitment, retention and engagement in inner city schools to the neighborhoods in which the schools are situated, to student cultures, and to parental involvement in schooling. Similarly, we plan to draw relationships between teacher beliefs and behaviors and the ways in which schools are organized.

The Center projects are situated, for the most part, in a common set of cities. These cities are diverse in size, geographical location, ethnic and racial composition, and in economic structures. This will allow us to generalize across different contexts as well as to understand the impact of specific inner city characteristics on the schools and their outcomes.

In short, the projects we propose are interconnected; they build on one another; and the projected Center throughout its existence will integrate the work and findings of seemingly discrete research. The Center will produce over the years of its work a series of monographs and research papers which explicitly link the projects of the three program areas.

The Time Line for Center projects is illustrated in Figure 2. As Figure 2 indicates, the initial projects span the five years of the Center

Figure 2
TIMEFRAME: OERI National Center on Inner City Schools Proposal Center Projects

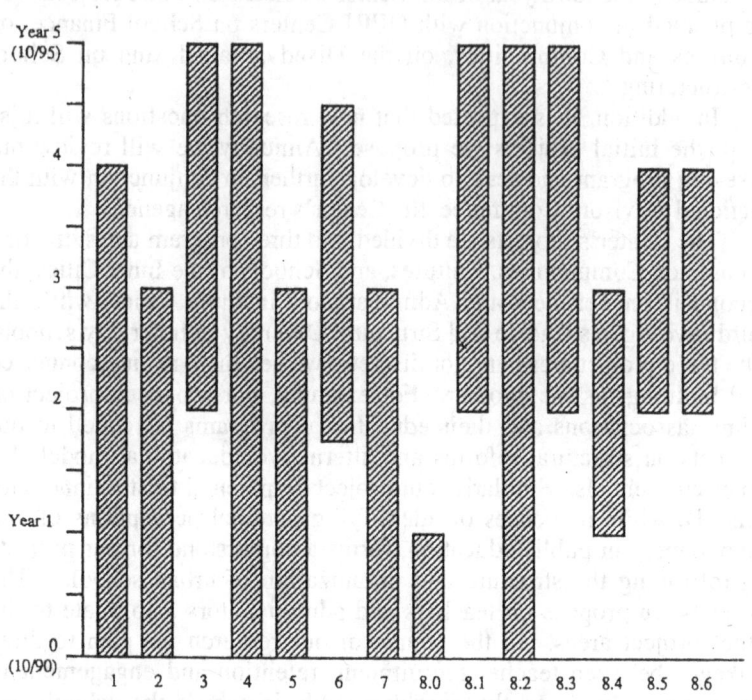

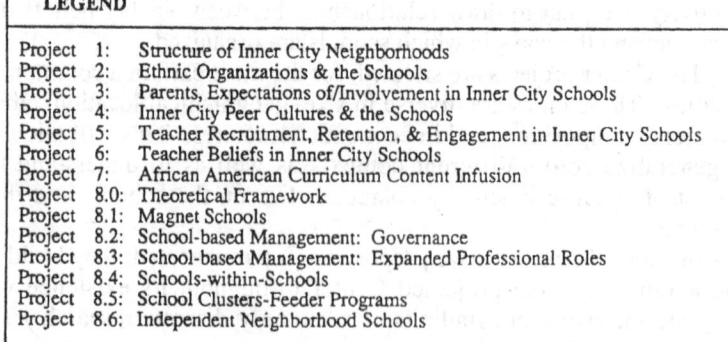

LEGEND		
Project	1:	Structure of Inner City Neighborhoods
Project	2:	Ethnic Organizations & the Schools
Project	3:	Parents, Expectations of/Involvement in Inner City Schools
Project	4:	Inner City Peer Cultures & the Schools
Project	5:	Teacher Recruitment, Retention, & Engagement in Inner City Schools
Project	6:	Teacher Beliefs in Inner City Schools
Project	7:	African American Curriculum Content Infusion
Project	8.0:	Theoretical Framework
Project	8.1:	Magnet Schools
Project	8.2:	School-based Management: Governance
Project	8.3:	School-based Management: Expanded Professional Roles
Project	8.4:	Schools-within-Schools
Project	8.5:	School Clusters-Feeder Programs
Project	8.6:	Independent Neighborhood Schools

and are phased in over time. Six begin in the first year; the remainder will begin in years 2 and 3. Figure 2 does not depict the projects the Center anticipates developing in the third year in conjunction with other OERI Centers or the mid-course corrections we expect emanating from the current research agenda.

Center Research Projects

Program Area 1. Communities, Cultures, and the Schools

The Center proposes four interrelated projects on the urban ecology and cultural context of inner city schools. The first asks about the structure of inner city neighborhoods and seeks to understand not only the impact of city size and location on neighborhood structures, but also how neighborhood structures influence support for public institutions like schools. Related to the questions posed in the Center's project on neighborhood structures is a project on inner city ethnic communities. The interest here is on understanding the types of educational programs inner city residents support and organize for their school-aged children and how those programs can be strengthened to support inner city schools.

Our first two projects concentrate on the urban ecology; other projects focus more directly on the schools. The third project centers on parental involvement in inner city schools. It asks how different inner city ethnic and racial constituencies perceive the public schools and their involvement or lack of involvement in the schools. It also asks whether and how different forms of school organization affect parental involvement.

Our fourth project is on student cultural forms, how those forms emerge in relation to schools, to community and neighborhood organization, and to families. Our interest here is in exploring how schools and communities can work with student peer groups to foster greater engagement in education.

The four projects we present here are truly multidisciplinary. They use methodologies derived from demographic/spatial analyses, anthropology, sociology, and social psychology. As cultural studies, most rely heavily on qualitative research, on in-depth interviewing, and on participant/observation. We expect these projects to give rise to additional research questions that the Center can develop in the third, fourth and fifth years of its existence.

(Ed. note. I have deleted projects for which Gail Kelly was not a principal investigator.)

Project 2. Ethnic Organizations' Educational Services in the Inner City

This project explores the educational services inner city ethnic organizations provide to school-age children. We seek to understand the role such organizations play in supporting as well as supplementing education given in inner city schools. This research is exploratory. While there are large numbers of these organizations and their cultural activities and roles in urban politics have been documented, little systematic research has explored their activities supplementing and supporting the education of inner city students. Our project surveys these organizations and their educational programs in four large urban areas. Our goal is to find ways in which these important community resources can best be used to help diverse inner city youth succeed in school. The project also will identify ways in which public and private inner city schools can cooperate with and enrich the educational programs ethnic organizations offer school-age children.

The research will use survey and interview techniques to study ethnic organizations in Philadelphia, a large eastern city; Buffalo, a mid-size "rustbelt" city; Minneapolis-St. Paul, a midwestern "American heartland" city; and Los Angeles, a large western city. We will focus on ethnic associations providing educational services for African Americans, Mexican Americans, Puerto Ricans, Native Americans, Chinese Americans, and recent immigrants from Southeast Asia and the Soviet Union. Associations serving each group will be studied in as many of the cities as possible, although some groups may not be represented in every city.

Significance of the Problem

The role of ethnic community associations in supporting and supplementing public education in inner cities is an area which has drawn little research attention. Historically immigrants and native-born American minorities—African Americans and Mexican Americans as well as Jews from Eastern Europe, Asians from China and Japan, etc.— have formed associations. Many of these centered on promoting the political and economic rights of their constituencies. Ethnic associations have historically not only acted as pressure groups seeking to make the schools "work" for their communities' children, they have also opened their own programs to supplement public education and to provide their members' children with greater understanding of their cultural and linguistic heritages in the face of Americanization programs which characterized U.S. public education in the late 19th and much of the 20th century.

Research on ethnic associations and their educational programs tends to be historical, for example, Maxine Seller (1988), John Daniels (1920, 1971), Chin-Ling Kuo (1977), Gilbert Osofsky in his book *Harlem: The Making of a Ghetto* (1966) provide useful histories of ethnic communities, their organizations and summaries of their educational programs.

Recent research on the topic has been sparse. The few studies available document the diversity of American ethnic associations and the wide range of educational, cultural, political, and economic activities, which they offer their constituencies. *The Harvard Dictionary of Asian American History* (Kim, 1986) and the *Encyclopedic Directory of Ethnic Organizations in the United States* (Wynar, 1975) both list thousands of organizations and provide brief listings of activities. Research on the current educational activities of these ethnic organizations, their clientele, and how they relate to inner city schools is virtually non-existent. Several works on specific minorities mention such activities and underline their importance (see, for example, Bukowczyk, 1987; Hendricks, Downing and Deinards, 1986; Fitzpatrick, 1987; Simon, 1985; Kelly, 1977; Tollefson, 1989). We, therefore, propose basic research on the educational programs of ethnic associations in U.S. inner cities. Our interest is not in providing compendia of such groups, but rather in studying what kind of programs such organizations offer inner city school-age children, the relation of those programs to those offered in inner city schools, and how better use might be made of these privately sponsored programs in enhancing public school programs. We also hope to see how inner city public schooling might effectively support the programs these organizations offer.

Research Questions

This research explores the roles of ethnic associations in supplementing the schooling of inner city youth. The research will focus on developing a typology of associations offering educational services to school-age students. We will do this by surveying organizations in four cities—Buffalo, Los Angeles, Minneapolis-St. Paul, and Philadelphia. The typology will classify associations by their size; the ethnic group with which they are associated; their stated functions; the extent of local, state, and federal funding; religious affiliation; and the extensiveness of their educational programs and the age groups to which they are offered. Once we have developed a typology, we will select a representative sample of organizations whose educational programs we will study in depth. These organizations will represent a range of associations sponsored by different ethnic groups and will include both government and non-government subsidized programs.

The specific research questions covered by the research include:

1) What are the ranges of educational services different kinds of ethnic associations offer to inner city children? Are there differences among ethnic groups as to the kinds of associations formed and the educational services they provide?

2) How and by whom are ethnic associations' educational programs and services initiated? How are they publicized?

3) What kinds of educational service and/or programs do specific ethnic organizations offer inner city children? To which age groups are they directed? Do they provide enrichment programs? Remedial programs? Help with homework? Cultural programs? Mother-tongue instruction? English language instruction? Health and drug programs? Vocational programs? Are there differences among ethnic organizations within and between cities as to what kinds of programs and services are emphasized?

4) How are the programs funded? To what extent do they rely on government grants, private donations, corporate donations, or user fees?

5) Who delivers the community based educational services? To what extent do ethnic organizations rely on certified teachers, social workers, and other professionals? To what extent do they rely on community volunteers and parents?

While the survey and typology we develop of ethnic associations will address the research questions posed above, we will select from our survey a number of organizations that we will study in depth. We will investigate how the ethnic associations under investigation select the programs they offer to inner city school students, the role of parents and educational professionals in shaping these programs, the relation of various programs to public and private schools, how such programs are supported and evaluated, the impact organizers, staff, and participants believe these programs have on students' engagement in school, and the ways in which these organizations believe they can best work with inner city public and private schools to promote common goals.

Methodology

A two tiered study is planned. The first involves a survey of ethnic associations in the four cities; the second will involve case studies of a representative sample of ethnic associations offering educational programs for primary and secondary school-age children. With the help of local "umbrella" groups such as the International Institute in Buffalo, the Balch Institute in Philadelphia, and the Immigration History Research Institute in St. Paul (see attached letters of support), we will identify all of the ethnic organizations in the specified cities.

Of particular interest will be organizations associated with African Americans, Puerto Rican Americans, Mexican Americans, Polish Americans, Asian Americans, and recent Eastern European and Southeast Asian immigrants. Once we have developed a list of organizations, a questionnaire will be mailed to the director of each eliciting the information needed to answer the research questions listed earlier and requesting relevant documentary material. Our staff will follow up the questionnaires through mail and through telephone calls until we have at least a 70 percent return rate.

Once we have developed a typology of ethnic organizations and their educational offerings, we will select a sample for in-depth study, taking care to include programs offered by different ethnic groups that will be comparable across cities. Tentatively, we hope to include programs sponsored by African Americans, Polish Americans, and Soviet Jewish immigrants in all four cities; by Native Americans in Los Angeles, Buffalo, and Minneapolis-St. Paul; by Vietnamese in Philadelphia, Buffalo, and Los Angeles; by Chinese Americans in Philadelphia and Los Angeles; by Hmong immigrants in Philadelphia and Minneapolis-St. Paul; by Mexican Americans in Los Angeles and Minneapolis-St. Paul; and by Puerto Rican Americans in Philadelphia and Buffalo.

The case studies of each ethnic organization and its educational program will be based on written documents and reports; site visits; semi-structured interviews with staff; observation of classes, educational activities, and parent meetings; analysis of curricular materials; and interviews with relevant community and school leaders.

The Balch Institute in Philadelphia, the Immigration History Research Institute in St. Paul, and the International Institute in Buffalo have expressed interest in assisting with the research in their respective cities. The project directors and graduate assistants from the Graduate School of Education at the University at Buffalo will conduct the interviews and site visits in Buffalo. The staff will be prepared to conduct interviews in Spanish, Russian, and Vietnamese as well as in English if it becomes necessary. Similar "umbrella" organizations and academic units will be identified to assist with the research in the remaining cities.

Time Line

The project will be conducted over a period of three years and will begin in Fall 1990. During the first year the ethnic organizations will be identified and the questionnaire will be developed and tested. Staff to follow up the questionnaire will be recruited and trained. The questionnaires will be mailed, and the staff will solicit responses from those that are not returned. A preliminary report will be written based on the results of this initial mail survey. A typology of ethnic organizations and their educational programs will be developed.

During the first six months of the second year, case studies will be selected and staff will be trained to conduct site visits and interview the directors. We anticipate that 50 case studies will be included across the four cities. In each city we will interview approximately two to three district administrators in the public schools.

The interview protocols will be developed in part from the results of the written questionnaires. The site visits and interviews will begin during the second year. In the third year, we will analyze our data and prepare a final report. The report will summarize our findings about the role of ethnic community organizations in supporting and supplementing the educational work of the inner city schools. The report will also recommend ways in which the schools and the ethnic organizations can work more together in the interest of better education for inner city children. At the end of the third year we anticipate a conference of ethnic associations and of urban school administrators focusing on strengthening relations between school and ethnic association programs.

Project 3. Parents, Communities, and the Schools

This project explores the perceptions and expectations that ethnic minority parents have of inner city schools their children attend. We ask first whether there are differences, stemming from cultural and historical experiences, between ethnic groups in the inner city in their expectations and perceptions of the schools, in their resulting trust or mistrust in the schools, and in their involvement in their children's schooling. Second, we will explore whether and how four forms of school organization found in inner cities affect parental perceptions and involvement in the schools: magnet schools, neighborhood schools within a centralized city system, open enrollment schools, or decentralized schools. Our goal in this research to develop a model for better communication among ethnically diverse parents of children who attend inner city schools and school teachers and administrators. The audience for this research consists of parents, parents' organizations, teachers, teachers' unions, school and district administrators and policy makers.

Significance of the Research

Research has long documented that parents of inner city students have little or no contact with their children's schools, are alienated from the schools and their children's teachers, and, as a result, do not become involved in their children's education (see, for example, Comer, 1984; Lightfoot, 1981; Becker, 1984, Ascher, 1988). Lack of parental involvement has been seen as a major reason for the underachievement of inner city children and for high drop-out rates in the inner city (McLaughlin, 1987; Medina, 1988; Ogbu, 1987; Ornstein, 1983; Slaughter and Epps, 1987; Swap, 1987). A number of strategies have been proposed to increase parental involvement (see, for example, Ascher, 1988; Constable and Walberg, 1988; Epstein, 1987; Heleen, 1988; McLaughlin and Shields, 1987; Morrow, 1989; Metropolitan Life Survey, 1987).

While this literature has documented the lack of involvement of parents in inner city schools, it has not looked at differences among different ethnic and racial groups in terms of parental involvement, which is what we propose to do in the research project outlined here. In addition, not all students in inner city schools are underachievers or dropouts. Research has indicated that the children of some ethnic groups do succeed well in inner city schools (see Seller, 1988) and we seek to understand whether that success is related to how parents perceive the schools, the trust they manifest in the schools, and their involvement with the schools.

In the late 1980s inner city schools began to undergo a number of organizational changes. Urban districts such as Los Angeles and Chicago have taken steps to decentralize education and, in some cases, have given parents more choice over their children's schooling. In some instances, districts like Minneapolis-St. Paul have provided open enrollment plans. The research we propose will ask whether different forms of school organization change inner city parents' expectations of, trust in, and involvement with the schools. This is an area, given the recentness of such experimentation in schools across the nation, research has yet to address systematically.

Research Questions

Our central research question focuses on whether and how different forms of school organization affect parents from different ethnic backgrounds, influencing their perceptions of, trust in, and involvement in inner city schools. The research question can be divided into a number of smaller questions, namely:

1) What views do parents of different ethnic groups hold of schooling in general, of inner city public schools in particular, and of the benefits of schooling to their children?

2) Do parents of the ethnic groups studied perceive the public schools their children currently attend as responsive to them as parents?

3) To what extent do parents of different ethnicities see the schools as supportive or hostile to their cultural heritage and moral values?

4) What specific demands, if any, do parents of different ethnic groups in inner cities make on the schools and why?

5) How much and what kind of contact do parents of different ethnic groups have with the inner city schools?

6) About what kinds of issues do parents of different ethnic backgrounds feel they can easily talk to school teachers and administrators?

7) Does the extent of parental trust in and/or contact with inner city schools depend on how the schools are organized? Do parents have greater trust in and/or contact with their children's schools if their children attend neighborhood schools, magnet schools, schools of choice, or schools recently decentralized?

8) What do parents think can be done to improve family/school relations?

Methodology

The research will be carried out in three cities, each with different patterns of school organization and large inner city ethnic communities. One site will be an urban area which has a well-developed system of magnet schools as well as neighborhood schools. A second site will be an urban area which has instituted an open enrollment plan. A third site will be a large urban district which recently implemented a school decentralization plan.

Each district in which the study will be situated will have appreciable ethnic populations consisting of African Americans, Hispanic Americans, ethnics from Eastern Europe, Native Americans, and recent immigrants from Southeast Asia and the Soviet Union. We believe that Buffalo, Minneapolis-St. Paul, and Los Angeles would be ideal sites for this research, since the Buffalo district has both magnet and neighborhood schools, Minneapolis-St. Paul has recently initiated an open enrollment plan, and Los Angeles has, like Chicago, decentralized the schools.

We will conduct in-depth interviews with a purposive sample of 420 parents of fifth and tenth graders. The table below describes the sample.

	Grade 5	Grade 10
1. Neighborhood Schools (probable site: Buffalo)		
African American	10	10
Hispanic (Puerto Rican)	10	10
Polish American	10	10
Recent Southeast Asian immigrants (Vietnamese)	10	10

Recent Soviet immigrants (Jews and Pentecostals)	10	10 n=100
2. Magnet Schools (probable site: Buffalo)	Grade 5	Grade 10
African American	10	10
Hispanic (Puerto Rican)	10	10
Polish American	10	10
Recent Southeast Asian immigrants (Vietnamese)	10	10
Recent Soviet immigrants (Jews and Pentecostals)	10	10 n=100
3. Open Enrollment (probable site: Minneapolis-St. Paul)	Grade 5	Grade 10
African Americans	10	10
Native Americans	10	10
Hispanics (Mexican Americans)	10	10
Polish Americans	10	10
Recent Southeast Asian immigrants (Vietnamese and Hmong)	10	10
Recent Soviet immigrants	10	10 n=120
4. Decentralized Schools (probable site: Los Angeles)	Grade 5	Grade 10
African Americans	10	10
Native Americans	10	10
Hispanics (Mexican Americans)	10	10
Recent Southeast Asian immigrants	10	10
Recent Soviet immigrants	10	10 n=100

Interview protocols will be developed and pretested. Interviews will, if necessary, be conducted in parents' mother tongue. Provided individual parents consent, we will tape all interviews. All tapes will be logged and coded and entered into the computer. Partial transcriptions of the tapes will be made. Those interviews conducted in Spanish, Russian, Vietnamese, etc. will be translated.

Time Line

The study will take place over three years and begins in the third year of the Center's existence. In the first year the interview protocols will be developed and pretested, interviewers and interviewer/translators trained, and a sample of parents of children attending neighborhood schools drawn. In the second half of the year we will conduct interviews with this sample. A preliminary report summarizing the findings will be produced.

In the second year of the project we will draw samples of parents of children in magnet schools, in schools under open enrollment plans, and in decentralized schools. Interviews of those parents will be conducted throughout the year.

In the third year of the project we will analyze the data, write up findings and prepare papers and articles for publication. Findings will be disseminated at a series of conferences for the targeted audiences.

References

Ascher, C. (1988). Improving the school-home connection for poor and minority urban students, *Urban Review,* 20(2), 109-123.

Becker, R. (1984). *Parent involvement: A review of research and principles of successful practice.* Urbana, IL: ERIC Clearinghouse on Elementary and Childhood Education. (ERIC Document Reproduction Service No. ED 247 032).

Bruno, J. (1986). Supply-demand model of teacher shortage in large urban school districts. *Journal of Education Finance* 11(4), 447-459.

Bruno, J. (1981). Design of incentive systems for staffing racially isolated schools in large urban school districts: Analysis of pecuniary and non-pecuniary benefits. *Journal of Education Finance,* 7(2), 149-167.

Bukowczyk, J. (1987). *And my children did not know me: A history of the Polish-American.* Bloomington, IN: Indiana Press.

Carnegie Foundation for the Advancement of Teaching (1988). *An imperiled generation: Saving urban schools.* Princeton, NJ.

Comer, J. (1984). Home-school relationships as they affect the academic success of children. *Education and Urban Society* 16, 323-37.

Committee on Policy for Racial Justice (1989). *Visions of a better way: A Black appraisal of public schooling.* Lanham, MD: Joint Center for Political Studies Press.

Constable, R. & Walberg, H. (1988, January). School social work: Facilitating home, school, community partnerships. *Urban Education,* 22(4), 429-43.

Corcoran, Walker & White (1988). *Final report of the study of teacher working conditions.* Washington, DC: Institute for Educational Leadership.

Daniels, J. (1971). *America via the neighborhood.* Montclair, NJ: Patterson Smith.

Epstein, J. (1987, February). Parent involvement: What research says to administrators. *Education and Urban Society,* 19(2), 119-36.

Fitzpatrick, J. (1987). *Puerto Rican Americans: The meaning of migration to the mainland.* Englewood Cliffs, NJ: Prentice Hall.

Heleen, O. (1988, Spring). Involving the hard to reach parents: A working model. *Equity and Choice,* 4(3), 60-63.

Hendricks, G., Downing, B. & Deinards, A. (1986). *The Hmong in transition.* Minneapolis, MN: Southeast Asian Refugee Studies of the University of Minnesota.

Kelly, G. (1977). *From Vietnam to America: Chronicle of the Vietnamese Immigration to the United States.* Boulder, CO: Westview Press.

Kim, H. (1986). *The Harvard Dictionary of Asian American History.* New York: Greenwood.

Kuo, Chin-Ling (1977). *Social and political change in New York's Chinatown: The role of voluntary associations.* New York: Praeger.

Lightfoot, S. (1981, Spring). Toward conflict and resolution: Relationships between families and schools. *Theory into Practice,* 97-104.

Mark, J. & Anderson, B. (1978). Teacher survival rates: A current look. *American Educational Research Journal,* 15(3), 379-383.

McLaughlin, M. (1987, October). Involving low-income parents in schools: A role for policy? *Phi Delta Kappan,* 69(2), 156-160.

McLaughlin, M. & Shields, P. (1987). Involving parents in schools. In B. Williams, P. Richmond, & B. Mason (Eds.) *Designs for compensatory education: Conference proceedings and papers.* Washington, DC: Research and Evaluation Associates, Inc.

MDC, Inc. for the Charles Stewart Mott Foundation. (1988). *America's shame, America's hope: Twelve million youth at risk.* Chapel Hill, NC.

Medina, M. (1988, August). Hispanic Apartheid in American Public Education. *Education Administration Quarterly* 24(3), 336.

Metropolitan Life Survey. (1987). *The American teacher, 1987: Strengthening links between home and school.* New York: Louis Harris and Associates, Inc.

Morrow, R. (1989, April). Southeast Asian parental involvement: Can it be a reality? *Elementary School Guidance and Counseling,* 234(2), 39-97.

Oakes, J. (1987). Tracking secondary schools: a contextual perspective. *Educational Psychology* 22, 129-153.

Ogbu, J. (1974). *The next generation: An ethnography of education in an urban neighborhood.* New York: Academic Press.

Ogbu, J. (1987). Variability in minority school performance: A problem in search of an explanation. *Anthropology and Education Quarterly,* 18, 312-334.

Ornstein, A. (1983). Community participation in large public school systems. *Urban Review.* 15(4), 245-54.

Osofsky, G. (1966). *Harlem: The making of a ghetto.* New York: Harper and Row.

Seller, M. (1988). *To seek America: A history of ethnic life in the United States.* Englewood Cliffs, NJ: J. S. Ozer.

Simon, R. (1985). *New lives: The adjustment of Soviet Jewish immigrants in the Unites States and Israel.* Lexington, MA: Lexington Books.

Slaughter D. & Epps, E. (1987). The home environment and academic achievement of black American children and youth: an overview. *Journal of Negro Education, 86:1, 3-20.*

Stevenson, R. (in press). Engagement and cognitive challenge in thoughtful social studies classes: A study of perspective. *Journal of Curriculum Studies.*

Swap, M. (1987). *Enhancing parent involvement in schools.* New York: Teachers College Press.

Tollefson, J. (1989). *Alien Winds: The seed of American Indo-Chinese refugees.* New York: Praeger.

Weis, L. (1990). *Working class without work: High school students in a de-industrialization economy.* New York: Routledge.

Wilson, B. & Corcoran, T. (1988). *Successful secondary schools.* London: Falmer Press.

Wynar, L. (1975). *Encyclopedic directory of ethnic organizations in the United States.* Libraries Unlimited.

The Education of Gail Paradise Kelly: A Memoir

David Kelly

I met Gail Paradise one evening in the autumn of 1961. She was in her senior year at the University of Chicago studying ancient and medieval history, interested in maintaining a stellar academic record and perhaps going on to graduate school. I and Mike Parker, a friend and comrade of hers in the Young People's Socialist League, were asking her to serve as the campus president of another organization, the Student Peace Union. (The SPU was rapidly becoming the largest white left-wing organization in the country, eventually to have three to four thousand members on three hundred campuses.) We argued to Gail that while the SPU was growing nationally and in the Chicago area, it was faltering on the U of C campus where it had originated. We wanted Gail not as an active leader, but as a figurehead, since she was well known on campus. (Gail had been active in student government and had been elected as one of the U of C delegates to the National Student Association. As such she had voted to support the student civil rights sit-ins against Woolworth's department stores and had played a major role in boycotts of Woolworth stores in the Chicago area in the spring of 1960.) Gail agreed to the figurehead role and was later elected.

While Gail retained a vivid memory of her election and of my giving her a powerful speech denoting this figurehead role, such was not to be the case. Late in the Fall of 1961 an independent student group at Harvard University, Tocsin, called for a mass demonstration in Washington, D.C. The SPU chapters in the northeast and our allies in New York (the National Committee for a SANE Nuclear Policy, the War Resisters League, the Fellowship of Reconciliation and the Committee for Non-violent Action) also supported the call. Although the national office of the SPU in Chicago questioned whether a national effort would undercut all other organizing goals, we were forced to go along. Gail was thrown into a frenzy of activity to keep the Chicago efforts under the SPU name and to make them successful. Seven busloads of students went from the Chicago area; they joined a total of 5,000 student marchers. It was the largest protest in Washington since the Depression of the 1930s and President Kennedy stole the headlines by sending the White House butler out to serve coffee to the demonstrators.

Gail finished her degree with distinction in the spring of 1962 but she did not enter graduate school; instead she became the national secretary of the Student Peace Union. (Philip Altbach and I served as National Co-Chairmen and spokespersons to the adult peace community, but Gail as secretary was the functioning and political head of the organization.)

The SPU rented a large townhouse across from the University of Chicago Law School; it served as the national headquarters and as a commune for staff, and was where Gail and I shared accommodations. The house had six bedrooms, three baths, and two half baths. The ground floor served as offices, while the basement provided space for printing and mailing machinery. The staff ranged from six to twelve people with rooms sometimes rented for income. In reality the national office functioned as a propaganda center with a monthly bulletin (most months of the school year) and an internal discussion bulletin, to prepare for national conventions, as a coordinating center for demonstrations, and as the home base for several field organizers. Politically the staff and others tried to respond to any foreign policy crisis: the China-India War, the Cuban missile crisis, the continuous arms negotiation failures, the Berlin wall, the beginning of the Vietnamese war. Because Gail knew French she became the SPU expert on Vietnam.

As a commune the national office functioned with rigid but equally assigned tasks of cleaning and cooking. It also was a melange of Antioch College co-op students, temporary college drop-outs, occasionally a high school runaway, transient radicals, all dedicated to either peace, socialist or civil rights activity and most going through adolescent sexual and sometimes psychological problems. Gail was in charge and everyone was working sixty to eighty hour weeks with no ability to escape from the work milieu. Our major entertainments included trips to the cheap ghetto movie house on 63rd street, trips downtown to see classic films at an all-night theater (usually as a three a.m. reward for finishing some task) and massive games of "Risk."

This commune experience left Gail with tolerance for communes but no enthusiasm. The content and structure of the nuclear family might need change, but not its existence. Gail came from strong family roots which included a good deal of social and political activity. She was born in Brooklyn and resided in that ethnic, Jewish enclave until she was eight. Her upwardly mobile parents, both lawyers, left Brooklyn when Gail's sixteen-year-old brother flirted with delinquency and Gail's twelve-year-old sister began flirting with the wrong boys. The family couldn't afford Westchester County and the move there was partly financed by Gail's paternal grandmother who lived with them for several years. However, in Westchester, her father's practice flourished. (When I first showed an interest in Gail, a friend who lived in her dormitory cautioned me that she was from a wealthy family out of my social class.) Gail's father, a lonely liberal in Westchester, helped organize the Democratic Party there; he also remained active in B'nai Brith and was vice-president of the Hillel Foundation. Gail's first political activity was campaigning for Adlai Stevenson in 1956. Her mother struggled against the suburban trap and eventually established her own law practice, partly through helping to found the Legal Aid Society of Westchester to serve the legal needs of the servant class of the rich. Gail's parents came to social activism by tradition: a maternal grandfather, who made a fortune in the 1920s and lost it refusing to collect rents in the 1930s was a lifelong socialist who escaped from Russia after the 1905 revolution. Her father had two younger brothers who were union activists in the 1930s and who were called up before the McCarthy committee in the early 1950s. (Gail also had a maternal uncle who was a wealthy contractor in Arizona and a stalwart Republican contributor.) Gail attended public school in Westchester with that same serving class (the wealthy of her area went to private school); only a handful of her classmates attended college. As school newspaper editor her liberal views constantly were repressed by school authority. Generally, she hated Westchester (and we were never to live in the suburbs) and she spent a good part of her youth practicing the piano.

In the summer of 1963, fearful of Gail's future (her mother never admitted to her working in the SPU and always told friends that Gail was working in the Peace Corps), her parents offered her a trip to Europe. Gail had toured France and Italy with a friend on her own funds in the summer of 1961. She needed a break from the hectic existence of the SPU national office, so she accepted the offer and with arrangements made through Norman Thomas set off on a tour of Western and Eastern European peace groups. The trip was not to include the Soviet Union, but after an alcoholic evening in Budapest, Gail found herself on the morning plane to Moscow, a guest of the Women's Peace Committee of the Soviet Union. Gail and the SPU were very critical of American foreign policy, but we were just as critical of the policies of the Soviet Union. After a speech at Moscow University to a stunned audience, she found a projected trip to Leningrad canceled and was sent back to Western Europe. (She did spend a charming evening with the poet Yevtushenko during which they picked up a couple of Ukrainian coal miners on holiday and ended up toasting the suppressed working class of the Soviet Union.)

In the fall of 1963 the Communist Party of Italy invited the SPU to send a representative to a planning conference for a youth peace meeting to be held in Bologna in the spring of 1964 and they were willing to fund the representative. (The SPU had no money—it was completely run by volunteers. The staff was paid only in the form of room and food, from the few dollars in cash that came in the daily mail. Its annual budget was about $20,000 a year.) Despite the funding we had little interest in the proposal until young friends in the English Campaign for Nuclear Disarmament urged us to attend to create a non-aligned presence. Gail went; her stance against both the U.S. and the USSR got her labeled in the Bologna press as "a daughter of the Chinese." We were sent no money to return to the actual conference. However, a call from an old friend who was international affairs vice-president for the National Student Association provided access to funds. (We assumed these were State Department moneys, but events in the 1970s demonstrated the source of funds was the Central Intelligence Agency, which had a policy of sponsoring independent American radicals and socialists to bring a different viewpoint to Communist dominated events. The same source offered to pay for a delegation we organized to the International Youth Conference in Algeria in the summer of 1965, but a coup in Algeria canceled the conference.) Gail did return to Bologna in the spring, accompanied by another representative—perhaps in some sense used, but from our viewpoint only speaking the same independent political stance we had always espoused.

The last major demonstrations coordinated by the SPU were pickets of Madam Ngo Dinh Nhu when she visited the U.S. in the fall of 1963 to bolster support for U.S. Vietnamese policy. She was greeted by student pickets in every major city. Gail was arrested in front of the South Vietnamese embassy in Washington on a disorderly conduct charge (no pickets are allowed near embassies). Annual conventions of the SPU held at Oberlin College, Princeton University and Antioch College had usually drawn from two hundred to four hundred delegates. In the spring of 1964 only twenty-five delegates came to the convention in Chicago. The 1963 test ban treaty and the fact that Vietnam was barely beginning meant student attention had shifted to domestic issues, the continuation of the civil rights struggle and, with the rise of Students for a Democratic Society, general anti-poverty organization. A few students tried to continue the SPU from a New York City base, but it was effectively moribund. In the summer of 1964 Gail and I married at her family home in Westchester with eight relatives, three friends and one infant nephew in attendance.

Gail's two-year stint of political activism finely tuned her organizational, bureaucratic, and political skills, gave her an assurance to speak before hundreds of people (she always considered herself a shy person although those around her never did; she had rejected a musical career because she hated performance and thought the training would be intellectually stultifying), introduced her to a lifelong study of the history of Vietnam, strengthened her commitment to social activism, and gave her a taste for international activity. However, she remembered other influences. When we were interviewed in the early 1970s for a Ph.D. dissertation on the origins of the new left, she could only speak to her experience as illustrative of sexism in the movement: only males were assigned as field organizers, there were discussions of horizontal recruitment, most women's talents were not fully appreciated or used, etc. The interview took place shortly after she had written the first article in this collection. The article and this memoir report different but accurate realities.

Finding a Career

In 1964 I had a year of undergraduate work to complete at the University of Chicago. Few job opportunities seemed available for women with B.A.s; Gail became a secretary to Frank Chase, Professor Emeritus of Education at the university. Gail, who was an incredibly rapid typist, 160 wpm after error deductions, did a good deal of reading as well as serving as a research assistant for the professor. We had a quiet year while the student world heated up around us, with the Berkeley free speech movement in the fall and the beginning of Vietnam teach-ins in the summer. Gail worked on her first real article, on the origins of the war for the journal *New Politics*. In a sense she saw the possibility of being an independent scholar.

Gail urged me to go to graduate school—there seemed an assured future in expanding higher education, and the role fit both a sense of social advocacy and purpose. Gail seemed to place herself almost in the female trap as I continued my studies at Indiana University in the fall of 1965. With the help of Frank Chase, Gail had arranged a position as an editorial assistant to the *Reading Research Quarterly*. When we arrived this position almost disappeared; The IU reading department thought she had agreed to a salary of $285 a month, Gail though they meant $2.85 per hour (about a $100 difference). She won the debate, but to pay at that level they had to make her a non-tenure track faculty member. Hence Gail entered education quite by accident and with sharply limited commitment.

The first years at Indiana were miserable for Gail: she was living in part through me rather than for herself. The idea of being an independent scholar or writer was smashed when the article in *New Politics* appeared with a new conclusion she had specifically rejected as historically and politically unrealistic. We did lead an active life. Bloomington, as lauded on the cover of the local phone book, was the cultural capital of Indiana. We had student subscriptions to the Sol Hurok attractions that toured the country and to the road companies of Broadway shows. We joined the local Students for a Democratic Society chapter and became part of the core group after attending our first meeting. (Because I dressed like a conservative graduate student we were taken as FBI spies at that meeting, but the National Secretary of the SDS happened to be visiting and as an old chum we took her out to dinner.) Gail also sewed and began quilting. She discovered a love for camping on a trip to Mexico in the summer of 1966, primarily because camping made travel inexpensive. But she also enjoyed wilderness camping and we took several backpacking trips to the Rockies and a canoeing trip in Canada. We hiked the local woods, but never in the fall after having walked into the sights of a disgusted rabbit hunter. We became avid flower and then vegetable growers. Gail loved not only preserving food she grew, but also collecting fruits and berries from the general environment. These pastimes remained part of Gail's life for the next twenty years (most of her family and intimate friends have been recipients of quilts) but they remained just pastimes. Gail did not really find peace at Indiana until she decided to return to school herself.

Her choice of comparative education was not simple. She thought about comparative literature (she always read widely), but an acquaintance described the paradigm of reconstruction that was becoming dominant and Gail viewed reconstruction as both arid and historicist. She was attracted to the philosophy of education and to economics by courses she took with Elizabeth Maisha and Sara Berry. Berry was doing studies of African market women that Gail saw as particularly exciting. However, she chose comparative education, which was a very weak field at Indiana. (Its very weakness allowed Gail to explore other areas at the university, hence the courses mentioned.) Twenty years later Gail claimed she entered education because there was a tradition of greater opportunity for women, but I feel that was a partial explanation. Neither Professor Maisha (in education) or Professor Berry (in economics) were having particularly easy careers. Phil Altbach was already part of the field and recommended it. Gail's real attraction to comparative education was its very intellectual breath: she could be theoretical, she could continue her interest in Vietnam and other areas of the Third World, and she could examine feminist issues. Additionally she already was in education and had credentials as an editorial assistant of the quarterly and as a research associate for the ERIC document system in reading. Finally, Gail recognized that education might actually provide some sort of service to people.

While finding a career, Gail also broadened and deepened her feminism at Indiana. As the daughter of a professional woman, as a strong individual who had assumed leadership roles, as an acute observer of her mother's and more recent women's struggles in the professions, she came to feminism quite naturally. While she might have flirted with the feminine mystique in our relationship, she had consciously rejected it before she met me (she had broken off an engagement to a young lawyer) and never seriously considered it while with me. While

Gail had natural inclinations to feminism, the late 1960s was when feminism became a major issue on campuses across the nation. As an activist Gail eagerly took part in consciousness raising groups, feminist reading circles, etc. These often led to our own long discussions of gender roles and knowledge of gender realities. (I received a lot of criticism for actions or lack of actions on the part of other men; ours had always been a fairly equal relationship at least in terms of time and work roles.) Gail's sense of "lived realities" and "politics as personal" were greatly enhanced by these discussions. But as indicated in the first essay, she questioned the life style revolution. One slogan she particularly resented was "smash monogamy," which was being used by a young professor to torture his wife with sexual affairs while they lived in a commune.

In 1969 the job market for young historians simply disappeared, and when I became a Ph.D. candidate in 1970 I found little interest in my teaching abilities. Altbach offered Gail a research assistantship at the University of Wisconsin and pressured for an answer; we agreed in April and Gail became a full-time student at Wisconsin that fall (having received an M.A. from Indiana). With the dearth of jobs we had stopped trying to have a child, but shortly after arriving at Wisconsin Gail realized she was pregnant.

Madison was a center of the national student movement. In the summer of 1970 before we arrived, the Army Math Research Center had been bombed, resulting in the death of one innocent student. While Gail and I had been active at Indiana in demonstrations against the Vietnam war and in a massive student strike opposing tuition increases, we always advocated nonviolence. Gail in part saw the left's violent turn as so much male "macho" nonsense; no real revolution of thought or personal relationship could depend on terrorism, but had to convince the vast majority.

Gail arrived in Madison a serious and very mature student. Lois Weis, who met her that Fall, recalled that Gail came up to her after a class discussion and said, "you're really very smart and will do well—don't let them get you down," quite like a junior professor, not a fellow student. Gail and Lois became lifelong friends as did Sheila Slaughter McVey, who also was working with Altbach and shared with Gail the fact of being pregnant. Coping with professors' attitudes toward pregnant graduate students and being concerned with a tenure fight going on in the school of education deepened the commitment to feminism of Gail and other female students. Gail and I also met a wider circle of Madison radicals who were studying in other areas, among them Paul and Mary Jo Buhle, who were then editing *Radical America* and were friends of the Altbach's and coincidentally our upstairs neighbors. We helped organize a food co-op and later a parent cooperative day care center. Hence we remained in touch with the left, even occasionally demonstrating, but very selectively because demonstrations in Madison tended to turn into stylized student riots: the National Guard would fire tear gas at students charging up the main hill of the campus, the gas would clear, the students would charge again, etc. When the demonstrators went the other direction down State Street toward the Capitol building, all the local merchants were prepared with custom-fitted plywood to cover their plate glass windows. Once when a fleeing demonstrator ran into the Student Union, police close behind swinging batons, Gail visibly pregnant attempted to intervene. Sheila also pregnant pulled her aside before the baton swung at her. (They were in the Union because Sheila knew the nature of Madison demonstrations and refused to let Gail attend because of the probable use of tear gas.)

Gail in Madison was primarily a student. She learned the full parameters of comparative education, delved deeply into Southeast Asian history, studied some sociology and political socialization theory, and independently learned the Vietnamese language. She was the type of student who read everything required, everything recommended and then asked for more. While she was a student she published her first real academic article in comparative education on the educational background of Vietnamese nationalists. Based on a published French archive, it contradicted the myth that Vietnamese learned communism in French metropolitan universities. Rather, the article demonstrated that Vietnamese noncommunist nationalists were the ones deeply imbued with French education. This was the beginning of Gail's lifelong study of the content and impact of French colonial education.

We had planned to spend one year in Madison, after which I would be employed somewhere and she would finish from a distance. But there remained a dearth of positions in history and one year became four. After the first year, Gail as a student was able to manipulate several student assistantships, and later an assistantship and a part time position as a planner with the State Department of Health. (I would do the work for one of the assistantships.) It was a lean but amusing existence—one winter we even shared a coat. With cooperative day care (our daughter Jennifer was born that first year) we both managed to have time for study and writing, work, parenting, and even a bit of fun.

A Career in Buffalo

In the early spring of 1974, in the midst of a move to escape a rapacious landlord, Gail was called for an interview at SUNY/Buffalo. She had only applied for the position because Phil Altbach had threatened never to speak to her again if she did not. (In his letter nominating Gail, Phil mentioned he was interested in leaving Wisconsin.) Gail got the job at SUNY/Buffalo, one of the last major positions in comparative education for a number of years. (SUNY/Buffalo, in the last throes of its great expansion also created a special line for Altbach, who came the next year.) Before moving to Buffalo we took the last of our meager savings and spent four months in Paris so that Gail could complete her dissertation research in the French national archives.

When Gail arrived at SUNY/Buffalo she was deeply immersed in her essentially historical scholarship. This scholarship was focused on a detailed political and social analysis of the meaning of education. Gail found ways of reaching into the classroom, schools and administrative arrangements of the past. She wanted to know and write about the processes as well as the outcomes of education. These were to remain lifelong themes and concerns. Gail spent most of the first year at SUNY completing her thesis, and for the next twenty years she would dip into that research to bring historical realities to contemporary debates on educational planning, teacher's career paths, the transfer of administrative technique, education for nation building, etc. She deepened and extended to French West Africa this historical research with a second extensive archival tour in 1982. Gail always searched for the impact of education on women and other gender issues in relation to this historical research, but this material contained only rare examples because the patriarchal attitudes of the French excluded most women from education in that time period.

In 1975, as the South Vietnamese government collapsed, a colleague of Gail's suggested they study the socialization of the new Asian immigrants to this country. Gail's knowledge of Vietnam and her language skills made her indispensable to the project. While the project started as a collaboration, the colleague wished to publish the interview data simply as oral history but Gail wanted to write up a completed history. They agreed he could publish the interviews after Gail used them, hence she completed the work on her own, publishing the seminal work on the Vietnamese immigration. From that point Gail was often asked to write on the subject, although in the long run it was not to be a major interest. The second item in this volume was a result of that research and showed clearly the dangers of ignoring or being ignorant of gender issues. Versions of this article have been Gail's most widely disseminated work.

Her book on the Vietnam immigration along with several articles on Vietnamese colonial education and a volume edited with Altbach on colonialism and education won Gail tenure after four years at SUNY/Buffalo. She also continued to push for women's issues within the university. In the fall of 1975, for example, Gail and Maxine Seller put together a graduate course on "Women's Education in Comparative

Perspective" which they co-taught in the Spring of 1976. In the spring of 1977, our second child, Elizabeth, was born.

In 1978 the comparative education program at SUNY/Buffalo made a bid to edit the journal *Comparative Education Review* from Buffalo with Philip Altbach as editor and Gail as associate editor. The bid was accepted. Gail and Phil also began a series of bibliography projects and a few years later, in collaboration with Robert Arnove at Indiana University, published the basic textbook in comparative education. These projects made the comparative education program at Buffalo one of the most notable in the nation. Being at one of the major centers in her field gave Gail immediate access to everything new in the field and provided an opportunity to comment in print and at various professional meetings on questions of feminism and women's role in education.

Gail's collaboration with Altbach was to be lifelong: recently a graduate student gave a paper at the Comparative and International Education Society annual meeting on the Altbach/Kelly approach to comparative education. He had difficulty making a distinction between the collaborators, but it is and was rather simple. Altbach's attraction has always been to issues in higher education, and to pioneering in areas like intellectual transfer, paths of knowledge, and world systems analysis. Gail was deeply concerned with internal issues of schools, questions of women in education, and she provided the systematic historical analysis of the field in which they both worked. However, their work was a true collaboration, in which they criticized each other's drafts and reached consensus. (One example of their work together is included in this volume.)

One result of having the *Comparative Education Review* at Buffalo was a request by the Ford Foundation to present a special issue of the journal on women. Although the woman who the foundation sponsored to edit such an issue, Carolyn Elliott (then at Wellesley), was a committed feminist, some of the papers they wished to be published reflected fairly conservative scholarship. Phil and Gail pushed for a broader representation of scholarship and Gail collaborated with Carolyn Elliott to bring out that special issue and subsequently to turn it into the well received volume from SUNY Press, *Women's Education in the Third World* (1982). (The summary article of that volume done with Carolyn Elliott is reprinted in this volume.) Just before Gail and Philip relinquished editorship of the *Review,* they and other colleagues began a new journal, *Educational Policy* (1986), hence helping SUNY/Buffalo to remain a center of scholarship.

While Gail was always an extremely active scholar, she also took on a full load of service to the university and occasionally to the community. She served as a teacher aide for our oldest daughter's first grade class in 1977 and later was active in escort services with the local pro-choice group. Her service to the university included all the usual committees—for searches, on undergraduate curriculum, on African, Asian and Canadian studies, on the library, etc. She also served on the Faculty of Education Executive Committee and in the Faculty Senate. Probably her most prominent activity in the early years was assuming the directorship of a major UNESCO grant that provided postbaccalaureate education for the faculty of a teacher training institute in Oweri, Nigeria. (She traveled back and forth several times a year for one or two week stays and once the whole family spent an extended winter break in Nigeria while she was teaching in the program.) In all this work she fought for the inclusion of feminist concepts and for equity for women and others not quite in the mainstream. She also forged links with women across the university. Indeed, she and other women, mainly in education but with occasional additions, took to eating lunch together on Thursdays simply to show a turn-about kind of solidarity.

Gail's broader activity in the university brought her into continuous contact with the women's studies area of the American studies department. This contact produced the most intensive collaboration of her career and resulted in *Feminist Scholarship in the Disciplines: Kindling in the Groves of Academe.* The five women who collaborated—Gail, Elizabeth Kennedy, Ellen DuBois, Carolyn Korsmeyer and Lillian Robinson—came from different disciplines (education, anthropology, history, philosophy and literature), but the primary division in the group was between those committed to women's studies as a field (Kennedy, DuBois and Robinson) and those more deeply attached to their own disciplines (Gail and Korsmeyer). This debate about the meaning of feminism and how it would develop in academe was intense and exciting to all involved. The fundamental notion of sisterhood and the moderating, consensus-building skills of Kennedy kept the group together and the product was such a true collaboration that I have not included any portion of the work in this volume. All the participants gathered several years later to present a colloquium on the book and all shared a deep memory of the work as among the most challenging of their careers.

Gail's sense of scholarship as shaped by collaboration was shared with her students. While she never dodged undergraduate courses and insisted while a chairperson that all teach the basic Social Foundations course, the growth of the SUNY program in comparative education meant that she usually taught graduate students. (SUNY/Buffalo is a center for graduate education.) From the outset she advised half a dozen thesis students and by the end of her career usually had a load of twenty graduate advisees and several doctoral theses going at the same time. Despite her own scholarship, travel and family responsibility, Gail had a firm rule that any material turned in on a thesis should be returned in two weeks. Her sense of collaboration and of mentoring students into the profession never let her forget that teaching has an authoritarian side—that the professor really does know more and that budding scholars need help to formulate and complete their ideas. Her students at one point surprised her by appearing in identical t-shirts with "but what is your question" emblazed on the front. (In class, Gail, after a long student presentation that might present data or refer to past theory, would usually make the quoted statement. The students had a similar t-shirt for Gail.) Because of her teaching, several of her students did doctoral work on the processes of education—textbook analysis, examining attitudes within a girls school, etc. (Her theoretical interests are represented in this volume by the inclusion of an article in criticism of David Angus from 1988.)

By the early 1980s Gail was notable enough to be invited to teach at other institutions, teaching summer courses at the Ontario Institute for Studies in Education in 1982 and 1984 and at Teachers College, Columbia University in 1986. She always made a presentation at the national meeting of the Comparative and International Education Society and often spoke before the French Colonial History Society. She was invited to speak at various universities (including the University of Missouri, University of New Hampshire, Duquesne University, University of Stockholm and Harvard University) and at major forums like the American Anthropological Association (where she confused people by not wearing symbols of the society she studied), the Nordic Studies Association (in Finland), and she gave the keynote address at the World Congress of Comparative Education Societies in Rio de Janeiro in 1987.

By the last lecture Gail was well known and felt in the position to counter-attack trends in comparative education that she thought dangerous for women. The scholarship in question was human capital theory, sponsored strongly by the World Bank. The theory's narrow definition of maximizing personal economic gain through education questioned the struggle for women's equality through education. Gail's last work in comparative education (reproduced here) was intended to look at intervening variables in that quantitative theory and to urge more careful attention to process in education as it affected women.

Aside from presenting scholarship before the Comparative and International Education Society and helping to edit its journal, Gail also acted in the society in an organizational sense. She served at various times on nominating committees and on its executive committee, and as president-elect organized its 1985 meeting in Toronto. Her presidential address of 1986 is reprinted here. The address sharply questioned the mood of pessimism felt by many educators regarding the slow pace of change in relation to education and social and political development.

While Gail was fighting these external struggles in 1986, she discovered a lump in her left breast. Urged to act by Ellen DuBois (who argued that lumps do not always mean cancer) Gail went to a physician to quiet her fears. Sometimes, however, lumps are malignant. After a semi-radical mastectomy (four lymph nodes were involved) Gail took a full course of chemotherapy followed by hormonal therapy, since the tumor was the type driven by hormones. The cancer went into a two-year remission and we continued our lives. (One dose of chemotherapy was given while we were on a faculty exchange to China and was given via careful medical instructions at a Beijing hospital that had never done outpatient chemotherapy.) In the spring of 1988 a new lump appeared in the neck and Gail had a second operation that summer. Again there was a period of remission but the blood cell counts indicating remission were never quite normal. In the spring of 1989 Gail underwent a bone marrow transplant at the Cleveland Clinic, from which she recovered enough so that we took a two week family jaunt to Scandinavia that summer. In the winter of 1989-90 she suffered a great deal of pain in her hip, which eventually just fractured. The cancer had spread to the bone. The hip was replaced and the pain treated through radiation therapy. Through all of these years Gail missed relatively little work and although during most of her last year she needed a wheelchair for any movement, she continued to be a fully engaged scholar, teacher and academic.

Gail's scholarly achievement led to an invitation to sit on the Fulbright commission for the international exchange of scholars. It also led to an invitation to tour South Africa early in 1989 under the aegis of the United States Information Service. In South Africa Gail lectured on transition to integrated education and attempted to aid those fighting for such changes. She also helped sponsor younger South African scholars who were identified as potential leaders for the new direction. That same year she also toured Vietnam as a member of Scholars for Reconciliation. While the tour was not officially sponsored, the group met with the American ambassador to Thailand before entering Vietnam. Gail subsequently arranged for the first Vietnamese student of the post-war era to study at SUNY/Buffalo and helped establish a language training connection between SUNY/Buffalo and the University of Hanoi. To negotiate that agreement Gail helped to host the first post-war delegation of Vietnamese education officials to the United States (the official sponsor of the group was the U.S. Committee on the International Exchange of Scholars). The article on Vietnamese women reproduced here was also a result of that journey.

While Gail was active on the international scene she continued her dedication to SUNY/Buffalo, serving in ever more important functions at the university, including the Graduate Fellowship Committee (which distributed all major university grants used to attract students) and the

Presidential Review Board (which reviewed all tenure and full professor decisions before the president of the university acted upon them). By 1988 Gail was the chair of one of the four departments of SUNY/Buffalo's School of Education. This department, which joined social foundations with educational administration, had formed a few years before. The focus of the department was supposed to be educational policy and Gail strove to bring the elements of the department together to really work on policy.

Years before, Maxine Seller and Gail had done a history of educational reform in New York State. Gail had continued her involvement with American educational reform in terms of feminism, and in her role in editing *Educational Policy*, through membership in the Holmes Group for teacher education and in working with Ellen Farrar on grant proposals for effective schools. (One review essay reflecting this interest is reprinted in this volume.) As chair Gail pulled together elements of the department, reached out across the university to the American Studies department and across the nation to create a multi-million dollar grant proposal to study and reform the American inner city school. (The portions of the proposal she was most directly responsible for have been reprinted here.) From her wheelchair, often in considerable pain, Gail realized she had educated herself to the point and gained enough stature and position that she had a chance at truly helping to shape the future of American education. She had little faith that the whole proposal would be funded by the conservative Bush administration, but there was no despair—the projects could be funded separately and still completed.

Unfortunately, this and other ongoing projects on Third World women and development were cut short by Gail's death in January of 1991. When she entered the hospital for a second hip replacement, her doctor warned me that long-term prospects were grim. When I told Gail that six or eight months were all we could reasonably expect, she resigned the chair to put the projects in order. However, she never recovered from the operation. Colleagues like Lois Weis, Philip Altbach and others continue work that she influenced, just as they had influenced hers. A memorial lecture series has been established at SUNY/Buffalo, the topic of which alternates between education and women's studies.

Her epitaph reads:
>Mother of two daughters,
>Teacher of educators,
>Wife, and lover of life.

Works of Gail P. Kelly

Books
Women's Education in Third World Nations: An Annotated Bibliography (with D. H. Kelly) New York: Garland Publishing, 1988.

Feminism and the Disciplines: Kindling in the Groves of Academe (with E. DuBois, E. Kennedy, C. Korsmeyer and L. Robinson) Champaign: University of Illinois Press, 1985.

International Bibliography of Comparative Education (with P. G. Altbach and D. H. Kelly) New York: Praeger, 1981.

From Vietnam to America: A Chronicle of the Vietnamese Immigration to the United States. Boulder, Colorado: Westview Press, 1977.

Monographs
"When I Become a Fonctionnaire": School Knowledge in French Colonial Africa, Buffalo: Comparative Education Center, 1984.

Franco-Vietnamese Schools. 1918-1938: Regional Development and Implications for National Integration, Wisconsin Papers on Southeast Asia, No. 6, April, 1982.

Women's Education in Developing Countries, (with D. H. Kelly) Geneva: International Bureau of Education, April, 1982.

The Distribution of Knowledge and the Professionalization of Teachers: Perspectives from Colonial Vietnam, Buffalo: Comparative Education Center, 1980.

Comparative Education: An Introductory Bibliography (with P. G. Altbach) Buffalo: SUNY/Buffalo Comparative Education Center, 1978.

Edited Volumes
Critical Perspectives on Early Childhood Education (with Lois Weis, Philip Altbach and Hugh Petrie, eds.) Albany: State University of New York Press, 1992.

Textbooks in American Society (with Philip Altbach, Hugh Petrie and Lois Weis, eds.) Albany: State University of New York Press, 1991.

Textbooks in the Third World: Policy, Context and Content (with Philip Altbach, ed.) New York: Garland Publishing, 1989.

International Handbook of Women's Education. Westport, Conn.: Greenwood Press, 1988.

Crisis in Teaching (with L. Weis, P. G. Altbach, H. Petrie and Sheila Slaughter, eds.) Albany: SUNY Press, 1988.

New Approaches to Comparative Education (with P.G. Altbach, ed.) Chicago: University of Chicago Press, 1986.

Excellence in Education: Perspectives on Policy and Practice (with P. G. Altbach and Lois Weis, eds.) Buffalo: Prometheus, 1985.

Education and the Colonial Experience (with P.G. Altbach, ed.) New Brunswick, New Jersey: Transaction Press, 1984.

Women's Education in the Third World: Comparative Perspectives (with C. Elliott, ed.) Albany: SUNY Press, 1982.

Comparative Education (with P. G. Altbach and R. Arnove, eds.) New York: Macmillan, 1982.

Education and Colonialism (with P. G. Altbach, ed.) New York: Longmans, 1978.

Book Chapters

"To Become an American Woman: Education and Sex Role Socialization of the Vietnamese Immigrant Woman," in Vicki Ruiz and Ellen DuBois (eds.), *Unequal Sisters: A Multi-Cultural Reader in U.S. Women's History,* 2nd ed. New York: (Routledge, 1994), pp. 497-507.

"The Politics of Textbook Selection and Control: The Case of Interwar Indochina and Africa," in P. G. Altbach and G. P. Kelly (eds.), *Textbooks in The Third World: Policy, Context and Content* (New York: Garland Publishing, 1989).

"Technological Transfers and Politics: The Care of the Transfer of School Management Systems from France to the Colonies," in Murray Thomas (ed.), *Educational Technology* (Oxford: Pergamon Press, 1988), pp. 233-252.

"Alternative Approaches in Comparative Education," (with P.G. Altbach) in Neville Postlethewaite (ed.), *International Encyclopedia of Comparative Education* (Oxford: Pergamon Press, 1988), pp. 877-891.

"Vietnamese, Cambodians, Laotians, Hmong and Mein—America's Most Recent Refugees: Resettlement and Adjustment," in Robert Hyung-Chan Kim (ed.), *Asian American History Dictionary* (Westport, Conn.: Greenwood Press, 1987), pp. 39-49.

"Comparative Education: Challenge and Response," (with P.G. Altbach) in P.G. Altbach and G.P. Kelly (eds.), *New Approaches to Comparative Education* (Chicago: University of Chicago Press, 1986), pp. 309-329.

"Education and Women: Equality Is Still Elusive," in Aisla Thomson (ed.), *The Decade for Women* (Toronto: The Canadian Congress for Learning Opportunities for Women, 1986), pp. 57-62.

"Educational Reform and Re-Reform: Politics and the State in Colonial Vietnam," in Colin Brock and Witold Tulasiewicz (eds.), *Educational Policy and Cultural Identity* (London: Croom Helm, 1985), pp. 6-19.

"School Reform in New York State: Historical Perspectives" (with Maxine Seller) in P. G. Altbach, G. P. Kelly and L. Weis (eds.), *Excellence in Education: Perspectives on Policy and Practice* (Buffalo: Prometheus Press, 1985), pp. 253-74.

"National Reports on Excellence: Setting Boundaries of the Debates about Education," in P. G. Altbach, G. P. Kelly and L. Weis (eds.), *Excellence in Education: Perspectives on Policy and Practice* (Buffalo: Prometheus Press, 1985), pp. 31-42.

"Failures of Androcentric Studies of Women's Education in the Third World," in Paula A. Treichler, Cheris Kramarae, and Beth Stafford (eds.), *For Alma Mater: Theory and Practice in Feminist Scholarship* (Champaign: University of Illinois Press, 1985), pp. 112-127.

"Colonialism, Indigenous Society, and School Practices: French West Africa and Indochina, 1918-1938," in P. G. Altbach and G. P.

Kelly (eds.), *Education and the Colonial Experience* (New Brunswick, New Jersey: Transaction Press, 1984), pp. 9-32.

"Factors Influencing Women's Access to Education in the Third World: Myths and Realities," in Sandra Acker (ed.), *World Yearbook of Education. 1983-84*, (London: Croom Helm Publishers, 1984), pp. 81-90.

"Orientations Toward the Study of Women's Education in the Third World" (with C. Elliott), in G. Kelly and C. Elliott (eds.), *Women's Education in the Third World: Comparative Perspectives* (Albany: SUNY Press, 1982), pp. 1-10.

"New Directions for Research" (with C. Elliott), in G. Kelly and C. Elliott (eds.), *Women's Education in the Third World: Comparative Perspectives* (Albany: SUNY Press, 1982), pp. 331-44.

"Schooling and the Reproduction of Patriarchy: Unequal Workloads, Unequal Rewards," (with A. Nihlen), in Michael Apple (ed.), *Cultural and Economic Reproduction in Education: Essays in Class, Ideology and the State* (London: Routledge and Kegan Paul, 1982), pp. 162-180.

"Teachers and the Transmission of State Knowledge: A Case Study of Colonial Vietnam," in P. G. Altbach, R. Arnove, and G. P. Kelly (eds.), *Comparative Education* (New York: Macmillan, 1982), pp. 176-196.

"Trends in Comparative Education: A Critical Analysis" (with Philip G. Altbach and Robert F. Arnove), in P. G. Altbach, R. Arnove, and G.P. Kelly (eds.), *Comparative Education* (New York: Macmillan, 1982), pp. 505-533.

"Comparative Education: A Field in Transition" (with P. G. Altbach), in P. G. Altbach, G. P. Kelly, and D. H. Kelly, *International Bibliography of Comparative Education* (New York: Praeger, 1981), pp. 1-28.

"I Am a Housewife: English Lessons for Vietnamese Women," in Maxine Seller (ed.), *Immigrant Women* (Philadelphia: Temple University Press: 1981), pp. 235-39.

"The Myth of Educational Planning: The Case of the Indochinese University," in I. Spitzberg (ed.), *Education and the New International Order* (New York: Praeger, 1980), pp. 93-108.

"Contemporary American Policies and Practices in the Education of Immigrant Children" in J. Bhatnagar (ed.), *Educating Immigrants* (London: Croom Helm Publishers, 1980), pp. 214-32.

"The Schooling of Vietnamese Immigrants: Internal Colonialism and Its Impact on Women," in B. Lindsay (ed.), *Comparative Perspectives of Third World Women* (New York: Praeger, 1980), pp. 276-96.

"Introduction" (with P. G. Altbach), in P. G. Altbach and Gail P. Kelly (eds.), *Education and Colonialism* (New York: Longmans, 1978), pp. 1-52.

"Colonial Schools in Vietnam: Policy and Practice," in P. G. Altbach and G. P. Kelly (eds.), *Education and Colonialism.* (New York: Longmans, 1978), pp. 96-121.

Articles

"Excellence in Teaching and Career Ladders: Reflections from Colonial Vietnam," *Educational Foundations*, Vol. 2, No. 1 (Winter 1988), pp. 23-47.

"Education and Political Development: Africa Since Independence" (with Claude Welch), *Africana Journal*, Vol. 16 (Spring 1988), pp. 387-402.

"Introduction to Perspectives in Affirmative Action" (with Sheila Slaughter), *Educational Policy*, Vol. 2, No. 2 (1988), pp. 113-115.

"Introduction to Special Issue on Women," *Higher Education*, Vol. 17, No. 5 (1988), pp. 475-477.

"Comparative Education and the Problem of Change: An Agenda for the 1980s," *Comparative Education Review*, Vol. 31, No. 4 (November 1987), pp. 477-489.

"Conflict in the Classroom: A Case Study from Interwar Vietnam," *British Journal of Sociology of Education*, Vol. 8, No. 2 (September 1987), pp. 191-212.

"Setting State Policy on Women's Education in the Third World," *Comparative Education*, Vol. 23, No. 1 (September 1987), pp. 95-102.

"Comparative Education: Challenge and Response" (with P. G. Altbach), *Comparative Education Review,* Vol. 30, No. 1 (February 1986), pp. 89-107.

"Learning to Be Marginal: Schooling in Interwar French West Africa," *Journal of African and Asian Studies* (Fall 1986), pp. 291-308.

"Coping with America: Refugees from IndoChina in the United States," *Annals of the American Academy of Social and Political Science* (September 1986), pp. 138-49.

"Education and Women: Equality Is Still Elusive," *Women's Education,* Vol. 4, No. 2 (Winter 1984), pp. 25-28.

"The Presentation of Indigenous Society in the Schools of French West Africa and Indochina, 1918 to 1938," *Comparative Studies in Society and History,* Vol. 26, No. 3 (June 1984), pp. 523-42.

"Reflection: Kindling for the Groves of Academe," *Academe,* (Sept.-Oct. 1983), p. 47.

"Interwar Schools and the Development of African History in French West Africa," *History in Africa,* Vol. 10 (1983), pp. 163-185.

"Schooling and National Integration: The Case of Interwar Vietnam," *Comparative Education,* Vol. 18 (June, 1982), pp. 175-195.

"Perspectives on the Education of Women in Third World Nations" (with Carolyn M. Elliott), *Comparative Education Review,* Vol. 22, No. 2 (Part 2) (June, 1980), pp. S1-S12.

"Women and Schooling in the Third World: A Bibliography" (with Y. Lulat), *Comparative Education Review,* Vol. 22, No. 2 (Part 2) (June 1980), pp. S224-63.

"The Relation between Colonial and Metropolitan Schools: A Structural Analysis," *Comparative Education,* Vol. 15, No. 2 (June 1979), pp. 209-216.

"Research on the Education of Women in the Third World: Problems and Perspectives," *Women's Studies,* Vol. 1, No. 4 (December 1978), pp. 365-373.

"Schooling, Gender and the Reshaping of Women's Social and Occupational Aspirations," *International Journal of Women's Studies*, Vol. 1, No. 4 (Summer 1978), pp. 323-335.

"The Myth of Educational Planning: The Case of the Indochinese University," *Occasional Paper. International Studies Program*, SUNY/Buffalo (October 1978), pp. 63-81.

"Introducing Vietnamese Adults to American Society: Adult Education in the Refugee Camps and the Possibility of Pluralism in America," *Journal of Ethnic Studies* (December, 1977), pp. 55-64.

"Colonial Schools in Vietnam, 1918-1938," *Proceedings of the Second Meeting of the French Colonial Historical Society*, (March 1977), pp. 96-106.

"School Health Service Needs in Wisconsin" (with Hilde Neujahr, Donald Verwayen, and M. J. Owen), *Journal of School Health*, Vol. 45, No. 10 (December 1975), pp. 595-598.

"Education and Participation in Nationalist Groups: An Exploratory Study of the Indochinese Communist Party and the VNQDD, 1929-1931," *Comparative Education Review*, Vol. 15, No. 2 (June 1971), pp. 227-237.

"Origin and Aims of the Viet Cong," *New Politics*, Vol. 5, No. 1 (Winter 1966), pp. 5-16.

Book and Essay Reviews

"Response to Angus's Conflict, Class and the 19th Century Public High School in the Cities of the Mid-West, 1845-1900," *Curriculum Inquiry*, Vol. 18, No. 1 (1988), pp. 87-93.

"Education and Intergroup Relations: An International Perspective" (ed. John N. Hawkins and Thomas J. Labelle), *Contemporary Sociology* (Winter 1987), 434-435.

"Schools for the Boys" (by Pat Mahony), *Educational Studies*, Vol. 18, No 1 (Spring 1987), pp. 162-164.

"The World Crisis in Education: The View from the Eighties" (by Philip Coombs), *Review of Education*, Vol. 11 (Fall 1985), pp. 295-98.

"Methods in Comparative Education: New Trends or Old Wine in New Bottles," *Comparative Education Review*, Vol. 26, No. 2 (June 1982), pp. 292-96.

"Philanthropy and Cultural Imperialism: The Foundations at Home and Abroad" (ed. R. Arnove), *Phi Delta Kappan*, (January 1982), p. 360.

"School Education of Girls: An International Comparative Study of School Wastage among Girls and Boys at the First and Secondary Levels of Education" (by Isabelle Deble), *Comparative Education Review*, Vol. 26, No. 1 (February 1982), pp. 127-128.

"Schooling for Women's Work" (by Rosemary Deem) *Comparative Education Review*, Vol. 25, No. 3 (October 1981), pp. 468-69.

"Introducing Comparative Education" (by A. Trethway), *Comparative Education Review*, Vol. 23, No. 3 (October 1979), pp. 461-62.

"Race and Education Across Cultures" (ed. by Gajendra K. Verma and Christopher Bagley), *Comparative Education Review*, Vol. 23, No. 3 (October 1979), pp. 473-74.

Index

academic performance 52
access to education 6, 7, 51, 62, 76, 157
access to power 176
achievement studies 53
activism 10, 11
Adler, Mortimer 188
administrators 205, 212
admissions requirements, 184
adult education 71
Afghanistan 164, 171
Africa 29, 33, 63, 76-76, 79, 92, 96, 100, 102, 164, 165, 168, 173-174
African Americans 200, 204, 208, 211, 214
age cohort 141
agricultural colleges 72
Algeria 164, 168, 176
Aligarh University 65
Altbach, Philip 91-92, 96, 100, 220, 225-228, 232
American Anthropological Association 230
American Business-Higher Education Forum 186
American culture 23-24
Angola 171
Annam 140, 144, 145, 147
Antioch College 222
Argentina 68, 83, 172, 175
Arnove, Robert 228
Arusha Declaration 128
Asia 29, 75-76, 79, 96, 100, 164, 165, 168, 170-171, 173-174, 175
Asian immigrants 227
Association of Secondary School Principals 183
AT&T 183
attitudes 122-123, 129

Australia 173, 177
Austria 169
authority and staffing patterns 45-46, 65-66
Bangladesh 96, 164, 168, 174
Belgian Congo 65
Belgium 170
Benin 164
Berry, Sara 224
bicultural 23
Botswana 168
Boyer, Ernest 185
Brazil 80, 93
Buffalo 198, 201, 208, 211, 214
Buhle, Paul and Mary Jo 225
Bulgaria 171
bureaucracy 139
Burkina Faso 164
Business Higher Education Forum 184-185, 189
Cambodia 154
Cameroons 36
Canada 80, 90, 164, 173-175, 177, 224
capitalism 10, 11, 13, 14, 16, 35, 37, 42, 77, 80, 83-84, 92, 94, 137
career and marriage expectations 33
Caribbean 164, 165, 168, 170, 171
Carnegie Foundation for the Advancement of Teaching 183-184, 198
Catholic schools 145
Central America 164, 168
Central Intelligence Agency 222
Chase, Frank 223

Chicago 198, 213
child bearing and raising 41, 50, 68, 153
child rearing 43-44, 68, 78, 81-82, 103, 125, 127, 175
Chile 36, 62, 64, 68, 76, 80, 96, 174
China 42, 84, 97, 137, 138, 148-149, 158, 164, 168, 169, 176, 179, 231
Chinese American 208, 211
class mobility 117
classroom interactions 6, 66
Cochinchina 140, 144, 145
College Board 183, 184, 186
Collège Dong Khanh 145, 146, 147
colonialism 29, 30, 65, 100, 137, 140, 141, 157, 226
Commission on Educational Issues of the National Association of Secondary Schools 192
Commission on Excellence 184
Communist party 148, 150, 156, 221
community organizations 14, 198
Comparative and International Education Society 230
comparative education 6, 89, 121
conflict theory 89, 95-96, 101, 129
Confucianism 139, 147
Congo-Brazzaville 171
Counseling procedures 50
cross-cultural research 31
cross-national research 29
Cuba 36, 84, 149, 169

cultural diversity 18, 25-26, 198, 204
curriculum 7, 53, 78, 130, 146, 187
curriculum innovation 37, 200, 204
Czechoslovakia 168, 171
day care centers 15
Democratic Party 221
dependency theory 100
development 31, 61, 76, 97, 123, 124, 127, 129, 138
Dien-Bien-Phu 148
division of labor 42, 140
Dow Chemical Company 183
Drop-out rates 185, 213
DuBois, Ellen 229, 231
Duồng Thi Duyen 156
Duquesne University 230
Eastern Europe 103, 126, 128, 137, 154, 171
Ecole Brieux 146
Ecole des Jeunes Filles Indigènes 146, 147
economic returns of education 5
Education Commission of the States 183, 184, 189, 190, 192
education of women 29, 30-31, 33-35, 37, 61
educational attainment 62, 64, 83
educational expansion 31, 125, 130
educational opportunity 76
educational planning 63, 96
educational processes 6-7, 30, 76, 94, 122, 129, 130, 178, 197
educational research 7, 30
educational statistics 34
educational vouchers 193
Egypt 175

Index

Elliott, Carolyn 228
English language education 18, 25
enrollments 7, 72, 80, 122, 126, 144, 150, 163
equality of educational opportunity 194
Ethiopia 163, 170, 171
Ethnic associations 208, 210
Europe 164, 165, 168, 169, 170, 171
expectations of women 30
extension of education 127
Federal Republic of Germany 75, 170, 172
feminism 5, 6-7, 30, 37, 55, 77, 79, 81, 84-85, 224, 225, 228
fertility 69, 77
Fiji 171
Finland 168, 171
Ford Foundation 102, 125, 208
formal education 49, 65, 77
France 92, 157, 168, 170-171, 177, 174, 176, 221
French Colonial History Society 230
Freud 11
Fulbright commission 231
Gabon 172
gender differences 5, 41, 141
Geneva Accords 148
German Democratic Republic 151, 169, 171, 172, 174
Gia-Long 139
Ghana 81, 104, 170, 171
Graham, Patricia 183
Great Britain 75, 92, 99, 102, 126, 128, 173-174, 177
Greece 169, 171
Harlem 199
Harvard University 219, 230
health-related professions 174

higher education 32, 47, 48, 51, 53, 62, 71, 97, 101, 116, 130, 141, 151, 158, 170, 175, 84, 228
Hispanic Americans 200, 214
historicism 6
Hmong 211
Ho Chi Minh 148, 150
Hong Kong 168, 171
Horner, Matina 54
human capital theory 68, 128
Hutchins, Robert 186
illiteracy 141
India 63-66, 69, 71, 80, 170, 174, 177
Indiana University 223
individual behaviors 122
Indochina 115
Indonesia 169
industrialization 35, 43, 52, 64-65, 76, 80, 82, 90, 124, 126, 128, 154, 165, 170, 175, 177
Republic of Germany, 172
inequality 41-42, 53, 80, 99
infant mortality 69
informal (or "hidden") curriculum 42, 45, 66, 81, 97
inner city 7, 197
inner city schools 199
institutions 95, 122, 123
instructional methods 188
international market 36
Iran 79, 172, 174, 177
Iraq 168
Islamic fundamentalism 177
Islamic societies 62, 79
Israel 172
Italy 172, 221
Ivory Coast 36
Japan 80, 97, 123, 128, 148, 165, 168

John D. and Catherine T. MacArthur Foundation 186
Jordan 168
Kennedy, Elizabeth 229
Kenya 76, 104, 174
Klawitter, Bob 11
knowledge distribution systems 96
knowledge transfer 96
Korea 168
Korsmeyer, Carolyn 229
Kuwait 79
labor force participation rates 69
Latin America 29, 62-63, 66, 75-76, 100, 102, 164-165, 168, 170-171, 174-176
Le Dynasty 139
Legal Aid Society 221
legitimation theory 89, 95, 129
Lesotho 172
Libya 168
lifestyle revolution 11, 12, 13
linguistic structures 25
literacy 72, 81, 104, 124, 141, 144, 149, 155
Los Angeles 198, 201, 208, 211, 213, 214
Macmillan 900 Series 21, 22, 26
Maisha, Elizabeth 224
Malawi 126
Malaysia 64, 168
Marxism 10-11, 13, 89, 90, 92, 94, 100-101, 113, 126, 129, 153
matriarchy 139
May the 15th School 151
McCarthyism 10
McVey, Sheila Slaughter 225
medical colleges 72
Medicine 153
merit pay 190

Mexican Americans 208, 211
Mexico 96, 174, 224
Middle East 36, 75, 164-165, 168, 170, 171, 173-174
Minneapolis-St. Paul 208-209, 211, 213-214
modernization 29, 34-35, 37, 61, 62, 89, 105, 121, 128
moral education 146
Moscow University 221
mothering 70
Mozambique 171
National Association of Secondary School Principals 185, 192
National Commission on Excellence 183, 185, 190-191
National Liberation Front 149, 150, 155
National Science Board 185, 187, 189, 191
National Science Foundation 83-184
National Student Association 219, 222
Native Americans 208, 211, 214
neo-colonialism 36
neo-Confucianism 149
Nepal 164, 168, 172
New Left 9-10, 12, 14
New York 198, 201
Nghe-An-Ha-Tinh uprisings 140
Ngo Dinh Diem 137, 148
Nhu, Madam Ngo Dinh 149, 222
Nicaragua 172
Nigeria 76, 96, 123, 174
nonformal educational 64, 104
Nordic Studies Association 230

Index

North America 164, 165, 168-169, 170-171
Norway 173
Oberlin College 222
occupational roles 20, 22, 49, 50, 116, 173
Old Left 13
Ontario Institute for Studies in Education 230
outcomes 6, 7, 67, 76, 79, 93, 94, 95, 97, 99, 115, 124, 125, 126, 129, 173, 178
Paideia Proposal 184, 186
Pakistan 168
Paraguay 68, 83, 175
parental involvement 200, 203, 212-213
patriarchy 5-6, 20, 41, 77-79, 82, 85, 116, 141, 157
Peru 174
Peterson, Paul E. 185
Pham Quynh 147
Phan Boi Chau 147
Philadelphia 208, 209, 211
Philippines 168, 170
Pittsburgh 198
Poland 151, 172, 173, 176
Polish Americans 211
political power 156
postprimary schools 145
poverty 199
primary education 63, 76, 104, 126, 130, 144, 164
Princeton University 222
principals 46
privatization 104, 158
processes of education 7, 230
professional women 33, 54
Puerto Ricans 208, 211
purdah 65, 79-80
quantitative measurement 90, 93
Quoc Hoc School 145, 150
regression analysis 128

Republic of Vietnam 148
research agenda 122, 207
Robinson, Lillian 229
Rudd, Mark 12
Rwanda 171
Sadler, Michael 34
school processes 6, 93, 99
schools' effectiveness 130
secondary education 32, 53, 71, 114, 117, 123, 144, 150-151, 165, 175, 184, 186
segregation by sex 19, 43, 41, 51, 141, 169, 172, 174, 178
Seller, Maxine 232
sex differences in education 30, 48, 66, 54, 99, 178
sex gender systems 79
sex role stereotypes 20, 66, 72
sexism 16, 223
significance of education 29
Singapore 168
Sizer, Theodore 183, 185, 188
social control theories 113-115, 118
social mobility 113
socialization 55, 64, 78, 114
South Africa 231
Southeast Asia 208, 214
Soviet Union 42, 103, 126, 128, 137, 154, 158, 174, 208, 214, 221
Spain 172
status hierarchy of schools, 32
structural functionalism 89, 90, 94, 97, 98, 100, 123, 126, 129
structural reforms 129
student achievement 185, 198
student alienation 186
student engagement 200, 203, 204
Student Peace Union 219, 220
student peer group cultures 200

Students for a Democratic Society 10, 222-223
Sub-Saharan Africa 165, 170-171
Sudan, 172
SUNY/Buffalo 226, 227, 228, 229, 231, 232
support groups. 13
Survival English 19, 20, 21, 22, 26
Sweden 75, 172, 174, 179
Switzerland 172
Syria, 172
Tanzania 84, 104, 128
teacher training 168, 190
teachers 7, 21-23, 46-48, 51-52, 66-67, 93, 130, 188-190, 192, 197, 199, 201, 203-205
Teachers College, Columbia University 230
teachers' unions 189
Teaching 153, 174
Texas Instruments 183
textbooks 49, 66, 80, 97
Thailand 231
theory construction 124
Third World 29, 30, 31, 35-37, 61, 67-68, 80, 84, 94, 124, 138
Togo 66-67, 81, 171
Tonkin 140, 144, 145
transmission of knowledge 130
Trung sisters 138
Tunisia 62, 63, 76, 79, 168
Turkey 172, 175
Twentieth Century Fund 183, 185, 188-193
UNESCO 229
United Arab Emirates 168
United Kingdom 171, 172
United States 30-31, 36, 62, 65-66, 80, 84, 89, 90, 92, 102, 126, 128, 137, 154, 171-175, 177, 200
universal primary education 91, 121, 164
universities 53, 145, 150
university administrators 47
University of Chicago 186, 219, 220, 223
University of Dalat 158
University of Hanoi 231
University of Missouri 230
University of New Hampshire 230
University of Stockholm 230
University of Wisconsin 225
Upper Volta 64, 81
USSR 148, 149, 151, 173, 174, 176, 179
Vietnam 11, 115, 177, 226
Vietnamese culture 19, 21, 23-24
Vietnamese Refugees 5, 17
Vietnamese Women's Union 148, 154-157
Vietnamese-American community 25
vocational education 168
Weis, Lois 225, 232
West Africa 115, 227
Westchester County 220
Western Europe 30, 36, 62, 65, 83-84, 103, 126, 128
Weisstein, Naomi 54
women access 30
women faculty 47
women's education 31, 32, 35, 89
Women's Liberation 12-15, 138, 148
women's life histories 127
Women's Movement 9
Women's Peace Committee 221
women's roles 33, 75

work force 35-36, 41, 44, 54-55, 67, 82, 153
working class 10
World Bank 102, 230
World Congress of Comparative Education 230
world systems analysis 89, 91-92, 96, 99, 100, 102, 228
Zaire 174
Zimbabwe 169